THE
COMPLETE GUIDE
TO
RUNNING
and
GROWING YOUR
BUSINESS

THE
COMPLETE GUIDE
TO
RUNNING
and
GROWING YOUR
BUSINESS

ANDREW J. SHERMAN

TIMES BUSINESS

RANDOM HOUSE

This book is dedicated to

my grandparents,

Helen and Bernie Hunter,

and in loving memory of

Tillie and Morris Sherman.

All rights reserved under International and Pan-American Copyright
Conventions. Published in the United States by Times Books, a division of
Random House, Inc., New York, and simultaneously in Canada by Random
House of Canada Limited, Toronto.

Library of Congress Cataloging-in-Publication Data

Sherman, Andrew J.
The complete guide to running and growing your business / Andrew Sherman.
    p.   cm.
Includes index.
ISBN 0-8129-2860-1
1. Small business—United States—Management.
2. Entrepreneurship—United States. I. Title. II. Series.
HD62.7.S5263 1997
658.02′2—dc21   97-6700

Random House website address: http://www.randomhouse.com/
Printed in the United States of America on acid-free paper

9 8 7 6 5 4 3 2

First Edition

Book design by Leon Bolognese

Acknowledgments

There are usually more people to thank than there is room on a page to thank them, and such is the case with this book. First, I'd like to acknowledge the hard work of John Mahaney and Ellie Wickland at Times Books and David Harrison at Kiplinger's for making this project possible. Second, I want to thank my fellow shareholders at Greenberg Traurig for their continuing support and encouragement, especially Larry Hoffman for believing in me and Cesar Alvarez for his patience. I am also thankful for the day-to-day efforts of the FLD Department at Greenberg Traurig and particularly Michele Lewis for keeping me focused and organized. Finally, I want to thank the source of my inspiration and motivation, my wife, Judy, and children, Matthew and Jennifer, for always putting up with me and being understanding when "one more chapter" meant time we couldn't spend together.

Preface

As we approach the year 2000, we are increasingly aware of the many recent trends that have triggered a surge in entrepreneurship, both nationwide and abroad. The growth of the Internet, the downsizing of American conglomerates, the gains in the stock market, and the improvements in computer and telecommunications technologies have all contributed to the swelling number of individuals who have chosen the entrepreneurial path as a means to support their family and to build a business. Yet the legal, competitive, financial, and strategic challenges to running and growing a business are also as strong as ever. The record number of new businesses started has also led to a record number of business failures.

Over the past twelve years, I have served as a strategic and legal adviser to over 200 entrepreneurs and growing companies in a wide variety of industries and at various levels in their stage of development. My experience has taught me that in order to mitigate the risks of business failure, owners and managers of small and growing companies must have the foresight to arm themselves with the knowledge and the advisers that will help them navigate through the murky waters of the competitive marketplace.

This book addresses many of the strategic, financial, and legal issues that are essential to understand in order to survive. It is about building a necessary foundation from which a growth strategy can be launched. And once the foundation has been built, there are chapters that address which growth strategies may be most appropriate for your business. The subjects addressed in the following chapters range from the basics of labor and employment laws to the fundamentals of business planning to how and when (and from where) to raise capital to marketing planning and strategy. From there, we look at certain key issues in growing a business, from mergers and acquisitions to franchising to joint ventures. Once the decision to grow the business is made there are many issues to address, such as

- What factors influence the selection of a particular growth strategy?
- What are the advantages and disadvantages of each strategy?
- How intellectual property and other intangible assets can be leveraged when or if access to capital may be too limited or too costly.
- What technological developments and current business trends influence the selection of a particular growth strategy?
- How a company avoids unprofitable growth or growth for growth's sake.
- How an entrepreneurial management team regulates the pace and rate of growth.
- What key interdependent relationships must be established in order to implement the growth strategy?

And since the path to grow a successful business will have bumps and detours along the way, there are also chapters on managing disputes and coping with financial difficulties.

The next millennium is a short three years away from this book's publication date. The trends affecting the way we now must do business, such as the virtual corporation, the global village, and the growth of electronic commerce, are among the issues examined in this book. We now live in a society where the "knowledge worker," "brand leveraging," and "technology-driven strategic business units," not smokestacks and heavy machinery, are the linchpins of industry. Recognizing the importance of protecting and managing these intangible assets, this book has devoted much attention to the protection and licensing of intellectual property.

This work is not intended as a substitute for the advice of a qualified lawyer, accountant, or consultant. Yet chapter 4 helps you to effectively manage these professional relationships, and it is certainly among the goals of this book to make these relationships more productive and efficient by sharing with you key information to better prepare you for reacting to the guidance offered by your professional advisers.

Finally, there is no greater challenge than the management and growth of a successful business. You must have the energy and the attitude to be dedicated to providing leadership to your staff and excellence to your customers and clients. You must have the tenacity to survive the challenges of your competitors and the frustrations of your failures. But as it is often said, "He who walks the path only when the days are sunny and the terrain is flat, will never reach his destination." I wish you the best of luck on your journey and hope that this book may serve as a compass and guide.

—Andrew J. Sherman
Bethesda, Maryland
April 1997

Contents

13 What to Do When Financial Problems Hit Your Company   275

14 Doing Business in Cyberspace and the Global Village: Opportunities and Challenges in the Twenty-First Century   288

15 Marketing and Sales Plans   309

Appendix   341

Index   353

THE COMPLETE GUIDE TO RUNNING and GROWING YOUR BUSINESS

Choosing the Right Structure for Your Business

One of the first major choices you must consider before starting a business, as well as throughout its growth, is the company's legal structure: a *proprietorship, partnership, corporation,* or *limited liability company.* Your choice should be based on a wide variety of factors, such as the need for flexible management, the level of interaction with the general public, the size of your staff, your personal goals, and the number of owners—to name just a few. Choosing the appropriate legal structure is a complex issue because of the inherent tax consequences and the liabilities of the owner or owners. This chapter will provide an overview and comparison of the basic business formats for you to consider, both at the outset of the new venture and periodically as you reach different stages of development.

Proprietorship

A proprietorship is a form of business entity that has not filed for the protection of a corporation or a limited partnership. It is owned and operated by one person who directly and personally owns the assets used in the company. To establish a sole proprietorship, you only need the state, county, or city licenses necessary to begin operations.

As the proprietor, you are personally responsible for all business liabilities. Therefore, creditors may force you to use your personal assets to satisfy the company's debts, although insurance may be available that will limit your personal liability for business debts. All profits and losses flow directly through to you as proprietor, and they appear on your federal tax returns. In lieu of Social Security taxes paid equally by an employer and employee, the net earnings of the company are subject to self-employment tax. Generally, any payments for personal coverage under group hospitalization, life insurance, or medical plans cannot be deducted as a business expense; however, payments for coverage of employees are deductible. A retirement plan may be established and contributions deducted as an adjustment to total gross income, though not as a deduction from income.

Although you will have to obtain the appropriate business licenses, no annual fees are required *solely* to maintain the form of ownership.

The primary *advantages* of proprietorship are:

- Owner's ability to exercise exclusive control
- Simplicity (compared with other forms of ownership)
- Lower start-up costs
- No "double taxation"—that is, no taxation of both the business and the owner

The primary *disadvantage* is the owner's unlimited personal liability (although, as noted, insurance is available that may limit such liability). The proprietorship is perhaps most appropriate for a typical "mom and pop" operation; however, if the business fails, you and your family could be faced with disastrous consequences, because you will be personally liable for all of the debts and obligations of the business. For most small businesses, other forms of ownership, which provide for limited liability, are more appropriate, particularly as the value of the business grows and there are greater stakes at risk.

Partnership

In a partnership, the assets used in the company are generally jointly owned by two or more parties who agree to share the profits, losses, assets, and liabilities proportionately. A partnership can be created by a written or an oral agreement, although a written agreement is preferred. Partners choose to work together for a wide variety of reasons, including the need to pool their resources and capital, to mitigate risk, and to share areas of expertise.

General Partnership

General partnerships are legal structures under which any or all of the individual partners may be liable for the debts and obligations of the partnership to third parties. For example, if three general partners form a business that then runs into financial difficulty, and only one has personal assets sufficient to satisfy the creditors, then this partner will be responsible for 100% of the obligations—*not* a pro rata share based on his or her actual proportion of ownership of the company. Although that partner may later seek reimbursement from the other partners, this will not affect his or her obligations to third-party creditors. Unless otherwise agreed, general partners have equal control regardless of their percentage of ownership. There are no formal officers, and the management functions are assigned by the partnership agreement. General partnerships are typically found in professions that are service-oriented (such as law, accounting, and medicine) and not capital-intensive. Many states have laws that require the filing of a certificate of partnership, or a similar document, as evidence of its existence in the state. Failure to file a certificate may prevent the partnership from availing itself of the courts of the state in which it conducts business. For this reason, it is advisable to check the laws of the state where the partnership intends to do business. Although the partnership must file a tax return, the partners (not the partnership) are subject to taxes. Income and expenses flow through the partners according to the partnership agreement, and the applicable payroll taxes must be paid directly.

The primary *advantages* of a general partnership are:

- There is a high degree of flexibility.
- Profits and losses can be shared disproportionately and flow through directly to the partners.
- There is no double taxation.

The primary *disadvantage* is the unlimited personal liability of each partner. Another disadvantage is that under partnership law, the partnership technically terminates upon the withdrawal of one partner; this complicates the impact of the entry or exit of any partner on the life of the company.

Limited Partnership

A limited partnership (LP) includes not only the general partners but also one or more partners who are not bound by the obligations of the partnership. As in a general partnership, the general partners are personally liable for all debts incurred by the partnership; however, a limited partner's liability for business debts is limited to his or her capital contribution to the partnership. All management functions—including the day-to-day operations of the business—are delegated to the general partners. The limited partners may *not* exercise any significant levels of control; otherwise (by law), their limited liability status is jeopardized. An LP is usually formed by a general partner to secure additional capital or to spread the risk of a venture without forming a corporation. LPs are common in real estate development, oil and gas exploration, and motion picture ventures. Virtually every state requires the filing of a formal certificate of limited partnership before an LP is legally valid. If such a partnership is not legally formed, the liability of the limited partners is the same as that of the general partners.

The primary *advantage* of the LP is that certain partners can limit their liability to the extent of their capital contribution. The primary *disadvantage* is the unlimited liability of the general partner or partners.

Corporation

A corporation is a separate legal entity that owns the assets of a business and is liable for its debts. Entrepreneurs should seriously consider the corporate form—or the limited liability company—either at the outset of the business or at the very least when the company is positioned for growth, following the initial start-up stage. Corporations are governed by state corporation laws. For federal income tax purposes, the distinguishing characteristics of a corporation include:

- *Continuity of life.* All state corporation laws provide that a corporation has perpetual existence and will continue to exist regardless of what happens to the owners (shareholders)—such as death, bankruptcy, or retirement—or when a shareholder or group of shareholders gives up any interest in the company;

- *Limited liability.* A shareholder is not personally liable for corporate debt or claims against the corporation, except in very special circumstances;

- *Free transferability of interest.* Shareholders may generally sell all or part of their interest to any buyer without the consent of the other shareholders.

- *Centralized management.* The board of directors (elected by the shareholders) is the body authorized to make independent business decisions on behalf of the corporation.

The specific aspects of forming a corporation vary from state to state; however, virtually every state requires the filing of articles (certificate) of incorporation. Once the state of incorporation is chosen, various registration requirements must be met initially and on an ongoing basis in order to obtain and maintain corporate status and to enjoy the protections afforded to corporations in that particular state. *It is important that all the legal formalities are observed in order to protect shareholders from personal liability.*

The *advantages* of the corporate form of ownership include limited liability for owners and the ability to continue the business easily, even if there is a change in the shareholders. Also, in some instances, a change of ownership is easier because all assets are owned in the name of the corporation and the company can be transferred to new ownership by a sale of the corporation's stock.

However, a disadvantage of corporate ownership is that it can be more expensive to form and maintain than other legal entities, primarily because of the filing and annual fees imposed by state agencies.

General Characteristics of Corporations

A corporation is owned by its shareholders—who may be individuals, partnerships, trusts, or other corporations—and there is no limit to the number of shareholders. The corporate entity is separate and distinct from its shareholders, and the personal assets of the corporation's shareholders are not available to satisfy corporate obligations; thus creditors of the corporation may look only to the assets of the corporation for payment. This is commonly referred to as the "corporate veil." If a corporation is involved in a number of activities, then separate corporate subsidiaries (corporations owned by another corporation) may be created to protect the assets of one business activity from the liabilities of any other activity.

The overall responsibility for management falls to the board of directors. The board is responsible for policy and elects officers to manage the day-to-day business operations. Unlike a partnership, a corporation is a taxpaying entity for which federal and state tax returns are filed, taxes paid are based on the profits of the corporation (unless the corporation elects an S status, as discussed below), and all applicable payroll taxes must be paid directly. Losses are not passed through but may be carried forward as an offset against the corporation's future income. The board may elect to distribute after-tax profits as dividends to the shareholders, who are then taxed at their individual rates (this is known as "double taxation"). The key document governing all aspects of the corporation is the *bylaws*. Bylaws may not exceed the scope of the articles of incorporation or the authority set forth in the state's statutes.

C Corporation versus Subchapter S

A corporation meeting certain requirements may (under the regulations of the Internal Revenue Service, IRS) elect S status. This affects the manner in which the corporation is taxed on the federal level. An S corporation (1) must have no more than 75 shareholders who (with very few exceptions) must be (a) individuals and (b) residents of the United States; and (2) cannot have two classes of stock with different financial interests. The responsibility for management is the same as in a Chapter C corporation. However, an S corporation does not pay federal tax on its income; rather, the profits and losses are passed along to the shareholders and are then declared on the individual's tax return.

The primary *advantage* of an S corporation is that the double taxation inherent in a Chapter C corporation is eliminated.

Managing the Corporation: Duties and Responsibilities

Each act or decision of the board must be performed in good faith and for the benefit of the corporation. The legal obligations of the directors fall into three broad categories: *duty of care, duty of loyalty,* and *duty of fairness.*

* *Duty of care.* The directors must carry out their duties in good faith with diligence, care, and skill, in the best interests of the corporation. Each director must actively gather information to make an informed decision regarding company affairs and in formulating company strategies. In doing so, the board member is entitled to rely primarily on the data provided by officers and professional advisers, *provided that the board member has no knowledge of any irregularity or inaccuracy in the information.* I have seen instances where board members have been held personally responsible for misinformed or dishonest decisions made in bad faith, such as a failure to direct the corporation properly or the board's knowing authorization of a wrongful act.

* *Duty of loyalty.* The duty of loyalty requires each director to exercise his or her powers in the interest of the corporation and

not in his or her own interest or in the interest of another person (including a family member) or organization. The duty of loyalty has a number of specific applications, such as the duty to avoid any conflicts of interest in the director's dealings with the corporation and the duty not to personally usurp what is more appropriately an opportunity or business transaction to be offered to the corporation. For example, if an officer or director of the company was in a meeting on the company's behalf and an opportunity to obtain the licensing or distribution rights for a new technology was offered at the meeting, it would be a breach of this duty to try to obtain these rights individually and not first offer them to the corporation.

• *Duty of fairness.* The third duty a director has to the corporation is that of fairness. For example, questions of the duty of fairness may come up if a director of the company is also the owner of the building in which the corporate headquarters are leased, and if the same director is seeking a significant rent increase for the renewal term. It would certainly be a breach of this duty to allow the director to vote on this proposal. The central legal concern under such circumstances is usually that the director may be treating the corporation unfairly in the transaction, since the director's self-interest and gain could cloud his or her duty of loyalty to the company. When a transaction between an officer or director and the company is challenged, the individual will have the burden of demonstrating the propriety and fairness of the transaction. If any component of the transaction involves fraud, undue overreaching, or waste of corporate assets, it is likely to be set aside by the courts. In order for an "interested" director's dealings with the corporation to be upheld, the director must demonstrate that the transaction was approved or ratified by a disinterested majority of the company's board of directors.

In order for each member of the board of directors to meet his or her duties of care, loyalty, and fairness to the corporation, certain general guidelines should be followed:

• Work with your attorney to develop for all officers and directors a set of written guidelines on the basic principles of corporate law. Keep the board informed about recent cases or changes in the law.

- Work closely with your corporate attorney. If the board or an individual director is in doubt as to whether a proposed action is truly in the best interests of the corporation, consult your attorney immediately—*not* after the transaction is consummated.

- Keep careful minutes of all meetings and comprehensive records of the information upon which board decisions are based. Be prepared to show financial data, business valuations, market research, opinion letters, and related documentation if a disgruntled shareholder later challenges the action as "uninformed." Well-prepared minutes will also serve a variety of other purposes, such as written proof of a director's analysis and appraisal of a given situation, proof that parent and subsidiary operations are being conducted at arm's length and as two distinct entities, or proof that an officer did or did not have authority to engage in the specific transaction being questioned.

- Be selective in choosing candidates for the board of directors. Avoid considering or nominating someone who may offer credibility but is unlikely to attend any meetings or contribute any real input to the management or direction of the company. In my experience, such a passive relationship will only invite claims by shareholders of corporate mismanagement. Similarly, don't accept an invitation to sit on a board of directors of another company unless you're ready to accept the responsibilities that go with it.

- In situations where a takeover is threatened, be careful to make decisions that will be in the best interest of *all* shareholders, not just the board or the officers or any particular shareholder. Any steps taken to defend against a takeover by protecting the economic interests of the officers and directors (such as lucrative "golden parachute" contracts, which ensure a costly exit) must be reasonable in relation to the threat.

- In order to avoid accusations of self-dealing or conflict of interest, any board member who independently supplies goods and services to the corporation should not participate in the board discussion or vote on any resolution relating to his or her deal-ings with the corporation. Proposed actions must be approved by a "disinterested" board after the material facts of the trans-action are disclosed and the nature and extent of the interested member's involvement is known.

- Questionnaires should be issued periodically to officers and directors regarding possible self-dealing or conflicts of interests with the corporation. Incoming board members and newly appointed officers should be provided with a more detailed initial questionnaire. Also, these questionnaires should always be circulated among the board members before any issuances of securities (such as a private placement or a public offering).

- The directors should be given, well in advance of a board meet-ing, all appropriate background and financial information relating to proposed board actions. An agenda, proper notice, and a mutually convenient time, place, and date will ensure good attendance records and compliance with applicable statutes regarding notice of meetings.

- Remember that a valid meeting of the board of directors may not be held unless a quorum is present. The number of directors needed to constitute a quorum may be fixed by the articles or bylaws, but it is generally a majority of board members.

- Board members who object to a proposed action or resolution should either vote "no" and ask that the vote be recorded in the minutes, or abstain from voting and promptly file a written dissent with the secretary of the corporation.

Limited Liability Companies

The limited liability company (LLC) is being touted by many as the business structure of the future, and no one has better access to it than a prospective entrepreneur. This concept, developed in Germany, was first introduced in the United States in 1977 by the state of Wyoming (although by then it had been popular in

Europe and Latin America for many decades). The LLC received its strongest endorsement when the IRS, in 1988, issued a formal opinion stating that an LLC would be treated as a partnership, not a corporation, for federal tax purposes, provided that certain criteria were met, as discussed below. This IRS ruling encouraged many states to pass legislation recognizing LLC status. At the time of this writing, the LLC structure has been approved for use in 48 states and the District of Columbia.

The flexibility, security, and tax savings of an LLC can be significant, and if you are just now starting your business, it's a good choice. However, if your business is already well established, the capital gains costs associated with liquidating your corporation and switching to an LLC may be too great.

Advantages of the LLC include the following:

• Members enjoy the same protection from personal liability as do officers and shareholders of a corporation. (There are some circumstances where officers and shareholders can be personally liable, and some states specify the same for LLCs.)

• The LLC itself does not pay federal income tax. If properly structured, it will be classified as a partnership for tax purposes, and it is also not subject to state income or excise tax. It allocates taxable income to members, who pay at their personal rates. The members can write off the losses of an LLC to the extent of their tax basis in it, including their share of its debts. In contrast, shareholders in an S corporation can write off losses only to the extent that such losses exceed the money they have contributed to the company in form of capital stock and loans.

• Management authority can be delegated to specific members, or to professional managers who are not members of the LLC.

• Once the operating agreement is formed, there are few other formalities that corporations must follow, such as holding annual meetings or issuing stock certificates.

• There are no restrictions on the number or type of owners (in this, an LLC is unlike an S corporation).

• There is no restriction on multiple classes of stock (again, this is unlike an S corporation).

- Distributions of property in kind can be made by an LLC (unlike an S corporation) without a recognition of taxable gain.

The following are *disadvantages* of the LLC:

- In most states, cessation of association of a member—by death, by withdrawal, or otherwise—will trigger the dissolution of the LLC. However, most operating agreements provide an option for the members to elect to continue the operation of the company, as they usually do.
- LLC statutes are not available in Vermont or Hawaii (as of this writing).
- A member who is also a manager may be required to treat his or her share of the income as "self-employment income," subject to additional taxes to fund Social Security and Medicare.
- In some states, an LLC cannot qualify for certain state tax credits or sales and property tax exemptions given to corporations.

The ability to form an LLC can offer clear advantages for the prospective entrepreneur who wants to form a new company; however, not every state recognizes an LLC for tax purposes. In fact, some states recognize *only* limited liability partnerships that are used by professional practices (lawyers, doctors, accountants), in which case an LLC would pay federal taxes as a partnership and state taxes as a corporation.

Structuring an LLC

It is best to structure an LLC so that it qualifies as a partnership under federal tax laws. The IRS will treat an LLC as a partnership for federal income tax purposes if it lacks at least two characteristics of a corporation (continuity of life, limited liability, free transferability of interest, and centralized management). Some states have adopted "bullet-proof" statutes providing that an LLC formed in the state will automatically lack at least two of the four characteristics and will always qualify as a partnership. The majority of states, however, have adopted "flexible" statutes allowing members to include some or all of these characteristics in designing LLCs, with the attendant risk that if the LLC has too many characteristics of a corporation, it will be taxed as a corporation.

If you establish an LLC, then you'll have tremendous flexibility in structuring economic and management arrangements. You'll get much more flexibility than will be afforded to you with an S Corporation, although you still get the liability protection and the "flow through" taxation. Members may elect to manage the LLC themselves or may designate one or more "managers" (who may or may not be members) to manage its business and operations. Capital contributions to the LLC may be in the form of cash, property, or services; and profits and losses may be allocated among the members in any manner they choose (subject to compliance with applicable state and federal tax law and regulations).

Regardless of which structure you choose, it is critical to have an effective board of directors. An effective board will be always informed, objective, active, attentive, accountable, independent, and be prepared to share risk with the company's shareholders when it comes to compensation and financial reward for their services. An objective board will regularly self-examine its performance by making periodic assessments of the track records of individual directors in areas such as attendance at meetings, commitment, lack of self-interest, and business acumen. A board should be made up of individuals with varying talents and insights, and not be too loyal to any given officer or shareholder. All acts should be governed by the company's best interests. Regular elections will force the board members to remain accountable to the company's shareholders. An excessive number of "inside" directors (e.g., major stockholders and key officers of the company) should be avoided to ensure objectivity. The board should be responsible for the review and approval of the company's long-term strategy and annual operating plans. For additional guidance, see the recently adopted expectations of the National Association of Corporate Directors included in Box 1-1 on the next page.

New Expectations for Directors

The National Association of Corporate Directors has issued new guidelines for enhancing the professionalism of board members. The key recommendations are that directors should:

- Become active participants and decision makers in the boardroom, not merely passive advisers.
- Budget at least four full forty-hour weeks of service for every board on which they serve.
- Limit board memberships. Senior executives should sit on no more than three boards, including their own. Retired executives or professional directors should serve on no more than six.
- Consider limits on length of service on a board to ten to fifteen years to allow room for new directors with fresh ideas.
- Immerse themselves in both the company's business and its industry while staying in touch with senior management.
- Know how to read a balance sheet and an income statement and understand the use of financial ratios.
- Own a significant equity position in the company.
- Submit a resignation upon retirement, a change in employer, or a change in professional responsibilities.

DATA: NATIONAL ASSOCIATION OF CORPORATE DIRECTORS

Evaluating Your Selected Structure

Once you've selected the legal structure and the company is growing, you must periodically examine and analyze the selected structure in order to ensure the company's viability as it grows. There are a number of reasons why the structure must be reconsidered from time to time:

- Need to raise additional capital for business expansion
- Changes in applicable tax laws

- Increase in risk due to additional dealings with creditors, suppliers, or consumers

- Shift in business plans that have an impact on the distribution and use of earnings and profits

- Opportunities to develop new technology, either in conjunction with others or under the umbrella of a separate but related subsidiary or research-and-development partner

- Retirement, death, or departure of an original founder

- Need to attract and retain additional top management personnel

- Mergers, acquisitions, spin-offs, or an initial public offering planned for the near future

These factors affecting the structure of a company often come into play as a business grows and evolves. For example, in its very early stages, a small retail business may start out as a sole proprietorship. Once the store is opened, the desire to give some ownership to a key employee may result in a shift to a general partnership. Then the need to bring in a passive investor to handle the cost of remodeling the store results in a shift to a limited partnership. As additional employees are hired and sales increase, the two general partners and the limited partner choose to incorporate, to better protect the assets of *all* partners against claims and liabilities to third-party creditors, but they elect S status to preserve "pass-through" taxation. When a decision is made to open a second store, legal counsel advises the three owners to form two additional corporations, one as a parent "holding company" and one for the operations of the new store. This type of structure prevents creditors of one store from proceeding against the assets of the other store. This structure also becomes helpful when a fourth individual is offered stock to help finance the second store but will not have an equity ownership in the first store. Finally, two years later, the company considers growth through business format franchising (see Chapter 9) and the decision is made to form an LLC to handle the franchise operations and to better insulate the assets of the two "company-owned" stores from the possible claims down the road by a disgruntled franchisee. The evolution looks as shown in Figure 1-1.

Making the best decision about business structure *early* could promote savings for you and avoid costs down the road. It is critical for anyone starting a new business venture to consult with qualified legal and tax advisers before making this decision.

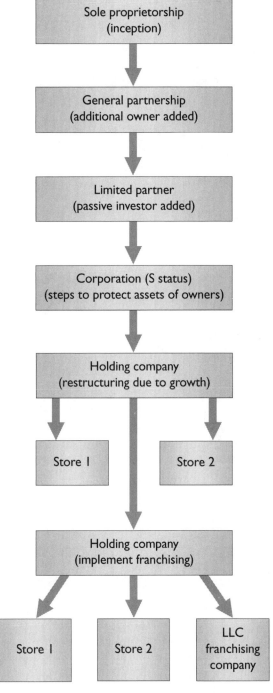

FIGURE 1–1.

People Power:
What You Need to Know About Your Employees

Ask small business owners or entrepreneurs about their greatest fear (other than running out of money) and they will almost invariably answer: *"Being sued by a current or former employee!"* This fear is not unwarranted. Whether it's sexual harassment, drug testing, or unjust termination, it seems as though there is an opportunity for litigation with each new hire. In fact, according to a recent survey of 850 companies conducted by a law firm based in New York City, the number of companies with employees in litigation against them rose to 63% in 1995, a 10% increase over 1993. The most common accusation was race discrimination; the next most common claims were allegations of age and gender discrimination and sexual harassment.

In fact, according to statistics compiled by the agency that investigates claims of discrimination, the Equal Employment Opportunity Commission (EEOC), claims of sexual harassment rose a staggering 154% from 1990 to 1995. In 1993, one year after the Americans with Disabilities Act of 1990 (ADA) went into effect, the EEOC reported 15,284 disability-related complaints; by 1995, the number of complaints rose by 30% to 19,795. This alarming growth is due in large part to the significant changes in federal employment laws that occurred at the beginning of the decade.

These are very alarming statistics. Our economy cannot

afford an environment where smaller companies are afraid to hire new staff because of the risk of litigation. This chapter will highlight the key aspects of many of these laws and offer steps for complying with them.

In addition to these legal challenges, smaller companies face especially difficult challenges in recruiting and retaining key employees because they do not have formal personnel departments or recruitment programs, owing to a lack of capital or time to spend searching for qualified workers. It is also often the case that entrepreneurs are fixated on marketing their products and services and on growing their businesses—so it's easy to lose focus on issues like hiring and firing, even though they are critical to the long-term success of the company. As a result, hiring decisions are often made hastily, and this can be especially damaging to a small company where most employees at almost every level will immediately be given significant responsibilities. Similarly, when capital is scarce, hiring decisions are delayed; this results in the overloading of current staff, which usually leads to disenchantment and lower morale. Also, the recruitment process is becoming increasingly more competitive, and many smaller companies simply cannot match the compensation packages offered by their larger competitors. Once key employees are finally recruited and trained, they may be hired away by a competitor offering a significant pay increase, potential for growth, and better employee benefits. To combat all these difficulties, you must be especially careful to take steps to protect your *key* assets with employment agreements and creative compensation and stock ownership plans.

Generally speaking, it is especially difficult for the smaller company to structure a compensation and benefits package that will enable it to compete with larger companies for qualified personnel. However, the competitive advantage offered by many entrepreneurial firms is that they are small. Many people prefer working in this type of environment. During the company's start-up stage, precious cash must be invested in the growth of the company, leaving little money for large officers' salaries or luxurious company cars. As a result, the compensation package often will include equity in the company from the outset, or a provision giving employees the right to acquire equity in the company through a stock option plan. A wide variety of employee benefit plans may be adopted, ranging from income-replacement programs (retirement and disability plans) to equity-oriented incentive compensation (stock option plans and stock appreciation rights) to fringe benefits (automobiles, club memberships, or even group legal services). These types of compensation plans are heavily regulated by the Internal Revenue Service, the Department of Labor, and in certain cases the Securities and Exchange Commission and the Pension Benefit Guaranty Corporation. As a result, the development and structuring of employee benefit plans has become a very dynamic and specialized field, dominated by compensation and benefit consultants who work closely with accountants and attorneys in ensure that the programs meet company objectives and comply with applicable laws.

Understanding the Basics of Employment Law

The doctrine of "employment at will" (which dates back to the Statute of Labourers in England in the 1700s) allows for termination of employment by either the employer or the employee at any time for any reason or for no reason at all. Today, however, the systems and procedures implemented by a company for hiring and firing personnel trigger a host of federal and state labor and employment laws. You must understand these regardless of the size of your company, but failure to understand them can be especially damaging to the smaller company because of the extensive litigation costs incurred in an employment-related dispute. Litigation between employers and employees continues to clutter our nation's tribunals. In fact, suits under federal employment laws currently make up the single largest category of civil filings in the federal court system. Federal and state legislatures have been equally active in designing new laws covering labor and employment, and small business groups have been quick to respond to the adverse impact of these laws.

The growing body of employment law encompasses topics

such as employment discrimination, comparable worth, unjust dismissal, affirmative action programs, job classification, workers' compensation, performance appraisal, disciplining and demotion of employees, maternity policies and benefits, recruitment techniques and procedures, employment policy manuals and agreements, age and retirement, plant closings and layoffs, sexual harassment and discrimination, occupational health and safety standards, handicapped employees, and mandated employment practices for government contractors. The most comprehensive federal statutes and regulations affecting employment include the following:

- *Equal Pay Act of 1963* prohibits unequal pay based on gender.

- *Title VII of the Civil Rights Act of 1964* prohibits discrimination based on race, color, religion, sex, or national origin.

- *Age Discrimination in Employment Act of 1967 (ADEA)* prohibits discrimination against individuals age 40 or older.

- *Rehabilitation Act of 1973* prohibits discrimination against handicapped individuals by all programs or agencies receiving federal funds and all federal agencies. This act also protects reformed or rehabilitated drug or alcohol abusers who are not currently using drugs or alcohol. In addition, it has been interpreted to cover people with AIDS and HIV infection and those perceived as having AIDS.

- *Vietnam Era Veterans' Readjustment Assistance Act of 1974* requires government contractors to take affirmative action to recruit, hire, and promote qualified disabled veterans and veterans of the Vietnam era.

- *Immigration and Nationality Act* prohibits employers from discriminating on the basis of citizenship or national origin.

- *Pregnancy Discrimination Act of 1978* prohibits discrimination against pregnant women.

- *Immigration Reform and Control Act of 1986* makes it unlawful for employers to recruit, hire, or continue to employ illegal immigrants to the United States and also contains nondiscrimination provisions similar to those of the Immigration and Nationality Act.

Following are some more recent federal statues and regulations:

- *Americans with Disabilities Act of 1990 (ADA)* prohibits discrimination against a qualified applicant or employee with a disability and applies to employers with 25 or more employees. The ADA is based on the Civil Rights Act of 1964 and Title V of the Rehabilitation Act of 1973. To fall within the ADA, a person's disability must be a physical or mental impairment that substantially limits at least one major "life activity." This covers a range of physical and mental problems, from impaired vision, speech, and hearing to cancer, heart disease, arthritis, diabetes, orthopedic problems, and learning disabilities such as dyslexia. HIV infection also is considered a disability. The ADA also prohibits discrimination based on a "relationship or association" with disabled persons; makes sure the disabled have access to buildings, etc.; and protects recovered substance abusers and alcoholics.

- *Civil Rights Act of 1991* expanded the legal rights and remedies to individuals who experience employment-related discrimination on the basis of their race, color, religion, sex, or national origin. Employees are now able to recover consequential monetary losses; damages for future lost earnings and nonpecuniary injuries, such as pain, suffering, and emotional distress; and punitive damages. The act also permits jury trials in these types of cases. Before the 1991 act, employees' remedies were essentially limited to monetary damages for lost back pay, reinstatement or promotion (if appropriate), and attorneys' fees.

- *Family and Medical Leave Act of 1993 (FMLA)* prohibits employers from interfering with, restraining, or forbidding employees to take reasonable leave for medical reasons; for the birth or adoption of a child; and for the care of a child, spouse, or parent who has a serious health condition. The leave is unpaid leave, or paid leave if it has been earned, for a period of up to 12 workweeks in any 12 months. During the leave period, the employer must maintain any group health plan covering the employee. At the conclusion of the leave, an employee generally has a right to retain the same position or an equivalent position with equivalent pay, benefits, and working conditions. Under the FMLA, an employer is defined as any person engaged in commerce, or in any industry or activity affecting commerce, who employs 50 or more employees for each working day during each of 20 or more calendar workweeks in the current or preceding calendar year.

In addition to these federal laws, many state legislatures have enacted antidiscrimination laws that go beyond the protection afforded at the federal level. These state laws must also be carefully reviewed in order to ensure that employment practices comply at both the federal and the state level.

Preparing the Personnel Manual

As the owner of your company, you are responsible for developing a personnel manual and handbook to communicate to *all* employees applicable management procedures and guidelines, and to define the employment relationship (rather than to enter into a formal employment agreement with each employee).

A well drafted personnel manual can serve as a personnel training program, a management tool for improving the efficiency of the company, a morale-builder for employees, and a guardian against excessive litigation. The personnel manual should be sufficiently detailed to provide guidance to employees on all key company policies; however, overly complex manuals tend to restrict the flexibility of management and lead to confusion and uncertainty among employees. It is also crucial that your attorney review the manual before it is distributed to staff members, especially since some courts have recently held that under some circumstances the employment manual can be treated as if it were a binding contract. And since the manual is also a written record of the company's policies for hiring, compensation, promotion, and termination, it could be offered as evidence in employment-related litigation. Recently, courts have seemed increasingly more willing to look at statements in the personnel manual (or every unwritten employment policy of the company) in disputes between employers and employees. Although the exact contents of the manual will vary, depending on the nature and size of the company as well as its management philosophies and objectives, all personnel manuals should contain the categories of information listed in Box 2-1.

Preparing Employment Agreements for Key Personnel

Although employment agreements are typically reserved for employees who either are senior managers or serve key technical functions, these documents serve as an important and cost-effective tool for safeguarding confidential business information and preserving valuable human resources. When combined with a well developed compensation plan, both provide an economic and legal foundation for employees' long-term loyalty.

There are many other reasons why employment agreements for key employees may be fundamental to a small company's existence and growth. For example, venture capital investors will often insist on employment agreements between the company and its founders or key employees in order to protect their investment. Also, individuals with special management or technical expertise may insist on an agreement as a condition for joining the company. In addition, such an agreement serves as an important tool for human resources management in terms of description of duties, bases for rewards, and the grounds for termination.

The essential provisions of an employment agreement for key employees include the following.

Duration

The crucial judgment that you must make when determining duration is whether the arrangement best suits the employer as a temporary, trial arrangement or as a long-term relationship. Other factors that should influence the decision about duration

B O X   2 - 1

What the Personnel Manual Should Contain

- Key goals and objectives of the company
- Background of the company and its founders
- Description of the products and services offered by the company
- Current organizational chart and brief job descriptions
- Compensation and benefits
  1. Hours of operation
  2. Overtime policies
  3. Vacation, maternity leave, sick leave, and holidays
  4. Overview of employee benefits (health, dental, disability, etc.)
  5. Performance review, raises, and promotions
  6. Pension, profit-sharing, and retirement plans
  7. Eligibility for fringe benefits
  8. Rewards, employee discounts, and bonuses
  9. Expense reimbursement policies
- Standards for employees' conduct
  1. Dress code and personal hygiene
  2. Courtesy to customers, vendors, and fellow employees
  3. Smoking, drug use, and gum chewing
  4. Jury duty and medical absences
  5. Personal telephone calls and visits
  6. Training and educational responsibilities
  7. Employees' use of company facilities and resources
  8. Employees' meals and breaks
- Safety regulations and emergency procedures
- Procedures for handling employees' grievances, disputes, and conflicts
- Employees' duties to protect intellectual property
- Term and termination of the employment relationship
  1. Probationary period
  2. Grounds for discharge (immediate versus notice)

(Box continued on next page)

3. Termination and resignation

4. Severance pay

5. Exit interviews

- Maintenance of employees' records

    1. Job application

    2. Social Security and birth information

    3. Federal and state tax, immigration, and labor or employment law documentation

    4. Performance review and evaluation report

    5. Benefit plan

    6. Exit interview

- Special legal concerns

    1. Equal employment opportunity

    2. Sexual harassment

    3. Opportunities for advancement

    4. Charitable and political contributions

    5. Garnishment of employees' wages

- Dealing with news media and distribution of press releases

- Summary and reiteration of the role and purpose of the personnel manual

- Employee's acknowledgement of receipt of manual (to be signed by the employee and placed in his or her permanent file)

---

are the nature of the job, the growth potential of the candidate, the business plans of the company, the impact of illness or disability, how the estate will be treated in the event of the death of the employee, and trends in the industry. A separate section should be added addressing what effect a subsequent merger or acquisition by the company would have on the agreement. The provisions should also specify the exact commencement and expiration dates of employment, the terms and procedures for tenure or renewal, and a specific discussion of the grounds for early termination.

Duties and Obligations of the Employee

The description of the nature of the employment and the employee's duties should include:

- Exact title (if any) of the employee.
- Statement of exact tasks and responsibilities and a description of how these tasks and duties relate to the objectives of other employees, other departments, and the company overall.
- Specification of the amount of time to be devoted to the position and to individual tasks.
- Where appropriate, a statement about whether the employee will serve on the company's board of directors, and if so, whether any additional compensation will be paid for serving on the board.

For certain employees, such as executives and managers, the statement of duties should be defined as broadly as possible (e.g., "as directed by the Board" so that the employer has the right to change the employee's duties and title if human resources are needed elsewhere), with a statement merely limiting the scope of the employee's authority or ability to incur obligations on behalf of the company. This will offer a company limited protection against unauthorized acts by the employee, unless apparent or implied authority can be established by a third party.

Compensation

The type of compensation plan will naturally vary, depending on the nature of the employee's duties, industry practices, and customs, compensation offered by competitors, the stage of the company's growth, market conditions, tax ramifications to both employer and employee, and the skill level of the employee. A schedule of payment, calculation of income, and a statement about the conditions for bonuses and rewards should be included.

Expense Reimbursement

The types of business expenses for which the employee will be reimbursed should be clearly defined.

Employee Benefits

All benefits and perquisites should be clearly defined, including these:

- Health insurance.
- Company cars.
- Education and training.
- Death, disability, or retirement benefits.
- Defined compensation plans.
- Pension or profit-sharing plans. In addition, any vacation or sick leave policies should be included in either the employment agreement or the personnel manual (or both).

Covenants of Nondisclosure

Trade secrets owned by a company may be protected with covenants that impose obligations on the employee not to disclose (in any form to any unauthorized party) any information the company regards as confidential and proprietary. This should include, among other things, customer lists, formulas and processes, financial and sales data, agreements with customers and suppliers, business and strategic plans, marketing strategies and advertising materials, and anything else that gives the employer an advantage over its competitors. This covenant should cover the pre-employment period (interview or training period) and extend through the term of the agreement into post-termination. The scope of the covenant, the conditions it contains regarding use and disclosure of trade secrets and sources, the forms of information it describes, and the geographic limitations it covers should be broadly drafted to favor the employer. However, a nondisclosure covenant will be enforceable only to the extent necessary to reasonably protect the nature of the intellectual property that is at stake.

Covenants Against Competition

Any company would like to be able to impose a restriction on its employees that should they leave the company, they will be absolutely prohibited from working for a competitor in any way, shape, or manner. Courts, however, have not looked favorably on such attempts to rob individuals of their livelihood, and have even set aside entire contract agreements on the basis of this section. The courts require that any covenants against competition be reasonable as to scope, time, territory, and remedy for noncompliance. The type of covenants against competition that will be tolerated by the courts vary from state to state and from industry to industry, but they must always be reasonable under the circumstances. It is crucial that an attorney with a background in this area be consulted when such provisions are being drafted.

Covenants Regarding Ownership of Inventions

Questions that might arise regarding the ownership of intellectual property developed by an employee during the term of employment should be expressly addressed in the agreement. If they are not specifically addressed, basic common-law rules regarding ownership of an employee's ideas, inventions, and discoveries will govern. These rules do not necessarily favor the employer, especially if there is a question of fact as to whether a discovery was made outside the scope of the employment, or if it is established that the employee did not utilize the employer's resources in connection with an invention. In the absence of a written agreement, the common-law principle of "shop rights" generally dictates that when an invention is made by an employee, if it utilizes the resources of the employer, even if it is made outside of the scope of the employment, ownership is vested in the employee—subject, however, to a nonexclusive, royalty-free, irrevocable license to the employer.

Protection of Intellectual Property upon Termination

The agreement should contain provisions regarding obligations of nondisclosure and noncompetition upon the termination of employment; and when an employee leaves, these obligations should be reaffirmed in an exit interview with at least one witness present. For example, a company should inform the exiting employee of his or her continuing duty to preserve the confidentiality of trade secrets and should reiterate specific information regarded as confidential as well as obtain assurances and evidence (including a written acknowledgement) that all confidential and proprietary documents have been returned and no copies retained. The name of the new employer or future activity should be obtained. Under certain circumstances, a new employer should even be notified of the prior employment relationship and its scope. These procedures put a new employer or competitor "on notice" of the company's rights and prevent it from claiming that it was unaware that its new employee had revealed trade secrets. Finally, the company should also insist that the employee not hire coworkers after the termination of his or her employment with the company.

Employers should carefully consider the long-term implications of the terms and conditions in the employment agreement. Once promises are made to an employee in writing, the employee will expect special benefits to remain available throughout the term of the agreement. Your failure to meet these obligations on a continuing basis will expose you to the risk of litigation for breach of contract.

Structuring a Recruitment and Selection Program

The Regulations Involved

Federal employment laws seek to protect each employee's right to be hired, promoted, and terminated without regard to race or gender. The agency enforcing these laws is the Equal Employment Opportunity Commission (EEOC). Under very limited circumstances, the EEOC will tolerate "discriminatory practices" in the recruitment and termination, but *only* if the criteria are based on a "bona fide occupational qualification" (BFOQ), or if requirement is reasonably and rationally related to the employment activities and responsibilities of a particular employee or a particular group of employees, rather than to all employees of the employer. For example, the EEOC upheld a postal agency's decision not to hire a seasonal carrier applicant on the basis of the applicant's medical examination and medical history. The agency had concluded that the functional requirements of the position (such as heaving lifting, heavy carrying, and repeated bending) would cause the applicant's medical condition to worsen. In another instance, the United States Supreme Court found that the Alabama prison system was justified in providing that only 25% of its positions as correctional counselors could be offered to women. The Court noted that in view of the peculiar nature of the prison system—in which the estimated 20% of the male prisoners who were sex offenders were scattered throughout the penitentiary's dormitory facilities—the board of corrections' limit on the number of female counselor positions was job-related and was a bona fide occupational qualification.

The equal opportunity laws do not require a company to actively recruit or maintain a designated quota of members of minority groups; however, they do prohibit companies from developing recruitment and selection procedures that treat an applicant differently because of race, sex, age, religion, or national origin. In determining whether a company's recruitment policies have resulted in disparate treatment of minorities, the courts and the EEOC will look objectively at the following:

- Nature of the position, and the education, training, and skill level required to fill it
- Minority composition of the current workforce and its relationship to local demographic statistics
- Prior hiring practices
- Recruitment channels (such as newspapers, agencies, industry publications, and universities)
- Information requested of the candidate in the job application and in the interview

- Any selection criteria or testing measure (or related performance measure) implemented in the decision-making process
- Any differences in the terms and conditions of employment offered to those who apply for the same job

Anyone alleging discrimination in the hiring process would need to demonstrate the following:

- That the applicant was a member of a minority class protected under federal law (such as an African-American)
- That the applicant was qualified for the job
- That the applicant was denied the job
- That the advertised position remained open after the applicant was rejected and that the company continued to interview applicants with the same qualifications as the rejected candidate

If these facts are successfully demonstrated by the applicant, then the burden usually shifts to the company, which must then present legitimate business reasons for not hiring the applicant.

Preventive Measures

There are several preventive measures you can implement to protect against discrimination claims. Ultimately, these measures will prevail when and if a disgruntled applicant files a discrimination charge.

First, a well-drafted job description that accurately reflects the duties of the position should be prepared before publicly advertising for the position. This should include the skills, ability, and knowledge needed to perform the job competently; compensation and related terms and conditions of employment; and the education, training, work experience, or professional certification (if any) that may be required. A well-prepared job description will not only help you determine the qualities you are looking for in an employee—and help you hire the right person—but will also serve as protection against a claim that the standards for the position were developed arbitrarily or in violation of applicable antidiscrimination laws.

Second, make sure that your advertising and recruitment program meets EEOC standards by insisting that all job advertisements include the phrase "Equal Opportunity Employer." The context of the advertisement should not indicate any preference for race, sex, religion, national origin, or age unless it meets the requirements of a BFOQ. If an employment agency is used, inform the agency in writing of the company's nondiscrimination policy. If applicants are recruited from universities or trade schools, be certain that minority institutions are also visited. When selecting publications for the placement of advertisements for the positions, target all potential job applicants and advertise in minority publications where possible.

Third, develop a job application form that is limited to job-related questions and meets all federal, state, and local legal requirements. There should be *no* questions in the application regarding an individual's race or religion. In court, the company will generally bear the burden of proving that any given question on the application—especially a question relating to handicap, marital status, age, height, weight, criminal record, military status, or citizenship—is genuinely related to the applicant's ability to meet the requirements of the position. Even questions regarding date of birth or whom to contact in the event of an emergency should be reserved for after an applicant has been hired.

Finally, an EEO compliance officer should be designated to monitor employment practices with the responsibility to: (1) structure position descriptions, job applications, and advertisements; (2) collect and maintain applicant and employee files; (3) meet with interviewers to review employment laws affecting what questions may be asked of an applicant; and (4) work with legal counsel to ensure that employment policies as well as recent developments in the law are adequately communicated to all employees.

The Interview

From a *legal* perspective, the questions asked in an interview must be substantially job-related and asked on a uniform basis to all candidates for the position. The exact types of questions that may be asked vary, depending on applicable state laws.

Therefore, state and local employment laws applying to the company should be consulted for further guidance. As a general rule, the following types of questions should be avoided:

- Do not ask: What is your marital status? How many children do you have? How do family responsibilities affect your ability to meet work-related obligations?

- Do not ask: What is your religious affiliation? What religious holidays do you expect will interfere with work-related obligations?

- Do not ask: What is your national origin? Where are your parents from? What is your native language?

- Do not ask: Do you have any specific disabilities? Have you ever been treated for any diseases?

- Do not ask: Does your spouse object to your traveling or to your anticipated relocation? Given the long hours of this job, will you be able to arrange for child care?

In addition, there are several topics that are not necessarily prohibited, but which nevertheless should be approached carefully to avoid an indirect claim of discrimination. These questions include an applicant's prior or current drug history, social clubs and hobbies, or career plans of an applicant's spouse.

Notwithstanding these stringent guidelines, several types of questions are still legally available for screening candidates. These include the following:

- Why are you leaving your current position? How does the position you are applying for resolve some of those problems or meet some of your unmet needs?

- What was the most challenging project that you were responsible for in your last position?

- Do you have any physical or mental impairments that would restrict your ability to fulfill the responsibilities of this position?

- Are there any criminal indictments currently pending against you? What is the nature of these charges?

- What are your expectations regarding this position? How do these expectations influence your short- and long-term career goals?

Drug Testing in the Workplace

Alcohol and drug abuse by employees is considered to be among the most common health hazards in the workplace. In addition to costing companies of all sizes millions of dollars in lost productivity, substance abuse by employees is perceived by employers as a threat to corporate security and an increased liability. Consequently, employers are fighting back by testing for substance abuse. While many of these testing programs have proved successful, private employers must be cautious of the potential legal problems involved in such testing.

Private-sector employees generally do not have a constitutional right protecting them from tests conducted by private employers as a condition of employment for applicants or a requirement for present employees. However, to withstand legal challenges, your policies should be carefully drawn and should be based on *legitimate business considerations,* accompanied by *reasonable safeguards,* and applied in a *nondiscriminatory fashion.*

Antidiscrimination Laws and Drug Testing

Abuse of, or addiction to, drugs or alcohol may be considered a protected handicap under federal or state law. Hence, when establishing a drug-testing program to detect substance abuse among applicants or employees, you must consider laws that prohibit discrimination against the handicapped.

The federal Rehabilitation Act includes recovered substance abusers within its definition of "handicapped." Although not directly applicable to private employers, the act applies to federal contractors and to some companies that provide goods or services to the federal government, or to a contractor with the federal government. The Rehabilitation Act will not protect

B O X   2 - 2

Drug Testing in the Workplace Checklist

1. *Initial Decision*
   Philosophy (disciplinary or rehabilitative). According to an extensive survey by the American Management Association, the most effective substance abuse policies combined four elements: (a) education of workers about the consequences of drug and alcohol abuse; (b) supervisor training; (c) drug testing; and (d) rehabilitation referrals.

2. *Notice*
   Any policy should be clearly stated in writing, should inform employees or applicants in advance of the penalties for violation of the rules, should outline the circumstances under which screening will be required, and should explain how the results will be used.

3. *Differentiation Between Alcohol and Drugs*
   If different philosophies or penalties will be applied to alcohol and drug abusers (e.g., alcoholics given opportunity for rehabilitation but drug abusers automatically fired), the policies relating to alcohol and drugs should be separate and a rationale for the difference should be stated (i.e., consumption of limited amounts of alcohol is not illegal).

4. *Description of Prohibited Conduct*
   At the very least, the policy should prohibit the following conduct: Use, possession, or sale of illicit drugs on company premises or company business or during work hours (prohibition can extend to lunch and break time). Unauthorized use or possession or sale of a controlled substance on company premises or company business or during work hours. Unauthorized use or possession or sale of alcohol on company premises or company business or during work hours.

5. *Testing*
   • Testing should be performed by a reputable, independent laboratory, using qualified and trained medical technicians or professionals.
   • The laboratory should be subject to periodic testing for accuracy.

6. *Procedure Before Testing*
   • Listing of all drugs taken in previous thirty days
   • Inquiry concerning possible drug or alcohol handicap
   • Public employees—Fifth Amendment concerns

(Box continued on next page)

7. *Opportunity to Explain*
   Employers should afford employees, and possibly applicants, some post-testing opportunity to explain or challenge "positive" test results.

8. *Employees Who Test Positive*
   - Referral to Employee Assistance Program. If an employee is given a chance at rehabilitation, the conditions of the rehabilitation should be explicitly stated in company policy; similarly, the conditions of post-rehabilitation should be expressly stated in company policy.
   - Discipline/Discharge:
     - For refusal to cooperate in testing
     - For positive testing

---

current alcohol or drug abusers whose problem either prevents them from performing the duties of their job or constitutes a threat to the safety or property of others. The federal Americans with Disabilities Act (ADA), which applies to private employers with 25 or more employees, also protects *recovered* substance abusers and alcoholics, since they are within its definition of "disabled."

In addition to federal legislation, many states have laws prohibiting employment discrimination by private-sector employers based on an individual's handicap. If you want to avoid running afoul of these laws, take the following steps:

- Relate any actions taken on account of results of a drug test to matters such as overall performance, violations of rules governing intoxication in the workplace, and the safety of the employee and other employees.
- Give individuals showing signs of alcohol or drug dependence an opportunity to seek and obtain rehabilitative treatment.
- When accommodating these "handicaps," do not distinguish between alcohol abusers and drug abusers.

It is important to note that these laws do not preclude employers from enforcing rules prohibiting the possession or use of alcohol or drugs in the workplace, provided that such rules are applied evenhandedly to all employees.

Defamation and Drug Testing

Employers must be careful to communicate information about employees only when it is accurate. If you publicly disclose to a third party untruths that are offensive and objectionable to a reasonable person of ordinary sensibilities, you may be liable for defamation. For example, an employer was held liable for damages for stating that an employee was terminated for drug use where the company's only evidence was a polygraph result indicating that the employee had lied when responding to a question concerning drug use.

Most states grant certain persons—such as personnel directors, supervisors, employees participating in an internal investigation, and unemployment compensation commissions—a qualified privilege to obtain information concerning employees' substance abuse. You can divulge such information to these people on a "need to know" basis as long as the information is not communicated with a malicious intent. This qualified privilege also applies when a prospective employer is checking references. The previous employer may supply information as long as it is completely accurate and not given for malicious purposes. It would be permissible to state that an employee tested positive on a drug test, but such an employee should not be described as an "addict." To avoid problems in this area, you may adopt a policy that, when responding to reference checks, the company will supply only the dates that former employees worked and the duties that they performed. Some companies have developed a limited waiver and release form (to release the employer against claims of defamation) if the former employee wants a more detailed reference.

Drug testing of applicants and current employees is increasing rapidly in private businesses. Consequently, private employers must be aware of the legal problems potentially involved when such tests are conducted. Given the complexity of the laws involved, private employers should closely monitor all judicial and legislative developments relating to drug testing as they pertain to employers' current policies and procedures.

ealing with HIV and AIDS in the Workplace

The human immunodeficiency virus (HIV), the virus that causes acquired immunodeficiency syndrome (AIDS), has led to great concern in the workplace in recent years. The majority of people infected with HIV and AIDS are between the ages of 20 and 45 and are employed, many by small and medium-size businesses. This raises questions regarding the measures an employer must take to accommodate these employees. Despite the ramifications of HIV/AIDS in the workplace, few companies have an established policy to guide their response to this issue.

Federal and State Legislation

At the federal level, two principal laws protect individuals with HIV/AIDS: the Rehabilitation Act and the Americans with Disabilities Act. When making decisions about hiring or promotion, you may not discriminate against an individual who is believed to be infected with HIV/AIDS. In a recent case, a New York State administrative agency found that the law firm of Baker & McKenzie (the world's largest law firm) discriminated against an associate attorney with AIDS when it terminated his employment, and the agency awarded the associate's estate $500,000 in compensatory damages. The award-winning film *Philadelphia* also dramatized the plight of an attorney, played by Tom Hanks, whose services were terminated once it was discovered that he was afflicted with AIDS.

The ADA also prohibits discrimination in places of public accommodation. This means that businesses such as restaurants and hotels may not deny goods or services to a person believed to be HIV- or AIDS-infected. Many states and local jurisdictions have passed laws similar to those on the federal level prohibiting discrimination against people with disabilities. A majority of these laws also include within the definition of "disabled" people who have tested positive for HIV/AIDS. For example, in Minnesota a dentist was found to have violated the state's Human Rights Act (similar to the ADA) for refusing to treat a patient who had tested positive for HIV.

HIV Testing As a Condition of Employment

Several states prohibit HIV/AIDS testing as a condition of employment, although others permit HIV/AIDS testing when the employer can show a legitimate reason. But merely suspecting that an employee is a homosexual or a drug user would not be a legitimate reason. To establish a legitimate reason, there must be some connection between HIV/AIDS and job performance or safety. This connection may exist when the job involves a risk of transmitting the disease. An employer who tests for HIV/AIDS without a legitimate reason may be liable for a claim of invasion of privacy.

Rights of Coworkers

Certain federal laws allow employees to discontinue working when they have a reasonable belief that their working conditions are unsafe. However, given the consensus in the medical profession that HIV/AIDS cannot be transmitted through casual contact, it would be difficult for an employee to refuse to work with an HIV/AIDS-infected coworker on such grounds. The reasonableness of the employee's demand may depend on how the employer has educated employees about HIV/AIDS. If the employees have been taught that HIV/AIDS cannot be transmitted through casual contact, their refusal to work may be found to be "unreasonable," and they could be discharged.

Accommodations for HIV/AIDS Employees

An issue has arisen with respect to whether an employer must make reasonable accommodations for an HIV/AIDS-infected employee. Federal legislation not only prohibits discrimination against handicapped persons but also requires employers to make reasonable efforts to accommodate handicapped applicants and employees where obstacles exist that would restrict their employment opportunities.

In addition, if your company is covered by the Rehabilitation Act and an employee has HIV/AIDS or develops it, you must make reasonable accommodations that permit the employee to continue working. Such accommodations can include leave policies, flexible work schedules, reassignment to vacant positions, and part-time employment. The criteria used to determine whether an employer is making reasonable accommodations for an HIV/AIDS-infected employee include the cost of the accommodations, the size of the business, and the nature of the employee's work.

Guidelines to Consider

Through advance education and preparation, an employer can avoid many of the problems associated with an employee infected with HIV. In 1987, the U.S. Surgeon General suggested that, when dealing with HIV issues, employers should do the following:

- Adopt an up-to-date HIV/AIDS education program that discusses how HIV is transmitted and explains the company's policies regarding employees with HIV/AIDS.

- Treat HIV/AIDS-infected employees in the same manner as other employees suffering from disabilities or illnesses are treated under company health plans and policies.

- Allow HIV/AIDS-infected employees to continue working as long as they are able to perform their jobs satisfactorily and their continued employment does not pose a threat to their own safety or that of other employees or customers.

- Make reasonable efforts to accommodate HIV/AIDS-infected employees by providing them with flexible work hours and assignments.

- Protect all information regarding an HIV/AIDS-infected employee's condition.

An employer must consider a broad range of legal issues when formulating practices and responses regarding HIV/AIDS. By educating your employees, you may be able to reduce work disruption, legal implications, financial implications, and other effects that HIV/AIDS can have on your business. Because of the complexity and changing nature of HIV/AIDS, an employer should always examine the applicable laws and consult an attorney when handling HIV/AIDS issues in the workplace.

Sexual Harassment in the Workplace

The problem of sexual harassment in the workplace has recently been brought to the forefront of national attention. According to a survey conducted by *Training* magazine, sexual harassment is the fastest-growing topic in workplace instruction and is now being offered by 70% of the companies polled. A wide range of sexual harassment claims against large and small companies has highlighted the importance of dealing carefully with this issue in developing personnel policies. Sexual harassment lawsuits are growing in number across the country; 15,549 sexual harassment complaints were filed with the EEOC in 1995, up from 6,100 in 1990. The Supreme Court, in *Meritor Savings Bank*, held that sexual harassment is a form of sex discrimination prohibited under Title VII of the Civil Rights Act of 1964. Other cases have held that both men and women may be victims and that both sexes have legal recourse under the statute.

The EEOC defines sexual harassment as any one of the following:

1. Unwelcome sexual advances, requests for sexual favors and other verbal or physical conduct of a sexual nature where, either explicitly or implicitly, submission to such conduct is considered a term or condition of an individual's continued employment.
2. Making submission to or rejection of such conduct the basis for employment decisions affecting the employee.
3. Existing where such conduct has the effect of unreasonably interfering with an individual's work performance, or creates an intimidating, hostile, or offensive work environment.

Points 1 and 2 are known as "quid pro quo" sexual harassment, meaning that sexual favors are requested in return for job benefits or retention of a job. Point 3 covers what is known as "hostile environment" harassment.

It is important to note that sexual harassment need not be overtly sexual in nature. Sexual harassment can encompass derogatory comments and abuse of someone's personal property. Furthermore, the victim need not be the person at whom the unwelcome sexual conduct is directed. If a person's work environment is adversely affected by sexual harassment toward a coworker, then sexual harassment is present. Some recent cases have expanded the definition of sexual harassment by holding employers liable for the actions of nonemployees when the employer knew of the harassment and failed to take any corrective measures to remedy the situation. In one case, a jury rendered a $7.1 million verdict against a major law firm (although the trial judge later reduced the award to $3.5 million). In this case, the jury found that a former partner of the law firm had been guilty of sexually harassing a newly hired paralegal and that the firm had taken insufficient steps to rectify the problem and prevent its recurrence, in spite of the fact that it had been put on notice concerning this attorney's inappropriate conduct.

Sexual harassment is actionable when it is sufficiently severe or pervasive to alter the conditions of the victim's employment or create an abusive working environment. Thus, a request for a date or a single sexual remark may not be sufficient to establish a claim of sexual harassment if the behavior is not repeated. A single remark or action that is particularly offensive may, however, be considered severe enough to constitute sexual harassment. To determine if a claim is valid, the court will first ask whether a reasonable person would find the conduct to have been sufficiently severe or pervasive to alter the claimant's work environment. Second, the court will examine the conduct in light of the totality of the circumstances. Thus, an insulting comment made by a coworker during the course of an argument would be viewed differently from the same comment made by a superior in a nonconfrontational situation.

Employers have a duty to provide a workplace free from sexual harassment and to protect employees from unwanted, unwelcome sexual overtures and invitations of a sexual nature whether such conduct originates with managers, fellow employees, or outsiders such as customers. In order to meet their responsibilities and to protect themselves against sexual harassment claims, employers should take the following defensive measures:

B O X   2 - 3

Examples of Sexual Harassment

Verbal

- Calling a person a hunk, doll, babe, or honey
- Turning work discussions to sexual topics
- Asking personal questions about social or sexual life
- Asking about sexual fantasies, preferences, or history
- Making sexual comments about a person's clothing, body, or looks
- Making kissing sounds, howling, smacking lips, whistling, or cat calls
- Telling lies or spreading rumors about a person's sex life
- Sexual comments or innuendos
- Repeatedly asking for a date from a person who is not interested

Nonverbal

- Staring at someone
- Blocking a person's path
- Restricting or hindering the other person's movements
- Looking a person up and down
- Sexual and/or derogatory comments about men or women on coffee mugs, hats, cartoons, posters, calendars, clothing, etc.
- Making facial expressions such as winking, throwing kisses, or licking lips
- Making sexual gestures with hands and/or body movements
- Letters, gifts, and/or materials of sexual nature
- Invading a person's body space; standing closer than appropriate or necessary for the work being done

Physical

- Massaging a person's neck, shoulders, etc.
- Touching a person's clothing, hair, or body
- Hugging, kissing, patting, or stroking
- Touching or rubbing oneself sexually around or in the view of another person

(Box continued on next page)

- Brushing up against a person
- Patting, goosing, caressing, or fondling
- Tearing/pulling/yanking a person's clothing
- Exposing oneself

- Maintain and enforce a written policy against sexual harassment.

- Educate all employees on the company's sexual harassment policy and be sure that they are aware of the consequences of violating the policy.

- Maintain a complaint procedure that allows the victim to file a complaint with a person other than his or her supervisor.

- Investigate all complaints thoroughly and confidentially.

- Take appropriate action following each and every investigation.

To avoid liability for a claim, the employer *must* take prompt and effective action that is reasonably calculated to end the harassment. When deciding a case, the court will analyze the investigation made by the employer and the effectiveness of the remedial action taken. Unfortunately, the court's determination of the effectiveness of your response is often based on whether the remedial action ultimately succeeded in eliminating the harassment. To survive this type of hindsight analysis, the employer should conduct a prompt investigation of all sexual harassment complaints. The investigation should be conducted by an officer outside of the department concerned and should commence within a week after the complaint is received. The investigator should then follow these guidelines:

- Carefully document when and how the claim first came to the attention of the company.

- Gather data to determine all relevant facts concerning the conduct in question.

- Treat all claims as valid until proved otherwise.

- Keep all discussions and information as confidential as possible.

- Involve legal counsel as early as possible in the fact-gathering process, to protect against claims of disparagement or defamation.

Once the investigation is complete, you must then take appropriate steps to remedy the situation. If the claim is substantiated, you must determine what discipline is appropriate. When the harassment occurred over an extended period of time or was severe, or if the harasser had been disciplined previously for such conduct, then terminating the harasser may be appropriate. However, if the conduct was less severe and other means may remedy the situation—such as transferring the harasser to a different department—you should probably wait until a second offense before terminating the employee. This puts you in a better position to defend your action if the discharged employee subsequently sues you for wrongful discharge. If the employee is not transferred, you should monitor the situation to make sure the harassment does not recur.

The laws pertaining to sexual harassment are still evolving and can be difficult for any business owner to grasp. Recent cases and guidelines do not draw clear distinctions between permissible behavior and illegal behavior that may subject your company to legal liability. The standards of behavior will vary depending on the specific facts of each case and the perceptions of the employee who was subjected to the alleged harassment. The key to protecting your business against liability is to develop a stated policy regarding the type of conduct that will not be tolerated, and to maintain standard grievance procedures. All complaints should be dealt with promptly and seriously; and if harassment has occurred, remedial action must be taken.

Guidelines for Hassle-Free Firing of Employees

The decision to terminate an employee can be both emotional and frustrating, and it can also result in expensive litigation if it is not handled properly. These days, a wrongful termination lawsuit is not an idle threat. According to a recent study conducted by Jury Verdict Research, recently fired executives who bring such suits are winning often and winning big. In a review of 1,700 verdicts rendered between 1988 and 1995, it was found that plaintiffs who were former executives won wrongful termination suits 64% of the time, as compared with only 42% for general laborers. Executives are winning in court, legal experts say, because they often have strong communication skills and can afford better legal representation.

When an employee wins a lawsuit for unfair termination, the remedies have ranged from simple reinstatement to back pay to actual damages, even to punitive damages for certain cases. Employers have also faced charges of discrimination or violation of federal statutes in connection with the termination of an employee. In order to successfully defend against these types of claims, you must be prepared to demonstrate that employee performance evaluations, policies contained in personnel manuals, and grounds for termination were implemented and enforced in a nondiscriminatory fashion and not as a result of any act contrary to applicable federal law. Specific, clear, and uniform guidelines should be developed for probation periods, opportunities to improve job performance, availability of training, and termination procedures.

Five steps for preventing lawsuits can be taken before, during, and after the termination of an employee:

Step 1

The first step (well before the actual termination) is careful record keeping. Comprehensive records should be kept on each employee, including any formal performance appraisal and any informal warnings, comments, or memos prepared by a supervisor to demonstrate the employee's poor work or misconduct. If a case ever gets to litigation, these documents and records may be the only evidence available to support the employer's claim that there were valid reasons for terminating the employee.

Step 2

The second step prior to termination is to ensure that you have a proper basis for termination. This involves a careful review of personnel manuals, policy statements, memoranda, and related documentation to ensure that no implied representation or agreement has been made regarding the term of employment, severance pay, or grounds for termination that may be inconsistent with the company's intentions. The various grounds for termination should be clearly stated in the personnel manual. These grounds should include, among other things: (1) discriminatory acts toward employees or applicants; (2) physical or sexual abuse; (3) falsifying time records or other key documents; (4) willful or negligent violation of safety or security rules; (5) violation of company policies; (6) unauthorized disclosure of the company's confidential information; (7) refusal to perform work assigned by a supervisor; (8) destroying or damaging company property; (9) misappropriation or embezzlement; or (10) substance abuse or gambling on company premises.

Step 3

The third step is to ensure that all alternatives to termination have been considered. An employee who has been performing poorly should be provided with plenty of advance notice of management's disappointment with his or her performance through personal and written evaluations, warning notices, and published employment policies. Where the cause for termination involves an act of insubordination, improper conduct, or related incidents, statements by witnesses, accident reports, customers' complaints, and related documentation should all be collected and reviewed. Even when a decision to terminate has been made by the immediate supervisor and the evidence supporting the cause has been collected, there should be an independent review of the proposed dismissal by a member of management at least one level above the direct supervisor of the employee. An opportunity to cure the defect in performance should be strongly considered. Before making the final decision, the reviewer should take the time to confront the employee and hear his or her side of the story. Written records of these meetings should be placed in the employee's file. The reviewer should question the supervisor and coworkers of the employee to gather additional facts and to ensure that all company policies and procedures have been followed, especially those regarding performance appraisal and discipline.

Step 4

Once the decision to terminate has been reached, the fourth step is to conduct an exit interview. During the exit interview, it is important to explain the reasons for the employee's discharge. The explanation should be candid and concise, in accordance with all available evidence, and consistent with any other explanation of the termination that will be provided to the employee. You should emphasize to the employee that the reasons for termination are legitimate and consistent with the company's past practices under similar circumstances. The employee should also be advised what will be told to prospective employers and reminded of any covenants not to compete and of his or her continuing obligation to protect the company's trade secrets.

Step 5

The fifth and final step is to prepare a comprehensive release and termination to further protect the company against subsequent litigation. The employee should be given an opportunity to have it reviewed by legal counsel. The release and termination agreement should: (1) be supported by valid consideration (e.g., some form of severance pay or covenants); (2) be signed by the employee knowingly and voluntarily; (3) include the grounds for termination in the recitals; (4) contain covenants against competition, disclosure, and litigation; (5) include all possible defendants in an employment action (company, officers, directors, subsidiaries, etc.); (6) avoid commitments regarding references to future employers; and (7) be checked carefully against all applicable federal and state laws.

The broad scope of federal and state antidiscrimination laws makes it imperative for owners (and their managers) to understand their obligations in structuring recruitment, selection, training, compensation, rewards, drug testing, and seniority programs. Charges of discrimination may be defeated if proper documentation is maintained, such as a complete personnel file of the former employee, detailed records of complaints of supervisors and coworkers related to the cause of termination, copies of actual work produced by the employee that was unsatisfactory, a written record reflecting the race and sex of other persons dismissed or disciplined for the same or similar purposes, and the name, race, and sex of the individual replacing the discharged employee.

Employees are clearly one of the most valuable assets of an emerging growth company. If they are treated unfairly in the hiring or termination process, however, they can become the largest liability. Employment agreements and personnel manuals are useful tools for defining the mutual rights and obligations of employer and employee. Owners (and their managers) are well advised to carefully structure personnel policies within the bounds of applicable labor and employment laws.

CHAPTER 3

Contracts and Agreements:
Getting It in Writing and
Getting It Right

Each year, businesses of all sizes, all across the country, enter into hundreds of thousands of written contracts. Millions of others have a "handshake"—a tacit, unwritten understanding of how business will be conducted among the parties. Yet most business owners (and their managers) do not understand the basics of contract law or the true role of contracts and agreements in the overall growth and planning of a business. Contracts come in all shapes and sizes, from employment agreements (as discussed in Chapter 2) to shareholder agreements (as discussed in Chapter 1) from distribution agreements to licensing agreements (as discussed in Chapter 9). The present chapter will not look at any particular type of agreement; rather, it will focus on the *process* of preparing a contract. It will also dispel some commonly held myths about contracts. In this chapter we will discuss:

- Basics of contract law
- Advantages and disadvantages of letters of intent and memorandums of understanding
- How to draft precise agreements
- Whether the term "oral contract" is an oxymoron (here we will dispel a myth)
- What to do in the event of a breach of contract

53

The most important rule to remember is that contracts are living, breathing, and evolving documents, which must be reviewed and even amended from time to time—not left on a shelf to collect dust. There are many different styles of drafting a contract. Some contracts are in traditional "legalese" and some focus on "plain English." Some try to anticipate every future event and contingency (this is the American style), and some tend to be shorter and more vague, recognizing that the parties will need to refine and supplement the document as facts and circumstances evolve (this style is more European). Contracts range from simple two-party agreements to very complex multiparty agreements. There are agreements to begin a relationship, change a relationship, or even end a relationship.

Basics of Contract Law 101

This section will highlight certain basics of contract law that you will find most helpful to your growing business. Your goal here is not to replace your business lawyer but rather to gain a better understanding of contracts and to be more prepared before a meeting with legal counsel. This improved understanding and preparedness will usually translate into direct savings of time and money.

What is a contract, and what is not? Most courts define a contract as a promise or a set of promises for the breach of which the law gives a remedy, *or* for the performance of which the law in some way recognizes a duty. There are several different types of contracts, differing primarily in the manner in which they are formed. These include the following:

- *Express contracts* are formed by *language* (either oral or written). Contrary to common belief, there *can* be an oral contract if all of the other tests for the creation of a contract are met (as discussed below).

- *Implied contracts* are formed by manifestations of assent (other than on the basis of written or oral language), such as one's *conduct*.

- *Court-imposed or quasi-contracts* are usually formed as a result of a *judicial act,* typically to prevent an unjust party from benefiting at the expense of an injured party. The court usually decides to award to the injured party the amount that was breached.

How do you know if you have entered into a binding contract? Here, the courts will look for three key elements to determine whether an enforceable contract has been formed between the parties:

1. Was there a "meeting of the minds" (mutual assent) as to the offer and the acceptance?
2. Was consideration (something of value) exchanged as a basis for the contract?
3. Are there any valid defenses to the creation of the contract?

With regard to the first element, mutual assent, the courts look for evidence that each party agreed to the same terms at the same time and intended to be bound by all objective standards. The offer creates the power of acceptance in the offeree and is based on a reasonable expectation that there will be a corresponding liability on the part of the offerer to be bound. To arrive at this conclusion of a valid and binding offer and acceptance, the courts will look for the existence of a mutual promise or commitment, certainty and precision on the essential terms, and confirmation of the communication of these terms among the parties. Among the other factors that a court may consider are the surrounding circumstances, prior practice, the relationship of the parties, industry custom, the method of communication, and the definiteness of the subject matter. The courts may consider special industry practices or special requirements for certain types of contracts, such as real estate, manufacturing "output" contracts, and employment contracts.

As a general rule, when working with counsel to prepare any type of contract, be certain that all essential terms are certain and definite. The court will not uphold a contract in which the key terms are vague. The essential elements include: (1) the parties; (2) the subject matter of the agreement; (3) the price and time of payment, delivery, and performance and the

B O X 3 - I

Common Myths About Contracts

MYTH I A good lawyer already has all of this stuff on computer, so a contract shouldn't cost so much.

REALITY Lawyers cannot merely "push a button" and get the right document. Naturally, an experienced business lawyer will not need to start from scratch with each contract, but he or she does make sure that the contract is appropriate for the proposed transaction or situation and adequately reflects the intent of the parties. To the extent that lawyers do use "forms," they are acceptable as a starting point, not as a "crutch."

MYTH 2 The best agreements are short and simple.

REALITY While I do not support an attorney's attempt to prove his or her worth by inserting the maximum number of "heretofores" and other impressive-sounding multi-syllabic words, some transactions genuinely do justify a larger and more complex document. Still, a contract should use a sufficient number of "defined terms" to ensure precision and then should be no larger or no more complex than it needs to be. If your business lawyer refuses to be guided by simplicity and clarity in drafting contracts, consider hiring another lawyer.

MYTH 3 "Oral contract" is an oxymoron.

REALITY As I will explain later in this chapter, a contract *can* be valid and binding even if it is not in writing, as long as all of the other elements of an enforceable contract are present.

MYTH 4 A letter of agreement is nonbinding.

REALITY Letters of agreement (those that are generally intended to be eventually superseded or supplemented with more definitive and detailed documents) may be drafted as either binding or nonbinding. In fact, some letters of agreement are structured with a binding section and a

(Box continued on next page)

nonbinding section. However, if it is clearly the intent that all or part of a preliminary agreement or letter of agreement will have no legally binding effect, then that intent should be clearly stated.

MYTH 5 **There's no harm in a handshake deal—we don't need to get the lawyers involved.**

REALITY Although the informality of certain circumstances or industry custom or even your own nature or personality may preempt a formal contract, the risks of relying on a mere "pressing of the flesh" may be significant. Generally, such an act leaves too much room for interpretation as to whether a legally enforceable agreement has been made. Just ask Texaco, which was held to an award of $10.6 billion in damages for allegedly interfering with a "handshake agreement" between Pennzoil and Getty Oil Company in the mid-1980s.

MYTH 6 **It's probably cheaper if the other side provides the first draft of the contract.**

REALITY The party who produces the first draft will have some minor strategic advantage in contract negotiations. The first draft generally sets the parameters of the agreement and establishes the tone of the negotiations.

---

nature of the work to be performed; and (4) where applicable, the quantity involved. In many cases, especially in contractual transactions by and among businesses and merchants for the sale of goods, the Uniform Commercial Code (UCC) may govern the interpretation of these issues. A detailed discussion of the UCC is beyond the scope of this chapter, but it should be carefully reviewed and understood by any high-volume transactional business.

The second element of a contract, the legal concept of "consideration," is often misunderstood by entrepreneurs in businesses of all sizes. Usually, to find the existence of valid consideration, the courts require two basic elements: that there was a negotiated exchange of items of value, and that whatever is bargained for is of legal value (not token or illegal). This exchange of valuable consideration is the "triggering event" that makes the contract enforceable.

The most widely recognized substitute for consideration is a legal concept known as "promissory estoppel"; this is used where the facts support enforcement of a promise in order to avoid an unjust result, even if the consideration is not mutual. This situation arises when a promise is made that the "promiser" should reasonably expect will induce action or forbearance by the promisee, which is often referred to as "detrimental reliance." An easily understood example of this concept would occur if Mr. Deep Pockets pledges $1 million to a local charity and the charity undertakes a series of acts and incurs expenses that Deep Pockets had reason to know would happen as a result of reliance on his pledge. If Deep Pockets then reneges on his promise, the charity may recover the $1 million.

Finally, the third element of a contract is that the courts must find that no defenses are available to either side that might prevent the creation of a valid contract. Most defenses fall into one of the following categories:

- *Defense to formation.* These defenses argue that the contract was never actually formed, either because there was no "meeting of minds" (such as mutual mistake, misunderstanding, misrepresentation, or fraud) or because there was no valid consideration. There may also be certain "public policy" defenses to the formation of the contract (such as contracts to undertake an illegal act).

- *Defect in capacity.* These defenses argue that one or more of the parties was legally ineligible to enter into a binding contract; either because of the age of the parties (typically, a party to a contract must be at least 18) or because of mental incapacity. Courts have also considered a party who is not acting voluntarily (one under duress or the subject of a fraud in the inducement) to be acting without capacity.

- *Defense to enforcement of certain terms.* These defenses apply to a specific term or aspect of the agreement that is sufficiently vague and sufficiently material to support a determination that no contract was formed. The courts may choose to refuse to enforce a particular provision or the entire contract, depending on the extent of the vagueness or unfairness of the terms in question.

Elements of Most Business Contracts

Throughout this book there are many references and drafting "checklists" for different types of business contracts. Regardless of the specific type of contract, certain key elements or "building blocks" apply to drafting virtually all business agreements. At first glance, some of these key elements seem fairly obvious, and some may seem to be issues that only your lawyer should worry about. But you do need to make many business decisions and gather certain information—and prepare, organize, and deliver it to legal counsel before the preparation and negotiations—to help ensure that the final contract is comprehensive and enforceable. The key elements include:

- *Parties.* If the essence of an agreement is "offer and acceptance" between the parties, then defining exactly *who* will be the participants to the relationship becomes critical. The agreement should clearly and correctly state each legal entity that will be a party to the agreement. When dealing with businesses, carefully consider a company's structure and its trade name versus its exact corporate name. Remember that you cannot enter into a contract with a nonlegal entity such as a trademark or an unincorporated subsidiary, so the exact corporate name should always be used in the agreement. When dealing with people, consider an individual's capacity and marital status.

- *Recitals.* Although not usually considered part of the "body" of the contract, the recitals (those dreaded "whereas" clauses), if drafted properly, tell the story that sets the stage for the more definitive contract. For example, in a technology licensing agreement, the recitals might explain the underlying technology and its benefits, explain why the licenser and licensee feel that working together will be productive (or even how they met one another), and describe each party's goals and objectives in entering into the agreement.

- *Subject matter.* This section goes to the core of the agreement: "Why are we doing this deal?" It defines the underlying asset (e.g., goods, services, parcel of land, technology) that is being sold, leased, or licensed between the parties. This section must be drafted with precision so that no party is unclear as to the scope of the agreement.

- *Form of payment.* In order to be enforceable (as we have seen) a contract must clearly state the "legal consideration." The amount of the initial fee, cost, or price; the amount of the ongoing fee, cost, or price; the method of payment; the type of consideration; the allocation (if multiple assets are involved); special tax issues; the timing of the payment; and any special formulae for payment—all these must be addressed in this section.

- *Representation and warranties.* These are a series of promises or statements that generally are used to refer to a past or present fact or circumstance affecting the terms of the agreement. These should be affirmative or negative, should generally refer to a party's promise to act (or not to act) in the future, and should be distinguished from the "covenants." A sample representation (and a critical one) in the sale or license of a tangible or intangible asset is that the seller or licenser actually has the ownership (or legal right) to sell or license the underlying asset that is the subject matter of the agreement.

- *Conditions.* Any specific conditions (either before or after the execution of the contract) should be clearly stated in the agreement. Each party should clearly understand any affirmative acts that must be performed before expecting the other side to perform. For example, if the buyer is not obligated to make payment until you, as the seller, have satisfied a series of performance conditions, don't expect a check until you've performed.

- *Ongoing obligations of the parties.* Some contracts have a limited "life" in that the subject matter of the contract is over relatively quickly. Other agreements—such as leases, licenses, and franchise agreements—anticipate a long-term relationship whereby each party has a set of clearly defined ongoing obligations.

- *Allocation of risk.* In some cases, the parties may attempt to contractually allocate responsibility for future risk, losses, or damages through sections that address indemnification, insurance, waivers, limitation of otherwise applicable warranties, disclaimers, limitations on liability, or even liquidated damages. These limitations and allocations are beyond the scope of this chapter but should be carefully discussed with legal counsel.

- *Default and termination.* The parties should anticipate which specific acts will be considered a default, reasonable procedures for notice, the appropriate time to cure the default, and the consequences and procedures of a failure to cure the default.

- *Term and conditions for renewal.* This section usually deals with the *time* that the contract begins, its length, and the procedures for renewal (if any). In some cases there may be conditions for renewal, such as the achievement of ongoing performance standards or a maximum number of defaults during the initial (or applicable) term of the agreement.

Strategies for Dealing with a Breach of Contract

Armed with the knowledge of what constitutes a valid contract, together with the guidelines for drafting and interpretation, you should now feel comfortable with the basics of preparation and negotiation of a contract. After a valid contract has been formed, however, it takes on a life of its own. Each party's performance should be carefully monitored, and the provisions dealing with default and termination should be followed in the event of a breach. Although an attorney should be consulted in the event of a breach of contract, it is helpful to know the basics of what constitutes a breach as well as understand whether there were any facts or circumstances that may have created a "discharge" of one party's duties or obligations.

What Is a Breach?

There are two key questions to consider before declaring a party to be in breach of contract. First, *"Has a present duty to perform arisen?"*—for example, has your obligation to perform matured? Second, *"Were there any facts or circumstances that may have discharged the duty to perform?"*—that is, are there any mitigating circumstances that may have created a waiver?

B O X   3 - 2

Tips to Consider When Preparing Contracts

It is critical to understand certain basic rules of interpretation and enforcement that most courts will follow when confronted with a contractual dispute. These rules should serve as guidelines in preparing and negotiating contracts.

- Contracts will be interpreted as a "whole"—specific clauses will be subordinated to the contract's overall intent. Therefore, do not rely on any "key section" to be enforced if it is inconsistent with the spirit and intent of the general agreement.

- Industry custom, usage, norms, and other trade practices will often be considered to the extent that they assist the court in understanding or interpreting the agreement. Therefore, if your industry has certain customs inconsistent with the terms of your agreement, be prepared to see those customs applied in the event of a dispute *or* state specifically that the parties have considered these customs and mutually rejected them.

- Understand the impact of the "parol evidence rule" on contract negotiation and drafting. The courts will be inclined to reject testimony offered by either party that contradicts or alters the contract's written terms. Where the parties have an "integration clause" clearly stating that they intend this document to be the full and final expression of their agreement, the courts will usually honor such a provision.

- Remember that courts prefer clear, simple agreements. Words will be construed to be within their common, everyday meaning unless the parties state otherwise, and the courts will generally interpret any vagueness or inconsistency *against* the party that prepared the contract.

- Do not disregard the boilerplate. Many entrepreneurs disregard those provisions, which they view as standard, dry, and boring. They assume that these clauses are for the lawyers to worry about and tend to focus only on the key economic or business terms. This can be a fatal mistake. Key decisions are often made in the "miscellaneous" section at the end of a business agreement, which should be just as thoroughly negotiated as the key business points. These issues

(Box continued on next page)

include methods for resolving disputes (see Chapter 5 for a more detailed discussion of alternative methods), the designation of the law to govern the interpretation of the contract, and how and when notices under the contract must be provided.

• When preparing and negotiating contracts, remember that many courts have interpreted or superimposed a "general implied covenant of good faith and fair dealing." In lay terms, this means that key facts or circumstances must be disclosed (to avoid a subsequent claim of fraud or misrepresentation in the inducement), and although the parties to a contract negotiation are free to cease the process at their discretion, be aware of the fact that this implied duty of conduct could subsequently be applied to the parties' failure to enter into (or renew) a contractual relationship. Do not be afraid, however, to always try to negotiate the best deal possible. The courts have acknowledged that "in a business transaction, both sides presumably try to get the best of the deal. That is the essence of bargaining and the free market . . . So one cannot characterize self-interest as bad faith" *(Indiana Hi-Rail Corp v. CSX Transport,* 818 F.Supp. 1254, S.D. Ind. 1993).

To answer the first question, the nondefaulting party must be certain that there were no express or implied conditions to the allegedly defaulting party's duty to perform. These external conditions may have (sometimes legitimately and sometimes not) led the other party to believe that his or her duty to perform had not yet come to fruition. These conditions or precursors to the obligation to perform may be express, implied, or constructive (read into the contract). The courts will also consider whether there are acts, facts, or circumstances that may have led a party to believe that the conditions had been waived or excused.

Once it has been determined that the duty to perform has in fact come to fruition, the courts will consider the second key question, whether the duty to perform may have somehow been discharged. A wide variety of circumstances may lead a court to determine that the duty to perform has been discharged, such as impossibility, incapability, illegality, death, physical incapacity, release, novation, cancellation, a substituted contract, a lapse, or by operation of law. Before acting too hastily to enforce a breach of contract, discuss the facts and circumstances with a business attorney to ensure that the duty to perform has in fact matured, that there is no evidence to support that the duty has been discharged, and that the breach is material.

Remedies in the Event of a Valid Breach

Once it has been determined that a valid and material breach has occurred, it is time to shift the analysis to the remedies available and the extent of the damages suffered. Remedies generally take two primary forms: (1) *equitable remedies* seek a specific action or forbid an action; (2) *legal remedies* seek a wide range of types of money damages. These two types of remedies are not mutually exclusive. The breach in question may give rise to both an award of money damages and an order of the court for the defaulting party to take a specific action or forbear from a given pattern of activity.

There are many types of money damages that generally seek to put the nonbreaching party where it would have been if the promise to perform had been kept. These are generally referred to as "compensatory" damages or "expectation" damages—that is, sufficient damages to substitute for the actual performance of the given contract. These are in contrast to "reliance damages," which award to the injured party the cost of *its* performance, in an attempt to restore the injured party to the position that would have existed if the contract had never been formed. "Consequential" damages are the third common type. They award to the injured party a reasonable forecast of future damages as a result of the breach. Less commonly awarded damages include "punitive" (to set an example), "liquidated" (pre-agreed by the parties in a contract), and "nominal" (where the breach is established but the extent of the damage is unclear). Remember that the nonbreaching party is generally under an obligation to mitigate or minimize its damages. An attempt to make matters even worse after notice of the breach will not be viewed favorably by the courts.

"Equitable" remedies are usually some type of order by the court to the defaulting party to take a specific act or forbear from an act as a result of the breach of the agreement. This is usually the case where mere money damages are viewed by the court as inadequate, as when the subject matter of the contract may be rare or unique. This kind of remedy, generally referred to as "specific performance," will not be applied to an obligation to perform under a services contract (courts tend to disfavor involuntary servitude!) and may be subject to other technical restrictions and equitable defenses. In general, before there will be an award of any type of damages, courts want to be reasonably certain of the nature and extent of the harm. A court will generally not award damages that are speculative in nature. Before bringing an action, regardless of the type of action, as discussed in Chapter 11, make sure that you have met with legal counsel and gathered sufficient evidence to meet your "burden of proof" and to demonstrate damages with clarity and precision. You should also carefully consider the many alternatives to formal litigation.

Defending Against a Claim of a Breach

If you find yourself on the "wrong end" of a breach of contract claim—that is, if you are the defendant—begin gathering a working file. Meet with defense counsel to discuss the following:

1. Was there clearly an offer, and was it acceptable?

2. Was there valid consideration?

3. Are any common contractual defenses available?

4. Are any pre-agreed (liquidated) damages applicable?

5. Were your duties to perform in any way excused, modified, or discharged?

6. Did the plaintiff immediately mitigate its damages?

7. Are there any counterclaims available for countersuing the plaintiff?

8. Are there any other, third parties that should be brought into the proceedings?

9. Has the plaintiff stated its damages clearly, or could the alleged damages be attacked as being nominal or speculative?

10. Are any UCC provisions or requirements applicable, or were any not followed?

11. Are there any other public policy reasons, facts, or circumstances—or reason having to do with industry custom—why this contract should not be enforced?

12. Were there any "conditions precedent" or "conditions subsequent" that have not been met by the plaintiff?

It has been said that a dog is man's best friend and that diamonds are a girl's best friend. I believe that clearly drafted business agreements can be an entrepreneur's best friend. They help define the foundation for the growth of the business by describing the company's obligations, expectations, risks, remedies; and in many cases they form the lion's share of the company's intangible assets on its balance sheet. The more enforceable the agreements, the greater the net worth of the company.

Managing Relationships with Professional Advisers

As your company grows and changes, there will be issues and problems for which you will want to seek outside advice and expertise in areas such as legal compliance, strategic planning, and capital formation. The needs of the company and the sophistication of the advisers will also change as new stages of growth are achieved. It is critical to periodically reevaluate the quality and effectiveness of these relationships to ensure that you are getting the attention and the expertise you deserve. Your management team will include an external team of professional advisers who are hired to assist with (1) the organization in the development stage; (2) implementation and monitoring of key goals and objectives; and (3) risk management. These advisers include attorneys, accountants, and consultants in a variety of business disciplines (such as marketing, sales, finance, administrative management, strategic planning, office automation, manufacturing, production, advertising, operations, and personnel). In all cases, these relationships must be *managed* in order to ensure cost-efficiency, to ensure compatibility among team members, and to ensure that tasks and problems are assigned to an adviser with the appropriate background and expertise.

Despite the fact that every business relies on key advisers to foster development and expansion, there remains a lot of mystery, confusion, and disenchantment among entrepreneurs and their advisers. Providers of professional services are constantly complaining about small-business clients who never pay their bills, never listen to their advice, and always wait until the last minute to discuss a task or problem. On the other hand, entrepreneurs have countless horror stories about advisers' inferior work, high fees, slow responses, lack of expertise, misunderstanding of the company's products and markets, insensitivity to business objectives, and lax attitude toward conflicts of interest.

Somewhere in all of the finger-pointing is the utopian entrepreneur-adviser relationship, toward which the owner or manager of a growing business must strive. The first step in understanding and improving relationships with outside advisers is to comprehend *why* the adviser is needed in the first place.

Identifying the Need for Professional Advisers

As a general rule, providers of professional services and business consultants are hired to fill a particular need of the company, such as:

- Expert advice in a particular field of knowledge
- A readily available pool of human resources when you can't (or prefer not to) hire full-time employees
- Identification and solution of specific problems or barriers to growth
- Stimulation or implementation of new ideas, technology, growth strategies, or business development programs
- A sounding board (or even a shoulder to cry on)
- Access to contacts and resources (the Rolodex lease)
- Insights on the successes and failures of other companies similarly situated
- The threat of potential litigation

- An excessive amount of governmental regulation of your industry

- Preparing to enter into new domestic or international markets

For example, many of my clients initially want to discuss the advantages and disadvantages of various growth strategies or how to raise additional capital. Others have a specific problem that must be solved, such as the need to protect their intellectual property or resolve a dispute. Once the exact reason has been identified, certain key questions must be addressed during the selection process, such as the following:

- How does the background, education, and experience of a particular adviser relate to the task or problem at hand?

- How does the professional adviser charge for its services? What billing options, if any, are available? How do rates vary among different members of the firm? How much will it cost to accomplish this specific project to resolve the problem?

- Which staff members will actually be assigned to this project? What is their expertise?

- What is the firm's anticipated timetable for completing the work? What progress reports will be provided? What input will the management team need to give to the service provider?

- What is the service provider's representative client base? What references can be provided? Does the firm have any actual or potential conflicts of interest? How does the client company compare with the firm's existing client base?

In addition, certain key misperceptions and myths regarding the use of outside advisers must be dispelled *before* the relationship begins. Common myths and fears include these:

- *Myth:* The need for an outside consultant is a sign of the management team's inability, business weakness, or failure.

- *Fear:* The internal management team will be too busy to have the time to work with external advisers.

- *Myth:* Consultants never really understand the special demands and problems of a particular company.

- *Myth:* Consultants are just too expensive, especially for what you get in return—a lot of advice about things already known.

- *The Classic Myth:* If this consultant really knew the industry well, he (or she) would be running his (her) own company.

You must, therefore, understand the exact reason *why* the adviser is being retained, ask the right questions before hiring the adviser, and enter into the relationship with the proper attitude.

The balance of this chapter is devoted to the dynamics of the attorney-entrepreneur relationship; however, these insights are equally applicable to relationships with accountants, business consultants, bankers, advertising agencies, and other key advisers.

Selecting a Business Attorney

As your company grows, it is likely to undergo a variety of changes in structure, in its products and services, in markets; and in its requirements for capital. A well-rounded business lawyer and adviser can assist in the protection of intellectual property, the restructuring of your corporation or LLC as additional capital is raised, develop effective growth strategies, and ensure compliance with key areas of law, such as securities, employment and related statues. Each change will raise a host of legal issues that must be considered before you implement your strategy to achieve your next level of growth. As a result, legal counsel must serve as a key member of the management team and as an active participant in your plan. When an experienced attorney is made an integral part of the outside set of management advisers, you will enjoy several benefits, including: (1) a genuine understanding of the legal hurdles and requirements raised by a particular proposed strategy or transaction *before* implementation or closing; (2) identification of the optimal legal structure and alternatives for achieving your objectives; and (3) the savings achieved as a result of the attorney's understanding of your basic goals, internal politics, and trends affecting your industry. The costs of having legal counsel participate in the growth planning and decision-making process will be far outweighed by these benefits.

Entrepreneur-attorney relationships have changed significantly in the 1990s. No longer is the strength of a personal relationship enough to sustain a long-term working relationship, and no longer is the ability to draft an effective contract the measure of a good advocate. Entrepreneurs in the 1990s do not maintain loyalty to their professional advisers the way they once did and seem more willing to leave a long-term relationship unless true insight, efficient performance, and a wide array of value-added services are brought to the table (and not just once in a while—it has to be all of the time). In the 1990s and presumably beyond, tolerance for mistakes, for exceeding budgets, or for lack of business acumen is gone. Opportunity exists for attorneys who are ready to deliver services in a manner that is cost-effective and strategy-driven, takes advantage of all available technologies, and focuses on problem solving and creative solutions. These are the attorneys that you must identify to represent you along your growth path. Mediocrity will be sufficient only for the small, dormant company. No longer are lawyers selected on the basis of blood relationships, fraternity memberships, or skill at golf. Today's attorney, to the successful entrepreneur, must be nimble and savvy, must have a genuine understanding of the entrepreneur's goals and objectives, and must do everything to help facilitate these goals and objectives every day. As one client told me, "I hate all lawyers, but I hate you a lot less . . ." as if this were supposed to make me feel better and more secure in the relationship. To earn this "compliment," we served as mergers and acquisiters counsel on three major transactions and continue to serve as the client's outside general counsel in the United States.

The Selection Process

The process of selecting, retaining, and knowing how and when to use an attorney is among the more important business decisions that an entrepreneur must make, both initially and throughout the growth of the company. Yet most entrepreneurs express frustration, dissatisfaction, and confusion when asked about selecting and retaining a law firm. Many owners cite as the sources of their ongoing problems with attorneys high fees, failure to meet deadlines, lack of business savvy, inaccessibility, inability to cut through red tape and mountains of paperwork, inexperienced staff, and a general inability to understand the business ramifications of legal decisions. As a result, attorneys are viewed as a necessary evil who do not understand the business considerations of proposed transactions. Therefore, entrepreneurs may take matters into their own hands, only to have the proposed agreement or strategy backfire—creating even larger legal problems.

An experienced attorney can and should be a key member of the management team of any company, but this does not mean that an attorney needs to be involved in every step of every transaction. The key to a prosperous and harmonious attorney-entrepreneur relationship is knowing how to select an attorney and when to seek advice from an attorney.

If your idea of an attorney with strong corporate legal skills and business acumen begins with an ability to keep your spouse away from key assets in a hotly contested marital dispute, think again. The days when your divorce lawyer could also handle a complicated corporate transaction are long gone. Because of the increasing complexity of the law and the ever-growing specialization of the legal profession, the division of assets in your family in a divorce or in estate planning and the division of assets in your corporation in a merger, acquisition, or shareholders' agreement must be handled by two very different types of lawyers. Although it is more than likely that the attorney who prepared your will could also assist in the performance of routine corporate tasks during the formation of the company, many general practitioners are quickly outgrown as the business expands and legal needs become more complex in areas such as capital formation, mergers and aquisitions, protection of intellectual property, taking your business abroad, and managing a large workforce. As a result, you must periodically assess whether your legal interests and requirements are best met by your current attorney or law firm.

You are likely to have personal preferences with respect to the age, experience, and interests of the attorney you hire. Priority may be placed on experience and clout (which would tend to favor an older, more seasoned lawyer) or on aggressiveness and cost control (which would tend to favor a younger lawyer). However, it is dangerous to place too great a priority on either experience or billing rates. For example, an older lawyer with time constraints is likely to assign a project to a younger, less experienced attorney; and a younger lawyer who offers lower billable rates may take twice as long to complete an assigned project. Similarly, age and reputation should be viewed with a grain of salt. An attorney practicing for three years who has devoted attention to a given area of law will probably know more about a specific matter than a general practitioner with 30 years' experience. Nonetheless, there are certain common denominators that a company should identify when selecting its legal counsel:

RESPONSIVENESS An attorney must be able to meet a client's timetable for accomplishing a particular transaction or implementing a particular strategy. An attorney with all the expertise in the world on a given legal topic is of no use to a company if the knowledge can't be communicated to the client in a clear and timely fashion. Make sure that deadlines are discussed and that the attorney has adequate resources set aside to meet those requirements in accordance with the schedule established.

BUSINESS ACUMEN Many attorneys are criticized by their clients as being unable to comprehend the business ramifications of legal decisions. Although a small company needs an independent and objective legal adviser, it also needs an attorney with business acumen, management and marketing skills, and a genuine understanding of the industry in which it operates. Legal decisions and strategies should not be made by attorneys with tunnel vision who lack the ability to understand the impact of the law on the client's business goals and objectives.

REPUTATION It goes without saying that a company will want to hire a law firm with a good reputation in the business community. However, reputation goes beyond a series of names on a door or letterhead. In considering the references of a prospective attorney, you should look closely at the *foundation* upon which the reputation has been built. Is the attorney's reputation primarily due to the accomplishments of named partners who have been dead for over 20 years? Or, on the other hand, maybe the lawyer enjoys a fine reputation as a golfer and a philanthropist, but no one can really give you an opinion as to the quality of his or her legal documentation.

PHILOSOPHY AND APPROACH   You need to understand the overall philosophy and approach of attorneys and firms. Are they more inclined to be "deal makers" or "deal breakers?" Are they truly trusted advisers, or are they more of a necessary evil? Do they understand the importance of value-added relationships (bringing more to the table than just good documents or accurate advice, such as strategic planning skills, access to a strong Rolodex, etc.)? Are they an asset or a liability to your company's growth and its ability to meet or exceed its business plan?

REPRESENTATIVE CLIENT BASE   An attorney's list of clients may read like a Who's Who of the Fortune 500, but this does not necessarily mean that the attorney will understand legal needs of a growing company. As has often been said, a small business is not a little big business, yet many corporate lawyers assume that because they have handled a $500 million acquisition, they can understand the legal needs of the parties to a $500,000 transaction. Although some of the legal planning and documentation may be similar, the business goals and philosophies of the parties are likely to be very different. The attorney's client base should also be evaluated to determine whether there are any actual or potential conflicts of interest or complementary resources, or whether the attorney has experience with matters that are relevant to your company.

BILLING RATES AND POLICIES   Managing legal costs is of especially great concern when your resources for legal expenses may be scarce. The good news is that increasing competition among lawyers for small-business clients demonstrating growth potential has created a certain amount of flexibility in billing policies. At the same time, however, attorneys at firms of all sizes expect to be paid for high-quality services rendered within the client's deadline. There is nothing more frustrating or offensive to any provider of professional services than to work nights and weekends for a client that does not pay its bills. Therefore, it is important that any mystery or confusion concerning the billing rates and policies be clarified before any legal work is begun.

One effective means of controlling billing rates and policies (as well as defining related rights and obligations of the attorney and the client) is the use of a retainer agreement. A retainer agreement is for the protection of both parties because it resolves any mystery about the relationship before any work starts. The components of a well drafted retainer agreement include:

- Nature of the services to be provided
- Compensation for services rendered
- Use of initial retainers or contingent fees
- Reimbursement of fees and expenses
- Conditions for withdrawal of counsel or termination of the relationship
- Counsel's duty to provide status reports
- Time limitations or timetables for completion of work
- Ceilings or budgets (if any) for legal fees
- Any special provisions needed in the agreement as a result of the nature of the project (e.g., rules governing media relations, court appearances, and protocol).

EFFICIENCY   You should quickly get out of the habit of relying on legal counsel for basic tasks such as routine corporate work, securities, or tax filings, which can be performed in-house at a far lower cost. It is the responsibility of counsel to train a legal compliance officer within the company who will be responsible for recurring legal and administrative tasks. You should also carefully monitor how projects are handled by the attorney in order to ensure that assignments are being completed in an efficient and cost-effective manner. For example, tasks that could be performed by a more experienced attorney in one day at $225 per hour should not be assigned to a more junior associate who will take three days at $135 per hour. Finally, a good lawyer will be the first to tell you when a matter may be outside his or her area of expertise or jurisdiction, at which point special counsel should be immediately retained.

KNOWLEDGE AND SKILLS The type of knowledge and skills that should be sought will naturally be influenced by the specific tasks, assignment, or transaction for which assistance is needed. If the task involves an adversarial dispute, then a skilled litigator will certainly be more useful than a transactional attorney. Conversely, a litigator may be inappropriate for a complex business deal where the skills of a more diplomatic attorney would be more effective in negotiating and closing the transaction.

CREATIVITY The identification and analysis of various alternative methods of structuring a particular transaction or achieving a particular objective are among the most important tasks that an attorney performs for an emerging growth company. The ability to develop creative legal solutions to a client's problems or disputes is clearly one trait that should be sought when selecting legal counsel.

Controlling Legal Costs

As your company grows, an increasingly larger portion of the annual budget must be allocated for the cost of legal services. As a result, many owners have attempted to control this expense either by avoiding lawyers or by avoiding the invoices sent by lawyers. Neither strategy is an effective way to manage a growing business. Completely ignoring lawyers is likely to result in problems that far outweigh the cost of retaining competent counsel. Similarly, ignoring legal invoices will lead to tension in the relationship, resentment by counsel toward tasks assigned by the client, and even litigation. The most effective way to control the cost of legal services is to work with legal counsel in an efficient manner, as follows:

• *Be prepared before calling or meeting with the attorney.* Remember that time is money. Gather all facts and review all documents before the telephone call or conference, and develop a specific agenda and list of questions.

- *Clearly define your goals and objectives.* Many entrepreneurs don't clearly tell (and lawyers don't ask about) their goals and objectives in a given transaction or strategy. If counsel understands your key objectives and negotiating parameters, then your company is likely to get much better value for its legal dollars.

- *Do not rely on the attorney for basic tasks* that could be performed more quickly and cheaply by you or your staff. Basic forms, correspondence, renewal filings, etc., can probably be handled by a designated legal compliance officer within the company.

- *Do not let executed contracts collect dust.* Most contracts are living, breathing documents that must be consulted periodically. Your failure to understand or perform obligations under a contract will usually lead to expensive litigation.

- *Do not be afraid to request that your attorney set a ceiling on fees* for a given project or transaction. Attorneys experienced in a given area of law should be able to predict the amount of time it will take to accomplish a specific task, absent any special problems, facts, or circumstances.

- *Monitor administrative and incidental expenses.* Ask your lawyer about travel, photocopying, postage, and related expenses. If these extra fees are too steep for your budget, ask your lawyer to make alternative arrangements for these services.

- *Review all bills and invoices carefully.* Insist on an itemized account that adequately explains the nature of the services rendered or out-of-pocket expenses incurred. Unfamiliar names or charges may be a sign that the billing system is not functioning properly or that invoices are not being carefully reviewed by the primary attorney for the matter. Be certain that the company is paying for services that were truly necessary and were actually rendered.

- *Do not tolerate paying for the education of an inexperienced attorney.* Although virtually every legal matter will entail a certain amount of legal research, this does not mean that your company should have to foot the entire bill to train an attorney who is handling a matter of this nature for the first time. There-fore, check the bills carefully to monitor exactly *which* lawyers or paralegals are working on your behalf.

- *Take a proactive, not a reactive, role in the preparation and nego-tiation of legal documents.* Insist on participating in the process of identifying alternatives and developing solutions. Request that periodic progress reports be provided to managers who are responsible for the given project or transaction.

- *Establish controls within the company* as to who may communi-cate with legal counsel and for what purposes. As the company grows, it is likely that a larger number of people will come into contact with legal counsel. If this is not properly controlled, it will result in mixed signals from the company to the attorney, in the assignment of unnecessary or duplicate tasks, or in handling of personal matters at the company's expense.

The relationship between the entrepreneur and the attorney must be one of synergy, ongoing communication, mutual respect and understanding, and trust and confidence. A shared goal of planning, implementing, and monitoring actions will ensure that business objectives come to fruition in a cost-effective and trouble-free manner. The best interests of the company—its employees, shareholders, assets, products, and services, and its future—must be given the highest priority by legal counsel. Selecting the right lawyer and other key profes-sionals to help your company grow is crucial to its long-term success.

The Practice of Preventive Law

Over the past few years, a concept known as "preventive law" has become very popular among corporations and their legal counsel. Preventive law is a "two-way street" that redefines the nature and purpose of the attorney-entrepreneur relationship. Under this approach, legal counsel must be *proactive* instead of reactive: identifying potential problems beforehand. By the same token, a system must be put in place under which the company's owners and managers (and, where applicable, its in-house legal counsel) are taught to work with their outside attorneys in order to recognize legal issues before they mature into more serious problems or conflicts.

The Legal Audit

Preventive law dictates certain periodic steps that enable legal counsel to properly assess the legal health of the company and prescribe a set of strategies and solutions for any problems identified in the checkup. This legal checkup is often referred to as a "legal audit."

In a legal audit, the company's management team meets with corporate counsel in order to: (1) discuss strategic plans and objectives; (2) review key documents and records; and (3) analyze and identify current and projected legal needs of the company. The legal audit also lays the groundwork for the establishment of an ongoing legal compliance and prevention program in order to ensure that the company's goals, structure, and ongoing operations are consistent with the latest developments in business and corporate law. Finally, the legal audit helps managers identify the legal issues that are triggered by changes in strategies, goals, or objectives and allows planning for the legal tasks that must be accomplished as a result of the issues identified.

A comprehensive legal audit will examine a wide range of issues, which may be as mundane as whether or not the company is qualified to do business in foreign jurisdictions or as complex as an analysis of the company's executive compensation and retirement plans in order to ensure consistency with current tax law and employment regulations. The topics that must be addressed include choice and structure of the entity; recent acts of the board of directors and documentation (or lack thereof) relating to those decisions; protection of intellectual property; forms and methods of distribution and marketing; pending and threatened litigation; estate planning; insurance coverage; hiring and firing practices; employment agreements; compliance with securities law; antitrust and related trade regulations; product liability and environmental law; and a review of sales and collection practices. Naturally, the extent and complexity of the legal audit will vary depending on the size and stage of growth of the company, the type of business (e.g., service versus manufacturing), the number of shareholders and employees, the extent to which the company does business in a "regulated industry," and a host of other factors.

A legal audit may be performed on a periodic basis as part of an ongoing compliance program or may be performed in connection with a specific event, such as a financial audit, or in connection with a specific transaction, such as an acquisition or securities offering. There are also specialized legal audits in such areas as taxes, labor and employment, estate planning and protection of assets, government contracts, franchising compliance, and environmental law. The mechanics of the legal audit and a sample questionnaire are set forth below.

Mechanics of the Legal Audit

Mechanics of a legal audit include the following:

- *Preliminary questionnaire.* The legal audit should begin with a comprehensive questionnaire for the company's management team to review and address before the arrival of the team of attorneys who are to conduct the legal audit. In the case of smaller companies, a simple checklist of issues or a formal agenda will be more than sufficient to prepare for the initial conference.

- *Initial conference.* Once the documents and related materials requested in the questionnaire have been assembled and problem areas tentatively identified, a meeting should be scheduled between audit counsel and the designated officers of the company who are well versed in the various aspects of its operations. Related members of the management team, such as the company's outside accountant and other professionals who play key advisory roles to the company, should be present during, at the least, the portion of the audit that relates to their area of expertise. This initial conference (or series of conferences) is basically an information-gathering exercise designed to familiarize the legal auditor with the most current information about all aspects of the company. In addition to such conferences with key personnel, the audit team should perform some on-site observations of the day-to-day operations of the company. The legal audit team should also review the current financial statements of the company and spend some time with the company's accounting firm.

- *Implementation of postaudit recommendations.* Once the legal audit team has issued its postaudit evaluation to the company's management team, you can implement the recommendations of the report. What you do will vary, depending on the growth planned by the company as well as on the specific findings of the report. At a minimum, you should schedule meetings with key personnel to review and discuss the postaudit recommendations; prepare internal memos to educate the rank-and-file employees; conduct employee seminars to educate employees about proper procedures and compliance; and, in certain cases, develop handbooks and operations manuals for continued and readily available guidance for the company's staff. If significant problems are discovered during the audit, counsel should be careful as to what is included in the final written report, in order to avoid potential adverse consequences down the road under the federal or state rules of evidence. In addition, you can establish a "tickler system" for periodic reporting and key dates and deadlines, as well as set a time for the next legal audit.

Failure to have an independent legal audit performed by qualified legal counsel can have a significant adverse impact on the company and its founders. The risks of noncompliance with the many laws and regulations include these:

1. Failing to keep proper books and records, or mixing personal assets with business assets, could allow third parties to "pierce the corporate veil," thereby removing the limited liability protection of a corporation or LLC (or leading to litigation among co-owners).

2. Failure to obtain all proper permits and licenses could lead to fines and penalties (and in come cases even to closure of the business) by governmental agencies.

3. Failure to comply with certain laws and regulations may lead to problems under federal law with agencies such as the IRS, the EEOC, the EPA, and even the SEC.

4. Failure to have employment applications, personnel handbooks, and general employment policies reviewed periodically could give rise to governmental and civil liability.

5. Failure by the directors of the company to keep accurate records and minutes of its decision-making procedures (e.g., proving that directors are exercising informed judgment) could subject the company and its board to liability to its shareholders and investors.

6. Failure to monitor the company's reporting requirements may put it into default with lenders or investors.

Topics Covered in the Legal Audit Questionnaire

CORPORATE MATTERS   Under what form of ownership is the company operated? When was this decision made? Does it still make sense? Why or why not? Have all annual filings and related actions (such as state corporate annual reports or required director and shareholder meetings) been satisfied? What are the company's capital requirements in the next 12 months? How will this money be raised? What alternatives are being considered? What issues are triggered by these strategies? Have applicable federal and state securities laws been considered in connection with these proposed offerings? Will key employees be offered equity in the enterprise as an incentive for performance and loyalty? Is such equity available? Has the adoption of such plans been properly authorized? Will the plan be qualified or nonqualified? Up to what point? Has anyone met with the key employees to ascertain their goals and preferences? Have all necessary stock option plans and employment agreements been prepared and approved by the shareholders and directors of the corporation? Will any of the founders of the company be retiring or moving on to other projects? How will this affect the current structure? If the company is a corporation, was an election under subchapter S ever made? Why or why not? If the entity is an S corporation, does it still qualify? Is such a choice unduly restrictive as the company grows (e.g., does it limit ability to attract foreign investment or does it affect taxation of undistributed earnings)? If the entity is not a subchapter S corporation, could it still qualify? Is this a more sensible entity under the applicable tax laws? Or should a limited liability company (LLC) be considered as an alternative? Have bylaws been prepared and carefully followed in the operation and management of the corporation? Have annual meetings of shareholders and directors been properly held and conducted? Have the minutes of these meetings been properly and promptly entered into the corporate record book? Have transactions "outside the regular course of business" been approved or ratified by directors (or where required by shareholder agreements or bylaws), and have the resolutions been recorded and entered into the corporate records? Are there any "insider" transactions or other matters that might constitute a conflict of interest? What "checks and balances" are in place to ensure that these transactions are properly handled? Have quorum, notice, proxy, and voting requirements been met in each case under applicable state laws? To what extent does the company's organizational and management chart reflect reality? Are customers and suppliers properly informed of the limits of authority of the employees, officers, or other agents of the company?

BUSINESS PLANNING MATTERS   Has a business and management plan been prepared? Does it include information about the company's key personnel; strategic objectives; realistic and well documented financial statements; current and planned products and services; market data, strategy, and evaluation of competition; capital structure and allocation of proceeds; capital formation needs; customer base; distribution network; sales and advertising strategies; facility and labor needs; risk factors; and realistic milestones and strategies for the achievement of these plans and objectives? How and when was the business plan prepared? Has it been reviewed and revised on a periodic basis, or is it merely collecting dust on a manager's bookshelf? Has it been changed or supplemented to reflect any changes in the company's strategic plans or objectives? To whom has the plan been shown? For what purposes? Have steps been taken to preserve the confidential nature of the document? To what extent have federal and state securities laws been reviewed to prevent violations due to the misuse of the business plan as a disclosure document?

COMPLIANCE WITH GOVERNMENTAL AND EMPLOYMENT LAW REGULATIONS Have all required federal and state tax forms been filed (employer's quarterly and annual returns, federal and state unemployment tax contributions, etc.)? Are federal and state record-keeping requirements being met for tax purposes? Have all payroll and unemployment tax accounts been established? Has the company been qualified to "do business" in each state where such filing is required? Have all required local business permits and licenses been obtained? Are the company's operational policies in compliance with OSHA, EEOC, NLRB, and zoning requirements? Has the company ever had an external environmental law compliance audit performed? Has the company developed policies and programs regarding smoking, substance-abuse testing, child labor laws, family leave, or child care that are in compliance with federal, state and local laws? Have modifications been made to the workplace in compliance with the Americans With Disabilities Act? Have steps been taken to ensure compliance with applicable laws governing equal employment opportunity, affirmative action, equal pay, wages and hours, immigration, employee benefits, and workers' compensation? When was the last time the company consulted these statutes to ensure that current practices are consistent with applicable laws? Has an employment manual been prepared? When is the last time that it was reviewed by qualified counsel?

EMPLOYEE BENEFIT PLANS Has the company adopted a medical reimbursement plan? Group life insurance? Retirement plans? Disability plans? If not, should they be adopted? If yes, have all amendments to the structure and ongoing management of these plans being made to maintain qualification? Have annual reports been filed with the U.S. Department of the Treasury and U.S. Department of Labor for pension and profit-sharing plans? Have there been any changes in the administration of these plans? Have there been any recent transactions between the plan and the company, its trustees, or its officers and directors?

CONTRACTUAL MATTERS   On which material contracts is the company directly or indirectly bound? Were these agreements drafted in compliance with applicable laws, such as your state's version of the Uniform Commercial Code? Is your company still able to meet its obligations under these agreements? Is any party to these agreements in default? Why? What steps have been taken to enforce the company's rights, mitigate damages, or both? To what extent are contractual forms used when selling company products and services? When is the last time these forms were updated? What problems have these forms triggered? What steps have been taken to resolve these problems? Are employees who possess special skills and experience under an employment agreement with the company? When was the last time the agreement was reviewed and revised? What about sales representatives of the company? Are they under some form of a written agreement and commission schedule? Has the scope of their authority been clearly defined and communicated to the third parties with whom they deal? To what extent does the company hire independent contractors? Have agreements been prepared with these parties? Have the issues of intellectual property law, such as "work for hire" provisions, been included in these agreements?

PROTECTION OF INTELLECTUAL PROPERTY   To what extent are trademarks, patents, copyrights, and trade secrets among the intangible assets of the business? What are the internal company procedures for these key assets? What agreements (such as ownership of inventions, nondisclosure, and noncompetition) have been struck with key employees who are exposed to the company's intellectual property? What procedures are in place for receiving new ideas and proposals from employees and other parties? What steps have been taken to protect the company's "trade dress," where applicable? Have trademarks, patents, and copyrights been registered? What monitoring programs are in place to detect infringement and ensure proper usage by third parties? Are documents properly stamped with copyright and confidentiality notices? Has counsel been contacted to determine whether a new discovery is eligible for registration? Does the company license any of its intellectual property to third parties? Has experienced licensing and franchising counsel prepared the agreements and disclosure documents?

RELATIONSHIPS WITH COMPETITORS How competitive is your industry? How aggressive is the company's approach toward its markets and competitors? What incentives are offered for attracting and retaining customers? To what professional and trade associations does the company belong? What types of information are exchanged? Does the company engage in any type of communication or have any cooperative agreement with a competitor regarding price, geographic territories, or distribution channels that might constitute an antitrust violation or an act of unfair competition? Has the company established an in-house program to educate employees about the mechanics and pitfalls of antitrust violations? Has an antitrust action ever been brought or threatened by or against the company? What were the surrounding facts? What was the outcome? Have you recently hired a former employee of a competitor? How was he or she recruited? Does this employee use skills or knowledge gained from the previous employer? To what extent has the previous employer been notified? What steps are being taken to avoid a lawsuit involving misappropriation of trade secrets or interference with contractual regulations? Does the company engage in comparative advertising? How are the products and services of the competitor generally treated? Are any of your trademarks or trade names similar to those of competitors? Have you been involved in any prior litigation with a competitor? Threatened litigation?

FINANCING MATTERS What equity and debt financing have been obtained in the past three years? What continuing reporting obligations or other affirmative or negative covenants remain in place? What triggers a default, and what new rights are created for the investors or lenders upon default? What security interests remain outstanding?

MARKETING AND DISTRIBUTION ISSUES Has the company clearly defined the market for its products and services? Who are the key competitors? What are their respective market shares, strengths, weaknesses, strategies, and objectives? What new players are entering this market? What barriers exist to new entry? What is the saturation point of this market? What are the key distribution channels for bringing these products to the market? Have all necessary agreements and regulations affecting these channels been adequately addressed (labeling and warranty laws, consumer protection laws, pricing laws, distributorship agreements, etc.)? If the company is doing business abroad, have all import and export regulations been carefully reviewed? Has a system been established to ensure compliance with the Foreign Corrupt Practices Act? Is the company considering franchising as a method of marketing and distribution to expand market share? To what extent can all key aspects of the company's proven success be reduced to an operations manual and taught to others in a training program? To what extent are competitors engaged in franchising? If franchising is appropriate for distribution of the company's products or business, have all necessary offering documents and agreements been prepared by experienced franchise legal counsel? What initial franchise fee will be charged? Ongoing royalties? Are these fees competitive? What ongoing programs and support are given to franchisees? What products and services must the franchisee buy from your company? Under what conditions may one franchise be terminated or transferred? Are any alternatives to franchising being considered? Has the company looked at dealer termination, multilevel marketing, or pyramid laws?

Legal audits offer the small, growing company an inexpensive yet comprehensive method of making sure that its plans and objectives are consistent with developments in the law. The process helps to identify problem areas, maintain legal compliance, offer legal solutions and alternatives for the achievement of the company's short- and long-term business objectives, and forces owners and managers to reevaluate the company's strategies in light of the legal costs, risks, and problems that have been identified in the audit.

Virtually every aspect of business development and growth is regulated or affected directly or indirectly by legal regulations and considerations. Owners must be familiar with the legal constraints and projections relevant to their particular enterprise. Each manager must understand the legal costs, benefits, and risks of each management, marketing, and financial decision.

The selection and retention of legal counsel that can meet the company's growing and changing legal requirements is crucial to the long-term success of the business. The interview and selection process should include a careful analysis of the attorney's reputation, billing policies, experience, understanding of smaller companies, efficiency, and responsiveness. Once selected, the attorney should serve as a key member of the management team responsible for strategic planning, implementation, and ongoing evaluation.

CHAPTER 5

Strategies for Resolving Disputes Among Cofounders of Small and Growing Companies

It's natural for small-business owners to look to others to start new ventures. You may want to pair up with other people for such reasons as the following:

- Friendship and having a "sounding board" for discussing ideas and strategies
- Pairing technical expertise with capital or other resources in which one cofounder may be deficient
- Sharing and mitigation of risk
- Bonding among family members or friends to start new ventures together

Regardless of why the cofounders were brought together, as in any business marriage, there will inevitably be bumps along the road. It may be for internal reasons, such as lack of communication, jealousy, or differing objectives; or for external reasons, such as the influence of a spouse or key employee, competitive conditions, or changes in technology or the marketplace.

Perhaps one of the most challenging hurdles for a growing company is a dispute among its cofounders. Virtually every company, as it achieves various stages of growth, will confront disagreements and problems—sometimes inevitable—among its cofounders. This chapter will look at the various reasons why cofounders have problems, and also look at some common and creative solutions to such problems. Some of these scenarios typically involve third parties or outside circumstances that none of the cofounders can control, yet that clearly have a direct impact on the ability of each cofounder to continue growing the business. As we shall see, basic agreements must be put in place in order to protect the cofounders from the outside world and each other. However, contracts are not enough; the agreements must be supplemented with sound management and business practices, a sensitivity to psychological and ego issues, and a clear, strategic development plan.

Common Problems

In my experience working with a variety of small and growing companies, I have encountered some common problems and situations that can arise as a result of disagreements and conflicts among cofounders. Here are the top ten:

1. *The "best friend in high school" or "college roommate" partner.* Many growing businesses in their early stages were founded by former college roommates or best friends in high school who grew up together. The mix of a personal friendship and a conflict in either business or personal relationships can make the resolution of disputes especially complex. Unable to separate the personal issues that may have come between them from the business issues that separate them, the partners can easily run into tricky situations.

2. *The "obsolete" partner.* Often, as a business grows, one or more of the cofounders are unable to keep pace with the level of sophistication or business acumen that the company now requires. Such a cofounder is no longer making a significant contribution to the business and in essence has become "obsolete." It's even harder when the obsolete partner is a close friend or family member. In this case, you need to ask: Will the obsolete cofounder's ego allow for a position of diminished responsibility? Can our overhead continue to keep him or her on staff?

3. *The "ego-clashing" partner.* Entrepreneurs, as leaders with strong values and integrity, also tend to have extra-large egos. Such egos tend to clash from time to time. Sometimes a clash is short-lived and easy to overcome, but at other times a continuing clash of the egos creates a problem that cannot easily be resolved. Often the challenge is how to make everybody feel important without creating too many chefs in the kitchen.

4. *The "we all have differing goals and objectives" partner.* One common situation is that the cofounders are all gradually moving in different strategic directions, with different visions and plans for the course the company should take and the markets it should enter. At this point, communication is strained and difficult, since each partner has his or her own ideas about where the company should be heading. I've even seen some lose the "fire in their belly" once the company reaches a particular stage of growth and when key goals and objectives had been met. When this happens, it's best for the cofounder to step down, be reassigned, or find new challenges or markets to pursue. Just as the flame in an old marriage can be rekindled, so the entrepreneurial spirit can be resparked.

5. *The "silent money" partner.* Few people that I have met have ever gotten wealthy by being stupid or being silent, but entrepreneurs still want to believe there's such a thing as a "silent partner." My experience has been that most silent partners are rarely silent and will go out of their way to interfere with the operations and management abilities of the operating partner or partners.

6. *The "I want to retire early" partner.* People tend to reach personal "comfort levels" or simply to "burn out" at differing stages of a company's growth. One partner may want to pursue a life on the tennis court; another may want to take a trip around the world; still others still may feel that they have accumulated sufficient wealth and "just want to take it easy." In addition, many growing companies, especially those founded by younger entrepreneurs, are established at a time when all of the cofounders are either unmarried or in the early stages of a marriage. As the size of the company grows, so does the size of the cofounder's family. Cofounders with young children may feel pressure to spend more time at home, but their absence will significantly cut their ability to make a continuous, valuable

contribution to the company's growth. Also, the new family may bring new income needs that the company may not be able to meet.

7. *The "hand caught in the cookie jar" or the "caught in the back room with a subordinate" partner.* When a cofounder is caught in an illegal or unacceptable act on the company's premises, it can be very, very difficult to handle the situation diplomatically. The issues—embezzlement, sexual harassment, discrimination, and other unacceptable or illegal acts—are sensitive, and the liability to the company is significant.

8. *The "I have an immediate need to cash out" partner.* Such a demand could result from normal and ordinary circumstances such as buying a home, or it could be related to less than acceptable circumstances like repaying a gambling debt. This situation puts a strain on the relations among the cofounders. More important, it puts a strain on the company's ability to provide the cash to repurchase that cofounder's shares. The company may not have readily available funds, and because nothing has happened by way of disability or death, there are rarely any insurance policies that could be drawn upon to fund this repurchase.

9. *The "we are being acquired and the buyer wants only me" partner or "the investor wants you out" partner.* In a rapidly growing business, the exit strategy is often either a sale of the company to a third party or the registration of the company's stock in a public offering. I have often seen that the buyer of a company wants only one or two of the cofounders. Many times the investment bankers who are handling an initial public offering (IPO) would prefer that one or more of the cofounders step down from the company, to ensure the success of the IPO. I have even seen this scenario in situations involving venture capital settings: two or three cofounders may be asked to either leave or modify their positions as a condition of the venture capitalist's closing the transaction. Naturally, such a situation creates divided loyalties among the cofounders. The post-closing status of each of the cofounders may put a damper on a transaction and add confusion to an already complex transaction, when it is necessary either to raise the necessary capital or to consummate the sale of the company.

10. *The "I think I am a cofounder" non-cofounder.* Often key employees (with or without stock options) are made to feel as if they
are cofounders, through open-book management styles, phan-
tom stock plans, stock appreciation rights, etc., and then get
downright "uppity" about it. These are key issues to consider
when developing a stock option or bonus plan. The "dark side"
of empowerment is that "making them feel like an owner" may
go too far. Suddenly, you may find yourself needing to justify
that new home, car, or adjustment in salary base to nonshare-
holders! Also, remember the impact, under corporate law, of
granting stock to a key employee when there are only two
cofounders. Guess who was just granted the "swing vote"—
probably *not* what the cofounders intended.

Why Problems Happen

There are several reasons why these common problems arise.

First, we often don't take the time to really get to know the
personality quirks of our cofounders until well into the development of the business. Many of us rush into business relationships with the same excitement and gumption and willingness to
overlook character flaws as we do in entering into various kinds
of personal relationships.

Second, no one likes to look into the crystal ball and see bad
things. It is very difficult to predict what problems may come up
in the future. Many business relationships start out as friend-
ships, and in business—as in any marriage—the negotiation of a
"prenuptial" agreement is not a pleasant thought in anybody's
mind.

Third, in the early stages many entrepreneurs don't have
enough capital to hire lawyers to draft the types of shareholders'
and partnership agreements that are necessary to protect
against certain kinds of problems, or to provide predetermined
solutions for these problems when and if they occur. At the point
when the company can afford to hire lawyers to draft these
agreements, or to purchase insurance policies, it is already too

late; the company is already too far along in its development. These time bombs must be defused before the company blows up.

Fourth, there are often significant disparities between how decisions are supposed to be made and how they are actually made. You can't predict each cofounder's styles of communication and decision making. Also, in rapidly growing, closely held companies decisions may not be properly documented or researched, and communication and key strategic decisions are ad hoc. Agreements—such as shareholders' and partnership agreements—can provide rules under which certain types of key decisions will be made.

Fifth, owners of smaller companies often find it hard to separate their roles as directors, officers, shareholders, and key employees because during the growth of a business, the cofounders initially wear many hats. It is important to know whether a meeting or decision has risen to the level of a board of directors meeting (which requires detailed minutes) or whether it is more of a strategic meeting at the officer or managerial level.

Sixth, management systems are often improperly documented (either contractually or procedurally). Issues of control, authority, and approvals are handled ad hoc with little guidance among cofounders or in the management of key employees.

Seventh, smaller companies often fail to provide for procedures in case of a "deadlock" among an even number of founders or directors. It is important to identify at an early stage how or by whom a deadlock will be broken.

Eighth, the old adage "failing to plan is planning to fail" often applies in disputes among cofounders. Lack of a clear, concise strategic development plan (not the boilerplate type used to raise capital) often leads to confusion and problems among cofounders.

Ninth, entrepreneurs often tend to approach problem solving reactively instead of proactively. By not understanding certain preventive techniques, such as the legal audits discussed and using your lawyer as a strategic adviser (both discussed in Chapter 4), entrepreneurs fail to heed another old adage: "An ounce of prevention is worth a pound of cure."

Tenth, entrepreneurs are often bad delegators, both among themselves and with regard to key employees. This difficulty in delegation can lead to problems among cofounders and stifle the company's ability to truly "departmentalize."

Preventive Measures

The best way to deal with these problems is *prevention.* The cofounders' willingness to communicate openly, prepare for the worst, and detect problems before they mature is at the heart of the solution. Following are some key preventive measures.

Valuations

Periodic valuations of the company, while expensive, are critical and can provide the cofounder with clear-cut, objective information. These valuations should be done annually, though that may vary, depending on the company's growth patterns and industry trends. Occasional financial and legal audits will give insights into the company's value and identify legal and financial problems before they mature.

Shareholders' and Partnership Agreements

It is critical to prepare a shareholders' agreement, a partnership agreement, or both early in the development stages of the business, in order to address decision-making procedures, restrictions on the transfer of stock, buyout provisions, and when a shareholder stops participating in the business. These documents should be *updated periodically* to reflect changes in law or circumstances. "Dust off" your old shareholders' and partnership agreements and ask: *Do these still work for us?* The cofounders can take mental comfort in knowing that these agreements are in place well in advance of a dispute.

Here, for example, are some of the decisions that might require unanimous approval in a shareholders' agreement:

- Changes to the company's articles of incorporation or bylaws
- Increases or decreases in the company's number of authorized shares of any class of stock
- Pledge of the company's assets (real or personal), or the grant of a security interest or lien that affects these assets
- Creating, amending, or funding a pension, profit-sharing, or retirement plan
- Signing any major contract or agreement
- Making substantial changes in the nature of the company

Insurance

Key-person insurance policies can provide a source of capital for the buyout of a cofounder's shares in the event of departure, death, or disability.

Employment Agreements

Employment agreements are needed for the cofounders, which will be separate and apart from the shareholders' or partnership agreements. The employment agreement will provide for conditions of termination, which are especially critical in some of the more sensitive problems discussed above, such as alcohol and drug abuse, sexual harassment, and discrimination. These agreements should also clearly set forth each cofounder's duties and decision-making authority.

If an accord can be reached in an agreement in the early stages of a company's growth, then the possibility that a third-party investor, venture capitalist, or investment banker will set forth these policies can be avoided. Taking a dose of *preventive* medicine can go a long way in saving you legal fees, anxiety, and the sense that you've wasted your efforts. It also helps to keep the relationship alive, avoiding the various types of breakups discussed below.

Managing a Breakup

The cofounders may recognize that the working relationship is truly over and that all reasonable alternatives have been considered. Following are different scenarios, with suggestions for administering the breakup smoothly.

Scenario 1

Once it has been decided that there are no solutions to the problems and discord among the cofounders, the clearest and most obvious choice is a repurchase of the departing cofounder's equity in the company, perhaps on a lump-sum basis or perhaps over a period of time. The payment may be cash, assets, contractual rights, intangibles, or a combination thereof.

Scenario 2

Several companies have resolved disputes among cofounders by splitting the business by function, essentially spinning off different operating divisions of the company on the basis of each founder's interest. To the extent that technology is involved, there can be cross-licensing arrangements among the various companies (or joint venture agreements between the now separate companies), which allow each cofounder to pursue his or her own interests and strategic objectives without losing some of the efficiencies and economies of scale that existed when the company was all under one roof. You should be as creative as possible. There may be ways to divide and subdivide the company by function, product line, market, territory, target customers, etc., that you are unaware of. Ask yourself: *How many different businesses are we really in?*

Scenario 3

Selling certain key assets (or even the company itself) to a third party may include a cofounder's transferring his or her interest to a separate company, providing a formal separation and an opportunity to pursue differing goals and objectives.

Scenario 4

Setting up a field office may create certain operational and overhead inefficiencies, but in the event that one or more cofounders feel a need to relocate, the field office might be an effective way for the business relationship to continue.

Scenario 5

If there is a suspicion of fraud or embezzlement, consider a court-ordered accounting of the books and records of the company.

Scenario 6

Seeking a dissolution of the company through a judicial decree may also be an alternative. The court would have to be convinced that the company should be dissolved because of a major event affecting it, such as the insanity of a cofounder, or because the company may *involuntarily* go out of business, or because it is operating at a financial loss.

Scenario 7

Consider arbitration, mediation, mini-trials, and other alternative techniques for resolving disputes that may be less expensive, less time-consuming, and often less emotional than full-blown litigation. See Chapter 11 for a detailed discussion. One may also try a less legalistic situation by appointing an advisory board to resolve disputes.

Scenario 8

If the cofounders cannot reach an amicable solution (as described in scenarios 1 through 7), then formal litigation is inevitable. The cofounders should be prepared for a lengthy and expensive battle in which cost-benefit analysis should be conducted at various stages of the litigation. However, it is possible to ask the court to appoint a receiver or independent trustee to manage the affairs of the company during the time that the litigation is still pending.

Thoughts and Advice to Consider Before a Breakup

In over 12 years of advising rapidly growing companies, I've found the following tips to be useful when facing a dispute with a cofounder:

- *Be creative in seeking and structuring solutions.* It's shortsighted of cofounders merely to repurchase shares when other strategies or more creative solutions would be a better choice.

- *Be civil.* What goes around comes around. It is a small world.

- *Be reasonable and realistic regarding price and structure.* Regardless of whether you are the departing cofounder or the cofounder who will remain, it is important to be creative in the structure of the departure—such as how and when payments are going to be made and whether they are going to be made in cash or with other assets or key licensing agreements. There are several instances of post-closing lawsuits by former cofounders who feel that information may have been wrongfully withheld from them concerning their buyout or the valuation used by the other cofounders. Such lawsuits are very difficult and complex and can go on for some time, at a significant cost both to the cofounders (past and present) and to the company. Consider an earn-out clause or some other participation right or post-sale adjustment to help avoid a future dispute.

- *When there are problems among cofounders, be sensitive to those around you.* It is important to recognize that the media, key vendors, key customers, creditors, and even employees all must be treated with sensitivity when cofounders are having a problem. Do not lose sight of the impact of these disputes on company morale and leadership in the company. The rumor mill can be cruel and can lead to the eventual demise of the company if certain kinds of problems are not treated properly.

- *Never litigate over matters of principle.* Be sure that the potential rewards and remedies outweigh the many expenses and opportunity costs.

- *Be patient and disciplined in your breakup negotiations with your soon-to-be former cofounder.* Be sure to deal with the difficult issues, such as notice to creditors, the extent of assumption by continuing cofounders of the liabilities of the company, the valuation of the withdrawing cofounder's equity in the company, indemnification, and protection from post-breakup obligations and liabilities. Do not let emotion or impatience interfere with your otherwise strong negotiating skills.

- *Govern yourself accordingly.* Remember that these problems and their solutions are as much psychological as they are legal and as much strategic as they are contractual.

- *Do not vacillate.* If you see a problem such as those discussed earlier in this chapter, don't avoid a confrontation or an unpleasant set of negotiations. Typically, the longer you wait, the worse it will seem. Few problems go away or cure themselves by being ignored.

Business Planning and Strategies for Raising Equity Capital

Creating a Business Plan

Owners and managers of growing companies have come to understand that meaningful and effective business and strategic planning is critical to the long-term success and viability of the company and its ability to raise capital. As a result, much has been written over the past two decades by bankers, accountants, consultants, and academics on the preparation of a business plan. Yet, the more that is written, the more confused the entrepreneurial community seems to become, not only with respect to the proper preparation and use of a business plan, but also as to what information should appear. There is no one "right answer." The business plan should tell a story, make an argument, and conservatively predict the future; and all companies have different stories to tell, different arguments to make, and different futures to predict.

Questions to Address in a Plan

Before turning to the various methods of financing available, it is crucial to understand the fundamentals of business planning. Regardless of what type of capital is to be raised, or by what method it will be raised, virtually any lender, underwriter, venture capitalist, or private investor will expect the manage-

101

ment team to be able to prepare a meaningful business plan. Since business plans are often prepared in order to raise capital, some of the key questions that must be addressed in the plan tend to be financial in nature. The following are examples:

- What market problems and financial opportunities have been identified?

- What services, products, and projects are planned to solve these problems or exploit these opportunities?

- How much capital will be needed to acquire the resources necessary to bring these projects to fruition?

- Exactly how will the capital be allocated? How will this infusion of capital increase sales, profits, and the overall value of the company?

- How will the company meet its debt service obligations or provide a meaningful return on investment to its investors and lenders?

- How much equity in the company is being offered to investors, and how is it being valued?

- What "exit strategies" will be made available to the equity investors?

Business plans are used by companies just starting up as well as established companies. For example, a company that has been operating for 15 years (or more) will still need to draft a business plan in order to raise the necessary capital to reach the next stage in its development because the investor will need to know how and where the capital will be allocated. In one recent case, clients of mine were forced to overhaul their business plan due to a rapid change in competitive circumstances coupled with the loss of a key supplier. The infusion of some fresh capital, together with the restructuring of their distribution channels, helped the company avoid bankruptcy. In any instance, the business plan should be prepared with the assistance of a financial consultant, the investment banker, and the internal management team, with input and editing by attorneys and accountants.

Myths and Realities of Business Plans

Be aware of some of the more common misperceptions when drafting your business plan.

MYTH 1 **"Business plans are only for companies starting up."**

REALITY Companies at *all* stages of development need to prepare business plans for planning and financing specific projects, for financing general expansion, for mergers or acquisitions, and for overall improvement of the company's financial and managerial performance.

MYTH 2 **"Business plans should be as detailed and slick as possible. The more is spent preparing a plan, the better the chance that a project will be financed."**

REALITY Sophisticated investors will not have the time to review hundreds of pages of text. Thus the plan must be *concise* and well written and should focus on the lender's or investor's principal areas of concern. Avoid overly technical descriptions of the company's processes or operations. Investors will commit funds on the basis of the quality and clarity of the document, not its bulk. Although business plans ought to be presented professionally, a very expensive binder or presentation will often imply inefficient resource management.

MYTH 3 **"Business plans should emphasize ideas and concepts, not people."**

REALITY Many entrepreneurs fear that if the success of a company depends too heavily on any specific person, investors will shy away. Although this is partially true, any experienced venture capitalists will tell you that ultimately they would prefer to invest in a company that has great people and only a good concept, rather than a great concept and a weak management team. Ultimately, lenders and investors will commit funds on the basis of the strength of the management team.

MYTH 4 **"Business plans should be prepared only by the founding entrepreneur."**

REALITY Most entrepreneurs are highly skilled in a particular profession or area of management. As a result, they may not necessarily possess the ability to prepare a business plan in a form to which prospective lenders or investors are accustomed. Ideally then, the plan should be developed by a team of managers within the company and then reviewed by qualified experts, such as accountants, attorneys, and the board of directors. Note that the business plan should never be prepared solely by outside advisers without the input of internal management. A venture capitalist will be quick to recognize a "cooked" plan or one that reflects the views and efforts of professional advisers rather than the management team responsible for running the company on a day-to-day basis.

MYTH 5 "Business plans should be distributed as widely as possible."

REALITY The business plan will invariably contain information that is proprietary and confidential. Therefore, distribution should be controlled and careful records kept as to who has been provided with copies of the plan. The cover sheet should make it clear that these are only the *plans* of the company, the success of which cannot be assured, as well as a notice of proprietary information. All applicable federal and state securities laws must be carefully considered if the business plan is intended as a financing proposal; however, it should not be used in lieu of a formal private placement memorandum (which is discussed later in this chapter). Finally, certain institutional investors will consider investments only in certain kinds of companies or industries. Do research on these criteria before sending a business plan in order to save the time and resources of everyone involved.

MYTH 6 "A business plan should follow a specified format, regardless of the industry in which the company operates."

REALITY While it may be true that all companies face certain common challenges in marketing, management, administration, and finance, companies at different stages of growth and companies operating in different industries face different problems and will require different sets of topics in the business plan. For example, plans for a manufacturing company that is just starting up may be far more concerned with financing the plant, equipment, patents, inventory, and production schedules than the plans of an established service-oriented company, which may be more focused on personnel, marketing costs, protection of trade secrets, and goodwill.

MYTH 7   **"Optimism should prevail over realism."**

REALITY   The business plan should demonstrate the enthusiasm of the founders of the company as well as generate excitement in the reader; however, it should be credible and accurate. Investors will want to know all of the company's strengths *and* its weaknesses. In fact, a realistic discussion of the company's problems, along with a reasonable plan for dealing with these various risks and challenges, will have a much more positive impact on the prospective investor. As a general rule, investors will feel more comfortable investing in someone who has learned from previous business failures rather in someone who has never managed a company. Finally, any budgets, sales projections, company valuations, or related forecasts should be well substantiated with accompanying footnotes, for both legal and business reasons. Unrealistic or unsubstantiated financial projections and budgets will reveal to an interested investor inexperience or lack of attention to detail, or even lead to litigation by disgruntled investors if there are wide disparities between what was represented and reality.

MYTH 8   **"A well written business plan should contain an executive summary, which should be written before the full text is prepared."**

REALITY   Institutional investors are exposed to hundreds of business plans in any given month and as a result will initially devote only a few minutes to the review of each business plan. It is true, then, that the *executive summary* (generally one to three pages in length) will be the first (and possibly the last) impression that the company makes on the investor. Thus, if the reader's attention is not captured in these first few minutes, he or she is not likely to complete the review of the plan. The executive summary should contain all of the information that will be critical in the investment decision, such as (a) the nature of the company and its founders; (b) amount of money sought; (c) allocation of the proceeds; (d) a summary of key financial projections; and (e) an overview of marketing considerations. However, the *mistake* often made by entrepreneurs is writing the executive summary first, before the main components have been drafted. To ensure consistency, it is much more effective to prepare the main body of the plan, *then* draft the executive summary last. The executive summary is then truly a preview of the details of the plan.

MYTH 9 "Business plans are written only when a company needs to raise capital."

REALITY Although most business plans are written in connection with a search for capital, a well-written business plan will serve a variety of beneficial purposes to the company and its management team. The completed business plan serves as (1) a road map for growth; (2) a realistic self-appraisal of the company's progress to date, as well as its projected goals and objectives; (3) a foundation for the development of a more detailed strategic and growth management plan (especially after the proposed financing has been successfully completed).

Strategies for Capital Formation

There are many different choices available to a small but growing company that is in search of capital, but most choices come down to dealing with two basic flavors: *debt* and *equity*. It is always a challenge to find the proper balance between the two in defining the "optimal" capital structure. It is also a challenge for smaller companies to find these sources of capital at affordable rates. The term "affordable" varies, depending on whether the company is pursuing debt versus equity. In the context of *debt*, "affordability" refers to the term of the loan, the interest rate, the amortization, and the penalties for nonpayment. In the context of *equity*, "affordability" refers to worth (known as "valuation") and dilution of the ownership interests of the current shareholders, as well as any special terms or preferences such as mandatory dividends or redemption rights.

Issuance of Securities

The first option available for obtaining capital is the issuance of securities. There are essentially three types of securities that may be issued: (1) debt securities; (2) equity securities; and (3) hybrid or convertible securities. Each type of security has certain fundamental characteristics, variable features, and attendant costs.

DEBT SECURITIES When a company authorizes the issuance of a debt security, it is usually in the form of a *bond*, a *note*, or a *debenture*. Typically, a bond is an obligation secured by a mortgage on some property of the company. A debenture or a note is unsecured (and usually carries a higher rate of interest), and therefore is issued on the strength of the company's reputation, projected earnings, and potential for growth. The terms of the debt security and the earnings (referred to as "yield") to the holder will be determined by an evaluation of the degree of risk to the holder and the likelihood of default. Growing companies that lack a high bond or credit rating will often be faced with restrictive covenants in the debenture purchase agreement or in the bond's indenture. For example, the covenants might restrict management's ability to get raises or bonuses or might require a certain debt-to-equity ratio be maintained at all times. For more examples of restrictive covenants in loan documents, see "Types of Commercial Bank Loans" in Chapter 7. The direct and indirect costs of these terms and covenants should be carefully evaluated with the assistance of qualified legal counsel before this option is chosen.

EQUITY SECURITIES   The various forms of equity securities include *common stock, preferred stock,* and *warrants and options.* Each type of equity security will carry with it a different set of rights, preferences, and potential rates of return in exchange for the capital contributed to the company. For example, the typical growing company (whose value to an investor is usually greatly dependent on intangible assets such as patents, trade secrets, goodwill, and projected earnings) will tend to issue equity securities before incurring additional debt because its balance sheet lacks the assets necessary to secure the debt and too much debt would be risky. The three types of equity securities are:

1. *Common stock.* Offering common stock is often traumatic for owners of growing companies because it will result in a realignment of the capital structure and a redistribution of ownership and control. Also, it is generally costly. However, it does offer the company an increased equity base and a more secure foundation upon which to build a company, and will increase the chance of obtaining debt financing in the future.

2. *Preferred stock.* Preferred stock carries with it the right to receive dividends with priority over dividends distributed to the holders of common stock, as well as a preference on the distribution of assets in the event of liquidation. Preferred stock may or may not have certain rights with respect to voting, convertibility to common stock, antidilution rights, or redemption privileges, which may be exercised either by the company or by the holder. Although the fixed-dividends payments are not tax-deductible (as interest payments would be) and ownership of the company is still diluted, a balance between risk and reward is achieved because the principal invested need not be returned (unless there are provisions for redemption). In addition, the preferred stockholders' return on investment is limited to a fixed rate of return (unless there are provisions for convertibility), and the claims of the preferred stockholders are subordinated to the claims of creditors and bondholders in the event of a failure to pay dividends upon the liquidation of the company. Convertible preferred stock is especially popular with venture capitalists.

3. *Warrants and options.* Warrants and options give the holder a right to buy a stated number of shares of common or preferred stock at a specified price and within a specific period of time. If that right is not exercised, it lapses. If the price of the stock rises above the option price, the holder can essentially purchase the stock at a discount, thereby participating in the company's growth.

CONVERTIBLE SECURITIES Convertible securities are stocks and bonds, such as convertible bonds, and convertible preferred stock that can be converted into common stock at some point in the future. The incentive for conversion is usually the same as for the exercise of a warrant: that the *conversion price* (i.e., the actual price the company will receive for the common stock when a conversion occurs) is more favorable than the current rate of return provided by the convertible security.

Convertible securities offer several distinct advantages to a growing company, such as these:

- An opportunity to sell debt securities at lower interest rates and with less restrictive covenants. In exchange, investors get a chance to participate in the company's success if it meets its objectives.

- A means of generating proceeds 10% to 30% above the sale price of common stock at the time the convertible security is issued.

- A lower dilution in earnings per share (usually because the company can offer fewer shares when convertible securities are offered than in a "straight" debt or equity offering).

- A broader market of prospective purchasers for the securities, since certain buyers may wish to avoid a direct purchase of common stock but would consider an investment in convertible securities.

Private Placement Offerings

Although there is a wide range of equity alternatives for raising growth capital, our focus in this section of the chapter will be on "private placements," a term that generally refers to any type of offering of securities by a small or growing company. The offer of these securities need not be registered with the Securities and Exchange Commission (SEC). With loan criteria for commercial bankers and investment criteria for institutional venture capitalists both tightening, the private placement offering remains one of the most viable alternatives for capital formation available to companies.

In order to determine whether a private placement is a sensible strategy for raising capital, it is imperative that you: (1) have a fundamental understanding of federal and state securities laws affecting private placements (an overview is provided below); (2) are familiar with the basic procedural steps that must be taken before such an alternative is pursued; and (3) have a team of qualified legal and accounting professionals.

The private placement generally offers reduced transactional and ongoing costs because of its exemption from many of the extensive registration and reporting requirements imposed by federal and state securities laws. Private placement usually also offers the ability to structure a more complex and confidential transaction, since the offerees will typically consist of a small number of sophisticated investors. In addition, a private placement permits more rapid penetration into the capital markets than a public offering of securities requiring registration with the SEC.

For example, a start-up company in St. Louis that sought to establish a retail "walk-in" advertising and marketing services business prepared a Rule 504 (discussed later in this chapter) offering for up to $1 million. Ownership interests in this limited liability company (LLC) were sold to local investors in increments of $25,000. The reputation and track record of the cofounders of the LLC were known in the business community and helped lead to the offering easily meeting its minimum, thereby allowing the cofounders to break escrow and proceed with the implementation of their business plan. The private placement memorandum (discussed later in this chapter) was the most effective way to raise this capital since: (a) no one single "angel" wanted to write a check for $1 million; (b) there were too many soft costs and it was too risky a project for traditional loans from a commercial bank; and (c) the project was generally at too early a stage for most venture capitalists.

**FEDERAL SECURITIES LAWS APPLICABLE TO PRIVATE PLACE-
MENTS**   As a general rule, Section 5 of the Securities Act of
1933 (the "Securities Act") requires you to file a registration
statement with the SEC prior to the offer to sell any security in
interstate commerce *unless* an exemption is available under
Sections 3 or 4 of the Securities Act. The company offering the
securities is referred to as the *issuer* or an *offerer.* The most
commonly recognized transactional exemption is a private
placement. The penalties for failing to register or for disclosing
inaccurate or misleading information under Sections 11 and 12
of the Securities Act are quite stringent. Registration under
Section 5 is an expensive and time-consuming process, and a
network of underwriters, brokers, and dealers must be assembled to make a market for the security. An issuer that registers
under Section 5 is also subject to strict periodic reporting
requirements.

To qualify for a private placement, you must work with
legal counsel to structure the transaction within the various
categories of exemptions available, such as: (a) *Section 4(2),*
considered the broad "private offering" exemption and
designed for "transaction(s) by an issuer not involving any
public offering"; (b) *Section 3(a)(11)* (an intrastate exemption);
and (c) the most common, *Regulation D,* which specifies three
specific transactional exemptions from the registration provisions within the framework of Sections 3(b) and 4(2) of
the Securities Act. Following is a brief discussion of these
options.

The statutory language of *Section 4(2)*—which allows for an
exemption from registration for "transaction(s) by an issuer not
involving a public offering"—has been a source of much
controversy and confusion in the legal and financial communities. Over the years, court cases have established that targeted
investors in a 4(2) offering must have *access to* the *same kind* of
information that would be available if the issuer were required
to register its securities under Section 5 of the Securities Act.
However, terms like "access to" and "same kind" generally leave
to the discretion of the company and its attorney the exact
method of presenting the necessary information. In relying on
an exemption under Section 4(2), the manner of the offering
should be structured in accordance with the following additional (although vague) guidelines:

1. The offering should be made directly to prospective investors without the use of any general advertising or solicitation.

2. The number of offerees should be kept as small as possible.

3. The offering should be limited to either insiders (such as officers of the company or family members) or sophisticated investors who have a preexisting relationship with you or the company.

4. The prospective investor should be provided (at a minimum) with a set of recent financial statements, a list of critical risk factors (which influence the investment), and an open invitation to inspect the company's facilities and records.

5. If in doubt as to whether Section 4(2) applies to a particular offering, *do not rely on it.* Rather, attempt to structure the transaction within one of the Regulation D exemptions.

The statutory language of *Section 3(a)(11)*—which allows for an exemption from registration for "any security which is part of an issue offered and sold only to persons resident within a single state by an issuer which is a resident and doing business within such state"—is not quite as controversial as Section 4(2). The key issue in relying on this exemption is ensuring that the offering is truly an intrastate offering. This test is deceptive; however, the SEC has adopted Rule 147 to assist in determining whether the requirements of Section 3(a)(11) have been met. Precautionary steps must be taken to ensure that *all* offerees are residents of the particular state, because even one nonresidential offeree will jeopardize the availability of the exemption. Steps should also be taken to ensure that all applicable state regulations have been satisfied.

Rule 504 under Regulation D permits offers and sales of not more than $1 million during any 12-month period by any issuer that is not subject to the reporting requirements of the Securities Exchange Act of 1934 (the "Exchange Act") *and* that is not an investment company. Rule 504 places virtually no limit on the number or the nature of the investors that participate in the offering. *But even if accreditation is not required, it is strongly recommended that certain baseline criteria be developed and disclosed in order to avoid unqualified or unsophisticated investors.* Even though no formal disclosure document (also known as a "prospectus") needs to be registered and delivered to offerees under Rule 504, there are many procedures that still must be understood and followed, and a *disclosure document is nevertheless strongly recommended.* An offering under Rule 504 is still subject to the general antifraud provisions of Section 10(b) of the Exchange Act and Rule 10b-5 thereunder; thus, every document or any other information that is actually provided to the prospective investor must be accurate and not misleading by virtue of its content or its omissions in any material respect. The SEC also requires that its Form D be filed for all offerings under Regulation D within 15 days of the first sale.

Finally, a growing company seeking to raise capital under Rule 504 should examine applicable state laws very carefully, because although many states have adopted overall securities laws similar to Regulation D, many of these laws do not include an exemption similar to 504. As a result, a formal memorandum (discussed later in this chapter) may need to be prepared.

Rule 505 under Regulation D is selected over Rule 504 (by many companies) because its requirements are consistent with many state securities laws. Rule 505 allows for the sale of up to $5 million of the issuer's securities in a 12-month period to an unlimited number of "accredited investors" and up to 35 non-accredited investors (regardless of their net worth, income, or sophistication). An "accredited investor" is *any person* who qualifies for one or more of the eight categories set out in Rule 501(a) of Regulation D (and *must* fall within one of them). Included in these categories are officers and directors of the company who have "policy-making" functions as well as outside investors who meet certain criteria for income or net worth. Rule 505 imposes many of the same filing requirements and restrictions as Rule 504 (such as the need to file a Form D), in addition to an absolute prohibition on advertising and general solicitation for offerings and restrictions on which companies may be an issuer. Any company that is subject to the "bad boy" provisions of Regulation A is disqualified from being a 505 offerer and applies to persons who have been subject to certain disciplinary, administrative, civil, or criminal proceedings, or sanctions that involve the company or its predecessors.

Rule 506 under Regulation D is similar to Rule 505; however, the issuer may sell its securities to an unlimited number of accredited investors and up to 35 nonaccredited investors. For those requiring large amounts of capital, this exemption is the most attractive because it has no maximum dollar limitation. The key difference under Rule 506 is that any nonaccredited investor must be "sophisticated." A "sophisticated investor" (in this context) is one who does not fall within any of the eight categories specified by Rule 501(a) but is believed by the issuer to "have knowledge and experience in financial and business matters that render him capable of evaluating the merits and understanding the risks posed by the transaction" (acting either alone or in conjunction with a "purchaser representative"). The best way to remove any uncertainty over the sophistication or accreditation of a prospective investor is to request that a comprehensive confidential offeree questionnaire be completed before the securities are sold. Rule 506 does eliminate the need to prepare and deliver disclosure documents in any specified format, if exclusively accredited investors participate in the transaction. As with Rule 505, there is an absolute prohibition on advertising and general solicitation.

STATE SECURITIES LAWS APPLICABLE TO PRIVATE PLACEMENTS Regulation D was designed to provide a foundation for uniformity between federal and state securities laws. This objective has been met in some states but still has a long way to go on a national level. Full compliance with the federal securities laws is only one level of regulation that must be taken into account when developing plans and strategies to raise capital through an offering of securities. Whether or not the offering is exempt under federal laws, registration may still be required in the states where the securities are to be sold under applicable "blue-sky" laws. You must consider the expense and requirements on both the federal and the state level.

Overall, there are a variety of levels of review among the states, ranging from very tough "merit" reviews (designed to ensure that all offerings of securities are fair and equitable) to very lenient "notice only" filings (designed primarily to promote full disclosure). The securities laws of each state where an offer or sale will be made should be checked very carefully prior to the distribution of the offering documents, and you must also be keenly aware of the specific requirements of each such state.

Although a comprehensive discussion of the state securities laws is beyond the scope of this chapter, be advised that every state in the nation has some type of statute governing securities transactions and securities dealers. When drafting an offering, these laws should be carefully reviewed in order to determine:

- Whether the particular limited offering exemption selected under federal law will also apply in the state

- Whether pre-sale or post-sale registration or notices are required

- Whether special legends or disclosures must be made in the offering documents

- What remedies are available to an investor who has purchased securities from a company that has failed to comply with applicable state laws

- Who may offer securities for sale on behalf of the company

NEW DEVELOPMENTS   Most states have now adopted the Small Corporate Offering Registration (SCOR), which, in accord with Form U-7, makes the use of Regulation D a more viable strategy for small businesses. Form U-7 simplifies and streamlines the preparation of disclosure documents for exempt offerings by allowing a disclosure document to have a question-and-answer format, which you can fill in directly with the assistance of your accountant or attorney. This new form significantly reduces the cost of compliance without sacrificing the information necessary to allow prospective investors to reach an informed decision. Interestingly enough, if Form U-7 is completed properly, it reads almost like an outline of a well written business plan. There are certain restrictions on the structure of offerings that can be made under the U-7, the details of which should be discussed carefully with your attorney.

PREPARING THE PRIVATE PLACEMENT MEMORANDUM You should work with legal counsel to prepare the document and exhibits that will constitute the "private placement memorandum" (PPM). The PPM describes the background of the company, the risks to the investor, and the terms of the securities being sold. In determining the exact degree of "disclosure" that should be included in the document, several factors affect the type of information that must be provided and the format in which the data are to be presented. These factors include:

- Minimum level of disclosure that must be made under federal securities laws (which depends, in part, on the exemption from registration being relied upon).

- Minimum level of disclosure that must be made under an applicable state's securities laws (which naturally depends on *in* which state or states an offer or sale of the securities is to be made).

- Sophistication and expectations of the targeted investors (e.g., some investors will expect a certain amount of information presented in a specified format regardless of what the law may require).

- Complexity or nature of the company and the terms of the offering (e.g., many offerers should prepare detailed disclosure documents—regardless of whether or not they are required to do so—in order to avoid liability for misstatements, fraud, or confusion, especially if the nature of the company and the terms of its offering are very complex).

Each transaction or proposed offering of securities must be carefully reviewed by legal counsel, first to determine the *minimum* level of disclosure that must be provided to prospective investors under applicable federal and state laws. Once this is established, the costs of preparing a *more detailed* document than may be required should be weighed against the benefits of the additional protection provided to the company by a more comprehensive prospectus. The key question will always be "What is the most cost-effective vehicle for providing the targeted investors with the information that they require and that both applicable law and prudence dictate they must have?" *There are no easy answers.*

The specific disclosure items to be included in the PPM will vary depending on the size of the offering and nature of the investors under federal securities laws and any applicable state laws. The text should be *descriptive, not persuasive,* and should allow the reader to reach his or her own conclusions as to the merits of the securities being offered by the company. Use the following as a checklist in preparing your PPM.

- *Introductory materials.* This section introduces the prospective investor to the basic terms of the offering. A *cover page* should include a brief statement about the company and its core business, the terms of the offering (often in table form), and all "legends" required by federal and state laws. The cover page should be followed by a *summary of the offering,* which serves as an integral part of the introductory materials and a cross-reference point for the reader. The third and final part of the introductory materials is usually a *statement of the investor suitability standards,* which includes a discussion of the federal and state securities laws applicable to the offering and the *definitions of an accredited investor* as applied to the offering.

- *Description of the company.* This is, obviously, a statement of the company's history (as well as its affiliates and predecessors) and should include, in addition to the company's history, principal officers and directors; products and services; management and operating policies; performance history and goals; competition; trends in the industry; advertising and marketing strategy; suppliers and distributors; intellectual property rights; key real and personal property; customer demographics; and any other material information that would be relevant to the investor.

- *Risk factors.* This is usually the most difficult section to write, but it is viewed by many as one of the most important to the prospective investor. Its purpose is to outline all of the factors that make the offering or the projected business plans risky or speculative. Naturally, the exact risks to the investors will depend on the nature of the company and on trends within the industry.

- *Capitalization of the issuer.* This section provides the capital structure of the company both before and after the offering. For the purposes of this section, all authorized and outstanding securities must be disclosed (including all long-term debt).

- *Management of the company.* This section should include: a list of the names, ages, special skills or characteristics, and biographical information on each officer, director, or key consultant; compensation and stock option arrangements; bonus plans; special contracts or arrangements; and any transactions between the company and individual officers and directors (including loans, self-dealing, and related types of transactions). The identity and role of the company's legal and accounting firms should also be disclosed, as well as any other "expert" retained in connection with the offering.

- *Terms of the offering.* This should describe the terms and conditions, the number of shares, and the price. If the securities are to be offered through underwriters, brokers, or dealers (to the extent permitted by federal and state laws), then the name of each "distributor" must be disclosed, as well as (1) the terms and nature of the relationship between the issuer and each party; (2) commissions to be paid; (3) obligations of the distributor (i.e., guaranteed or "best efforts" offering); and (4) any special rights (such as the right of a particular underwriter to serve on the board of directors), any indemnification provisions, or any other material terms of the offering. *Note:* The terms and structure of the offering should be based on a series of preliminary and informal meetings with possible investors (without those discussions qualifying as a formal "offer" as that term is defined by the securities laws) as well as research on current market conditions and recently closed similarly situated offerings.

- *Allocation of proceeds.* This must state the principal purposes for which the net proceeds will be used and the approximate amount intended to be used for each purpose. You should give careful thought to this section because any material deviation from the use of funds as described in the PPM could trigger liability. If no exact breakdown has been prepared, then try to describe why additional capital is being raised and what business objectives are expected to be pursued with the proceeds.

- *Dilution.* This should include a discussion of the number of shares outstanding prior to the offering, price paid, net book value, and effect on existing shareholders of the proposed offering, as well as dilution effects on new purchasers at the completion of the offering. Often the founding shareholders (and sometimes their key advisers or the people who will help promote the PPM) will have acquired their securities at prices substantially below those in the prospective offering. As a result, the book value of shares purchased by prospective purchasers pursuant to the offering will be substantially diluted.

- *Description of securities.* This section should explain the rights, restrictions, and special features of the securities being offered, and any applicable provision of the articles of incorporation or bylaws that affect its capitalization (such as preemptive rights, total authorized stock, different classes of shares, or restrictions on declaration and distribution of dividends).

- *Financial statements.* Statements to be provided by the issuer will vary depending on the amount of money to be raised, applicable federal and state regulations, and the company's nature and stage of growth. Provide a discussion and explanation of these financial statements and an analysis of the company's current and projected financial condition.

- *Exhibits.* Articles of incorporation and bylaws, key contracts or leases, brochures, news articles, marketing reports, and résumés of the principals are examples of material that may be appended as exhibits to the PPM. These documents will generally be examined by attorneys and accountants during the due diligence process (which is discussed in Chapter 10).

SUBSCRIPTION MATERIALS   Once the prospective investors and their advisers have made a decision to provide capital to the company in accordance with the terms of the PPM, a series of documents must be signed as evidence of the investors' desire to "subscribe" to purchase the securities offered by the PPM. The various subscription materials that should accompany the PPM serve several purposes. The two key documents are the "offeree and purchaser questionnaire" and the subscription agreement.

The *offeree and purchaser questionnaire* is developed in order to obtain certain information from prospective offerees and then serves as evidence of their level of sophistication and their ability to fend for themselves as required in a PPM. You may also wish to attempt to obtain information regarding the prospective purchasers' background, citizenship, education, employment, investment, and business experience.

The *subscription agreement* is the contract between the purchaser (investor) and the issuer for the purchase of the securities. It should, therefore, contain acknowledgments of the following:

1. Receipt and review by the purchaser of the information given about the offering and the issuer.

2. Restricted nature of the securities to be acquired and the fact that the securities were acquired under an exemption from registration.

3. Any particularly significant suitability requirements (such as amount of investment or passive income, tax bracket, and so forth) that the issuer feels may be crucial to the purchaser's ability to obtain the benefits of the proposed investment.

4. Awareness of specific risks disclosed in the information furnished.

5. Status of the purchaser representative (if one is used).

The subscription agreement should also contain a reconfirmation by the purchaser of the accuracy and completeness of the information contained in the offeree and purchaser questionnaire; the number and price of the securities to be purchased and the manner of payment; and agreement to any special elections that may be contemplated (such as S corporation elections, accounting methods, and any relevant tax elections). The subscription agreement often contains a stipulation on the part of the purchaser to indemnify the issuer against losses or liabilities resulting from any misrepresentations on the part of the prospective purchaser that would void or destroy the exemption from registration that the issuer is attempting to invoke. The subscription agreement should also contain representations on the part of the purchaser with respect to its authority to execute the agreement.

Joint Ventures and Corporate Partners

Another avenue for raising equity capital is from joint venture partners or through the formation of a strategic alliance. In a nutshell, *joint ventures, strategic partnering, strategic alliances, cross-licensing, co-branding,* and *technology transfer agreements* are all strategies designed to obtain one or more of the following: (1) direct capital infusion in exchange for equity, intellectual property, or distribution rights; (2) a "capital substitute" where the resources that would otherwise be obtained with the capital are obtained through joint venturing; or (3) a shifting of the burden and cost of development (through licensing) in exchange for a potentially more limited upside.

When embarking on a search for a joint venture partner, you should conduct a thorough review of the prospective candidates, and extensive "due diligence" should be done when the final few are being considered. A list of key objectives and goals to be achieved by the joint venture or licensing relationship should be developed along with a comparison of your final candidates. Take the time to understand the corporate culture and decision-making process within each company by: (1) asking how this fits with your own processes; (2) asking each prospective partner about his or her previous experiences and track record with other joint venture relationships; and (3) asking why these previous relationships succeeded or failed.

In many cases, smaller companies looking for joint venture partners may wind up selecting a much larger Goliath, which offers a wide range of financial and nonfinancial resources that will allow the smaller company to achieve its growth plans. Under these circumstances the motivating factor for the larger company is to get access and distribution rights to new technologies, products, and services. The larger company will often offer access to pools of capital, research and development, personnel, distribution channels, and general contacts that the small company desperately needs.

Try to distinguish between what is being promised and what will actually be delivered. If your primary motive is *only* capital, then consider and explore alternative (and perhaps less costly) sources of capital. A larger joint venture partner should ideally offer a lot more than money. If your primary motive is *access* to technical personnel, then consider the alternatives to the level of control and ownership that will be given up in the joint venture and at what price. If the resources can be purchased separately, it's not worth embarking on a joint venture and giving up control and ownership. Explore whether strategic relationships or extended payment terms with vendors and consultants can be arranged in lieu of the joint venture. *But proceed carefully.* Be sensitive to the politics, red tape, and different management practices that may be in place at a larger company, which will be foreign to many smaller firms.

In identifying joint venture objectives, selecting the right partner, and structuring the appropriate documentation, the following key questions should be asked:

- Can this relationship be built in multiple stages? Should a consulting or cross-licensing agreement be considered as a preliminary step to a formal joint venture?

- Exactly what types of tangible and intangible assets will be contributed to the joint venture by each party? Who will have ownership rights in the assets contributed by the partners during the term of the joint venture and thereafter? Who will own the assets developed as a result of joint development efforts?

- What covenants of nondisclosure or noncompetition will be expected of each joint venturer during the term of the agreement and thereafter?

- Will the joint venture be structured as a partnership, corporation, or (the recently established) limited liability company?

- What timetables or performance quotas for completion of the projects contemplated by the joint venture will be included in the agreement? What are the rights and remedies of each party if these performance standards are not met? What "reversion" rights can be maintained in the technology to avoid "shelving" problems?

- How will issues of management and control be addressed in the agreement? What will be the respective voting rights of each party? What are the procedures in the event of a major disagreement or deadlock? What is the fallback plan?

Once all of these preliminary issues have been discussed by the joint venturer, a formal joint venture agreement or corporate shareholders' agreement should be prepared with the assistance of counsel. The precise terms of the agreement between the joint venturer and the company will naturally depend on the specific objectives of the parties. At a minimum, however, the following topics should be addressed in as much detail as possible:

- *Nature, purpose, and trade name of the joint venture.* The legal nature of the parties' relationship should be stated along with a clear statement of purpose, to prevent future disputes. If a new trade name is established for the venture, provisions should be made for the use of the name and any other trade or service marks should the project be terminated.

- *Status of the respective joint venturers.* Clearly indicate whether each party is a partner, shareholder, agent, independent contractor, or any combination thereof.

- *Representations and warranties of each joint venturer.* Standard representations and warranties will include obligations of due care and due diligence as well as mutual covenants governing confidentiality and anticompetition restrictions.

- *Capital and property contributions of each joint venturer.* A clear schedule of all contributions—whether in the form of cash, shares, real estate, or intellectual property—should be established. Detailed descriptions will be particularly important if the distribution of profits and losses is to be based on overall contribution. The specifics of allocation and distribution of profits and losses among the venturers should also be clearly defined.

- *Management, control, and voting rights of each joint venturer.* If the proposed venture envisions joint management, it will be necessary to specifically address the keeping of books, records, and bank accounts; the nature and frequency of inspections and audits; insurance and cross-indemnification obligations; and responsibility for administrative and overhead expenses.

- *Rights in joint Venture property.* Each party must be mindful of intellectual property rights, and the issues of ownership use and licensing entitlements should be clearly addressed—not only for the venturers' presently existing property rights but also for future use of rights (or products or services) developed in the name of the venture itself.

- *Default, dissolution, and termination of the joint venture.* The obligations of the venturers and the distribution of assets should be clearly defined, along with procedures in the event of bankruptcy and grounds for default.

Negotiating Venture Capital Transactions

A rapidly growing company that cannot qualify for debt financing from a commercial bank should strongly consider institutional venture capital as a source of equity financing. This is especially true for growing companies, whose capital needs are often "soft costs" such as personnel and marketing, for which debt financing may be very difficult to obtain.

The term "venture capital" has been defined in many ways but generally refers to relatively high-risk, early-stage financing of young emerging growth companies. The professional venture capitalist is usually a highly trained finance professional who manages a pool of venture funds for investment in growing companies on behalf of a group of passive investors. Another major source of venture capital for growing companies is a small business investment company (SBIC). An SBIC is a privately organized investment firm specially licensed under the Small Business Investment Act of 1958 to borrow funds through the Small Business Administration, for subsequent investment in the small business community. Finally, some private corporations and state governments also manage venture funds for investment in growth companies.

1997 has been a banner year for venture capital investments thus far. A Coopers & Lybrand survey demonstrated that venture capital investments totaled $3 billion to 584 U.S.-based entrepreneurial companies in the second quarter of 1997, compared to one record already set and then broken in the first quarter of $2.3 billion to 489 companies.

CENTRAL COMPONENTS OF THE VENTURE CAPITALIST'S INVESTMENT DECISION Regardless of the company's particular stage of development, primary products and services, or geographic location, there are several key variables that all venture capital firms will consider in analyzing the business plan presented for investment. The presence or absence of these variables will ultimately determine whether capital will be committed to the project. These variables generally fall into four categories: (1) management team; (2) products and services offered; (3) markets in which the company competes; and (4) anticipated rate of return on investment. In determining whether a growing company would qualify for venture capital, its management team must be prepared to answer the following questions:

- *Management team.* What are the background, knowledge, skills, and abilities of each member? How is this experience relevant to the specific industry in which the company competes? How are the risks and problems often inherent to your industry handled by the members of the management team?

- *Products and services.* At what stage of development are the company's products and services? What specific market opportunity has been identified by the company? How long will this "window of opportunity" remain open? What steps are necessary for the company to exploit this opportunity? To what extent are the company's products and services unique, innovative, and proprietary?

- *Growing company's targeted markets and stage of development.* At what stage of the life cycle is the industry in which the company plans to operate? What is the size of the company's targeted market? What is its projected growth rate? What methods of marketing, sales, and distribution will be utilized in attracting and keeping customers? What are the strengths and weaknesses of each competitor (be it direct, indirect, or anticipated) in the targeted market? From a timing perspective, is this the appropriate stage of development for the company to receive a venture capital investment?

- *Return on investment.* What are the company's current and projected valuation and performance in terms of sales, earnings, and dividends? To what extent have these budgets and projections been substantiated? Has the company overestimated or underestimated the amount of capital required for the growth and development of its business plan? How much money and time has already been invested by the owners and managers?

NEGOTIATING AND STRUCTURING THE INVESTMENT   Assuming that the financing proposal is favorably received by the venture capitalist, the company must then assemble a negotiation team. The negotiation and structuring of most venture capital transactions revolve around the need to strike a balance between the concerns of the founders (such as dilution of ownership and loss of control) and the concerns of the venture capitalist (such as return on investment and mitigating the risk of company failure). The typical end result of these discussions is a *term sheet* that specifies the key financial and legal terms of the transaction and then serves as a basis for the negotiation and preparation of the definitive legal documentation. The company should ensure that legal counsel is familiar with the many traps and restrictions that are typically found in venture capital financing documents. The term sheet may also contain certain rights and obligations of the parties, which may include an obligation to (1) maintain an agreed valuation of the company; (2) be responsible for certain costs and expenses in the event the proposed transaction does not take place; or (3) secure commitments for financing from additional sources prior to closing. Often these obligations will also be included as part of the "conditions precedent" section of the formal investment agreement.

Negotiation regarding the *structure* of the transaction between the company and the venture capitalist will usually center on the types of securities to be used and the principal terms, conditions, and benefits offered by the securities. The type of securities ultimately selected and the structure of the transaction will usually fall within one of the following categories:

- *Preferred stock* is the most typical form of security issued in connection with venture capital financing because of the many advantages offered to an investor (such as convertibility into common stock, dividend and liquidation preferences over common stock, antidilution protection, mandatory or optional redemption schedules, and special voting rights and preferences).

- *Convertible debentures* are often preferred by a venture capitalist in connection with higher-risk transactions because he or she is able to enjoy the elevated position of a creditor until the risk of the company's failure has been mitigated.

- *Debt securities with warrants* (preferred by venture capitalists for the same reasons as convertible debt) protects against downside by conferring the elevated position of a creditor and protects against upside by including warrants to purchase common stock at favorable prices and terms. The use of a warrant enables the investor to buy common stock without sacrificing the position of creditor, as would be the case if only convertible debt was used in the financing.

- *Common stock* is rarely preferred by venture capitalists (especially at early stages of development) because it does not offer the investor any special rights or preferences, any fixed return on investment, any special ability to exercise control over management, or any liquidity to protect against downside risks. One of the few situations in which common stock might be selected is if the company wishes to preserve its subchapter S status under the Internal Revenue Code, and that status might be jeopardized if a class of preferred stock (with different economic terms) were to be authorized.

Once the type of security is selected, steps must be taken to ensure that the authorization and issuance of the security is properly made under applicable state corporate laws. For example, if the company's charter does not provide for a class of preferred stock, then the articles of amendment must be prepared, approved by the board of directors and shareholders, and filed with the appropriate state corporation authorities. The articles of amendment will be the focus of negotiation on voting rights, dividend rates and preferences, mandatory redemption provisions, antidilution protection (also called "ratchet clauses"), and related special rights and features. If debentures are selected, then negotiations will typically focus on term, interest rate and payment schedule, conversion rights and rates, extent of subordination, remedies for default, acceleration and prepayment rights, and underlying security for the instrument, as well as the terms and conditions of any warrants that are granted along with the debentures.

The legal documents involved in venture capital financing must reflect the end result of the negotiation process and must contain all of the legal rights and obligations. These documents generally include the following:

- Preferred stock or debenture purchase agreement ("investment agreement")
- Stockholders' agreement
- Employment and confidentiality agreements
- Warrant (where applicable)
- Debenture or notes (where applicable)
- Preferred stock resolution (to amend the corporate charter; where applicable)
- Contingent proxy
- Legal opinion of company counsel
- Registration rights agreement

Following is a brief overview of the nature and purposes of some of these documents.

The *investment agreement* describes all of the material terms and conditions of the financing. It also serves as a type of disclosure document because certain key historical and financial information is disclosed in the representations and warranties made to the investors. The representations and warranties (along with any exhibits) are designed to provide full disclosure to the investors, which will then provide a basis for evaluating the risk of the investment and the structure of the transaction. The investment agreement will also provide for certain conditions precedent which must be met by the company prior to the closing. These provisions require the company to perform certain acts at (or prior to) closing as a condition to the investor providing the venture capital financing. The conditions of closing are often used in negotiations to mitigate or eliminate certain risks identified by the investor (such as a class-action suit by a group of disgruntled employees) but usually are more of an administrative checklist of actions that must occur at closing, such as the execution of the stockholders', employment, and confidentiality agreements.

The *stockholders' agreement* will typically contain certain restrictions on the transfer of the company's securities, voting provisions, rights of first refusal, and co-sale rights in the event of a sale of the founder's securities; antidilution rights; and optional redemption rights for the venture capital investors. Venture capitalists will often require the principal stockholders to become parties to the stockholders' agreement as a condition of closing on the investment. Any existing stockholders or buy-sell agreements will also be carefully scrutinized and may need to be amended or terminated as a condition of the investment. For example, the investors may want to reserve a right to purchase additional shares of preferred stock (in order to preserve their respective equity ownership in the company in the event that another round of the preferred stock is subsequently issued). This is often accomplished with a contractual preemptive right (as opposed to including such a right in the corporate charter, which would make these rights available to *all* holders of the company's stock).

Employment and confidentiality agreements will often be required of key members of the management team as a condition of the investment. As discussed in Chapter 2, these agreements define the obligations of each employee, the compensation package, the grounds for termination, the obligation to preserve and protect the company's intellectual property, and post-termination covenants (such as covenants not to compete or not to disclose confidential information).

Contingent proxy provides for a transfer of the voting rights attached to any securities held by a key principal to the venture capitalist upon the death or disability of such personnel. The proxy may also be used as a penalty for breach of a covenant or warranty included in the investment agreement.

The *registration rights agreement* would require the venture capital investors to convert their preferred stock or debentures prior to the time that a registration statement is approved by the SEC; it is often required, since these registration rights are limited to the company's common stock. Many venture capitalists view the eventual public offering of the company's securities (pursuant to a registration statement filed with the SEC under the Securities Act) as the optimal method of achieving investment liquidity and maximum return on investment. As a result, the venture capitalist will protect his or her right to participate in the eventual offering with a registration rights agreement. The registration rights may be in the form of "demand rights" (which are the investors' right to *require* the company to prepare, file, and maintain a registration statement) *or* "piggyback rights" (which allow the investors to have their investment securities included in a company-initiated registration). The number of each type of demand or piggyback rights, the percentage of investors necessary to exercise these rights, the allocation of expenses of registration, the minimum size of the offering, the scope of indemnification, and the selection of underwriters and broker-dealers all will be areas of negotiation in the registration rights agreement.

A well-prepared business plan, an understanding of the analysis conducted by the venture capitalist, and an understanding of the legal documents typically prepared in a venture capital financing will significantly increase your company's ability to gain access to this growing capital market.

Debt Financing for Growing Companies

No small or growing company survives and prospers without some debt component on its balance sheet. Whether it is a small loan from family or friends at the outset of the business or a sophisticated term loan and operating line of credit from a regional commercial lender, most companies end up borrowing some amount of capital along their path to growth. The use of debt in the capital structure (commonly known as "leverage") will affect both the valuation of the company and its overall cost of capital. The determination of the proper debt-to-equity ratio in any given entity will depend on a wide variety of factors. These include, among other things:

- Risk of business distress or failure created by the contractual obligation to meet debt-service payments
- Direct and indirect costs to the company of obtaining the capital
- Need for flexibility in the capital structure in order to respond to changing economic or market conditions
- Ability of the company to get access to various sources of financing (access to capital issues)
- Nature and extent of the tangible (or intangible) assets of the company that are available to serve as collateral to secure the loan

- Level of dilution of ownership and control that the shareholders (and managers) of the company are willing to tolerate
- Certain tax considerations (interest payments are a deductible expense, whereas dividends are not)

The maximum debt capacity that an emerging company will ultimately be able to handle will usually involve the balancing of the costs and risks of defaulting a debt obligation against the desire of the owners and managers to maintain control. Many entrepreneurs prefer preservation of control over the affairs of the company in exchange for the higher level of risk that is inherent in taking on additional debt obligations. The ability to meet debt-service payments must be carefully considered in the company's financial projections.

If the forecasted projections and analyses reveal that the ability to meet debt-service obligations will put a strain on the corporation's cash flow (or that insufficient collateral is available), then equity alternatives should be explored. It is simply not worth driving a company into voluntary (or involuntary) bankruptcy solely to maintain a maximum level of control. As is often said, 60% of something is worth a whole lot more than 100% of nothing. Also, the level of debt financing selected by a company should be compared against key business ratios for the particular industry (such as those published by Robert Morris Associates or Dun & Bradstreet). Once the optimum debt-to-equity ratio is determined, you must be aware of the various sources of debt financing as well as the business and legal issues involved in borrowing funds from a commercial lender.

Debt Financing: Bank Loans and Alternative Sources

Although most small companies turn to term loans and operating lines of credit (the traditional form of financing from commercial lenders), there exists a wide variety of alternative sources of debt financing such as trade credit, equipment leasing, factoring, and other sources of nonbank financing.

- *Trade credit.* The use of credit with key suppliers is often a means of survival for rapidly growing companies. When a company has established a good credit rating with its suppliers, but as a result of rapid growth tends to require resources faster than it is able to pay for them, trade credit becomes the only way that growth can be sustained. A key supplier has a real economic incentive for helping the growth and prosperity of a loyal customer and, therefore, may be more willing to negotiate credit terms that are mutually acceptable.

- *Equipment leasing.* Most rapidly growing companies need the *use* but not necessarily the *ownership* of certain key resources to fuel and maintain growth. Therefore, equipment leasing offers an alternative to ownership of the asset. Monthly lease payments are made in lieu of debt-service payments. There are many forms of equipment leasing, such as *operating leases* (which are generally shorter-term and include repair and maintenance services) and *capital leases* (which are generally longer-term, do not include ancillary services, and virtually transfer ownership to the lessee, partly through an attractive option to purchase the asset at the end of the lease term).

- *Factoring.* Under the traditional factoring arrangement, a company sells its accounts receivable to a third party in exchange for immediate cash. The third party—the "factor"— assumes the risk of collection in exchange for the ability to purchase the accounts receivable at a discount. The amount of the discount is usually determined by the level of risk that debtors will default and the prevailing interest rates. Once notice has been provided to debtors of their obligation to pay the factor directly, the seller of the accounts receivable is no longer liable to the factor in the event of a default. As factoring has become more commonplace in a variety of industries, less traditional forms of factoring have emerged (which are more akin to pure accounts receivable financing), whereby (a) the lender does not assume the credit risk; (b) the accounts are assigned to the lender without notice to the debtors; and (c) the accounts receivable merely become the principal source of collateral to secure the loan agreement.

- *Miscellaneous sources of nonbank debt financing.* Debt securities (such as bonds, notes, and debentures) may be offered to venture capitalists, private investors, friends, family, employees, insurance companies, and related financial institutions. Many smaller companies turn to traditional sources of consumer credit (such as home equity loans, credit cards, and commercial finance companies) to finance the growth of their business. In addition to the loan programs offered by the Small Business Administration (SBA), many state and local governments have created direct loan programs for small businesses.

Although all available alternative sources of debt financing should be strongly considered, traditional bank loans from commercial lenders are the most common source of capital for small growing companies. These are discussed in the following sections.

Understanding the Lender's Perspective

Before attempting to understand the types of loans available from commercial banks, it is important to understand the perspective of the average commercial bank when it analyzes a company's loan proposal.

A lot of confusion and resentment can exist in the relationship between bankers and small-business entrepreneurs. Entrepreneurs may believe that the banker does not understand and appreciate their business requirements, while a loan officer may have had bad experiences with entrepreneurs who expect to borrow $1 million collateralized only by a dream or a foreclosure.

Given these problems, it is crucial to understand the lender's perspective. Banks are in the business of selling money, and *capital* is the principal product in their inventory. Bankers, however, are both statutorily and personally averse to risk. The bank's shareholders and board of directors expect that in each transaction loan officers will take all necessary steps to minimize the risk to the institution and maximize its protection in the event of default. Therefore, the types of loans available to growing companies, the terms and conditions of loan agreements, and the steps taken by the bank to protect itself all have a direct relationship to the level of risk perceived by the lending officer and the loan committee.

Preparing for Debt Financing

The management team assigned to obtain debt financing from a commercial bank must immediately embark on a program to mitigate and manage risk, in preparation for the negotiation of the loan documentation.

1. The Loan Proposal

Mitigation and management of risk will always have a direct result on the favorability and affordability of traditional debt financing. For a small, growing company, this means that a loan proposal package should demonstrate the presence of a strong management team; an aggressive internal control and accounts receivable management program; financial statements and projections that demonstrate ability to service the debt; well-developed relationships with suppliers, distributors, and employees; and an understanding of the trends in the marketplace. In addition, many commercial loan officers will apply the traditional test of creditworthiness, the "four C's": *character* (reputation and honesty), *capacity* (business acumen and experience), *capital* (ability to meet debt-service payments), and *collateral* (access to assets that can be liquidated in the event of a default). All of these elements will be assessed by a loan officer in determining a company's creditworthiness and the relative risk to the bank in making the proposed loan.

Although the exact elements of a loan package will vary depending on the size of the company, its industry, and its stage of development, most lenders will want answers to the following fundamental questions:

- Who is the borrower?
- How much capital is needed and when?
- How will the capital be allocated and for what specific purposes?

- How will the borrower service its debt obligations (e.g., application and processing fees, interest, principal, or balloon payments)?

- What protection (tangible and intangible assets to serve as collateral) can the borrower provide the bank in the event that the company is unable to meet its obligations?

Although the answers to these questions are all designed to assist the bank in its assessment of the risk factors in the proposed transaction, they are also designed to provide the commercial loan officer with the information necessary to persuade the loan committee to approve the transaction. You must understand that the loan officer, once convinced of your company's creditworthiness, will then serve as an advocate on behalf of your company in presenting the loan proposal to the bank's loan committee. The loan documentation, terms, rates, and covenants that the loan committee will specify as a condition of making the loan will be directly related to the ways in which your company is able to demonstrate its ability to mitigate and manage risk as described in its business plan and formal loan proposal.

The loan proposal should include the following categories of information, many of which can be borrowed or modified from your business plan:

- *Summary of the request.* Overview of the history of the company, amount of capital needed, proposed repayment terms, intended use of the capital, and collateral available to secure the loan.

- *History of the borrower.* Brief background of the company, its capital structure, its key founders, its stage of development, and its plans for growth; list of key customers, suppliers, and service providers; management structure and philosophy; plant and facility; key products and services offered; and an overview of any intellectual property owned or developed by the company.

- *Market data.* Overview of trends in the industry; size of the market; the company's market share; assessment of the competition (direct and indirect); proprietary advantages; marketing, public relations, and advertising strategies; market research studies; and future industry prospects.

- *Financial information.* Pro forma financial statements, federal and state tax returns, appraisals of key assets or company valuations, current balance sheet, credit references, and a two-year income statement. The role of the capital requested (with respect to the company's plans for growth), an allocation of the loan proceeds, and the company's ability to repay must be carefully explained. There should also be a discussion of the company's ability to service the debt, supported by a three-year projected cash flow statement on a monthly basis.

- *Schedules and exhibits.* Schedule of supporting documents (such as agreements with manufacturers or letters of intent for planned operations, insurance policies, key contracts, employment agreements, and leases) must be made available to the lender for inspection upon request. Résumés of the company's principals, recent articles about the company, a picture of the company's products or site, and an organizational chart of the management structure should also be appended as exhibits to the loan proposal.

2. Types of Commercial Bank Loans

During the process of planning the capital structure and preparing the loan proposal, it is important for you to understand the various types of loans that are available from a commercial bank (one or more of which could be tailored to meet your specific requirements). Loans are usually categorized by the term of the loan, the expected use of proceeds, and the amount of money to be borrowed. The availability of these various loans will depend on the nature of the industry as well as the bank's assessment of the company's creditworthiness.

Types of loans traditionally available include the following.

SHORT-TERM LOANS A short-term loan is ordinarily used for a specified purpose with the expectation by the lender that the loan will be repaid at the end of the project. For example, a seasonal business may borrow capital in order to build up its inventory in preparation for the peak season; when the season comes to a close, the lender expects to be repaid immediately. Similarly, a short-term loan could be used to cover a period when the company's customers or clients are in arrears; when the accounts receivable are collected, the loan is repaid. Short-term loans are usually made in the form of a promissory note (see the discussion of loan documentation below) payable on demand. They may be secured by the inventory or accounts receivable which the loan is designed to cover, or they may be unsecured (under which no collateral will be required). Unless the company is just starting up or is operating in a highly volatile industry (thereby increasing the risk in the eyes of the lender), most short-term loans will be unsecured. This minimizes the loan documentation and the bank's processing time and costs. Lenders generally view short-term loans as "self-liquidating" in that they can be repaid by foreclosing on the current assets which the loan has financed. The fact that the bank's transactional costs are low, along with its perception of lower risk during this short period of time, makes short-term borrowing somewhat easier for a growing business to obtain and serves as an excellent means for establishing a relationship with a bank and demonstrating creditworthiness.

OPERATING LINES OF CREDIT   An operating line of credit consists of a specific amount of capital that is made available to the company on an "as needed" basis over a specified period of time. A line of credit may be short-term (60–120 days) or inter-mediate-term (one to three years), renewable or nonrenewable, and at a fixed or fluctuating rate of interest. You should be especially careful to negotiate ceilings on interest rates, to avoid excessive commitment, processing, application, and related "up-front" fees, and to ensure that repayment schedules will not be an undue strain for the company. The company should also ensure that its obligations to make payments against the line of credit are consistent with its own anticipated cash flow projections.

INTERMEDIATE-TERM LOANS   An intermediate-term loan is usually provided over a three- to five-year period for the purpose of acquiring equipment, fixtures, furniture, and supplies; expanding existing facilities; acquiring another business; or acquiring working capital. The loan is almost always secured, not only by the assets being purchased with the loan proceeds but also by other assets of the company, such as inventory, accounts receivable, equipment, and real estate that may be available to serve as security. The loan usually calls for a loan agreement, which typically will include restrictive covenants that govern the operation and management of the company during the term of the loan. The restrictive covenants (discussed in greater detail below) are designed to protect the interests of the lender and ensure that all payments are made on a timely basis, *before* any dividends, employee bonuses, or noncritical expenses are paid.

LONG-TERM LOANS   A long-term loan is generally extended for a specific, highly secured transaction, such as the purchase of real estate or a multiuse business facility, in which case a lender will consider extending a long-term loan to a small company for 65% to 80% of the appraised value of the land or building. As a general rule, commercial banks do not provide long-term financing to small businesses. The risk of market fluctuations and business failure over a 10 or 20-year term is simply too high for the commercial lender to feel comfortable.

LETTERS OF CREDIT   Until recently, letters of credit were issued primarily by commercial banks solely in connection with international sales transactions as a method of expediting the shipping and payment process. In a typical scenario, the seller of goods demands that payment be made in the form of a letter of credit and the buyer of the goods must then make arrangements with its bank to issue the letter. The buyer's bank, often in conjunction with a corresponding bank, will then communicate with the seller of the goods, explaining the documents that it requires (such as a negotiable bill of lading) as a condition of releasing the funds. It is important to understand that a bank issuing a letter of credit may be liable to the seller of the goods for payment if the bill of lading and related documents are properly presented, even if there are problems in the performance of the underlying contract between the buyer and the seller. Any defenses available to the buyer relating to the underlying contract are generally not available to the bank issuing the letter of credit.

In more recent years, the *standby letter of credit* has emerged as an indirect form of debt financing that serves as a guaranty of performance. Standby letters of credit are often issued by a bank on behalf of a customer in order to secure payments to a builder, landlord, or key supplier. The operative term of such an instrument is "standby" because if the transaction goes as planned, the instrument will never be drawn upon.

3. Negotiating the Loan Documents

Negotiating the financing documents requires a delicate balance between the requirements of the lender and the needs of the borrower. The lender will want to have all rights, remedies, and protection available to mitigate the risk of loan default while, on the other hand, the borrower—the company—will want to minimize the level of control exercised by the lender (generally through the affirmative and negative covenants of the loan agreement) and achieve a return on its assets that greatly exceeds its debt-service payments.

The actual documents typically involved in debt financing are discussed later in this chapter. Here, however, it is important to understand some general rules of loan negotiation.

INTEREST RATES Interest rates will generally be calculated in accordance with prevailing market rates, the degree of risk inherent in the proposed transaction, the extent of any preexisting relationship with the lender, and the cost of administering the loan.

COLLATERAL Collateral may be pledged that has a value equal to or greater than the proceeds of the loan. Under such circumstances, you should attempt to keep certain assets of the business outside of the pledge agreement so that they are available to serve as security in the event that additional capital is needed at a later time. Beyond the traditional forms of tangible assets that may be offered to the lender, companies should also consider intangibles (such as assignment of lease rights, key-person insurance, intellectual property, and goodwill) as candidates for serving as collateral. Naturally, these assets could be very costly to a firm in the event of default and should be pledged only when the ability to repay is readily available.

RESTRICTIVE COVENANTS   Restrictive covenants are designed to protect the interests of the lender, and the typical loan agreement will contain a variety of such covenants.

Affirmative covenants encompass the obligations of the company (and its subsidiaries, except as otherwise provided) during the period that the loan is outstanding, and may include (among others) the following affirmative acts by the company:

- Furnishing audited financial statements (income and expenses and balance sheets) *at regular intervals* (usually quarterly and annually, with the annual statement to be prepared and certified by an independent certified public accountant).

- Furnishing other information regarding the company's business affairs and financial condition.

- Furnishing copies of all financial statements, reports, and returns that are sent to shareholders or to governmental agencies.

- Giving access to its properties and to its books of accounts and records.

- Keeping and maintaining proper books of accounts.

- Complying with all applicable laws, rules, and regulations.

- Maintaining its corporate existence (as well as that of any subsidiaries) and all rights and privileges.

- Maintaining all property in good order and repair.

- Maintaining any agreed dollar amount of net worth (or any agreed ratio of current assets to current liabilities).

- Keeping and maintaining proper and adequate insurance on all assets.

- Paying and discharging all indebtedness and all taxes as due (except such as are contested in good faith).

- Purchasing and paying premiums as due on life insurance on named key personnel (wherein the company is named as beneficiary).

- Maintenance of existing management.

Negative covenants (generally negotiable) encompass certain actions for which the company must obtain the lender's consent.

These depend in large part on the company's financial strength and economic and operational requirements. The company must obtain the lender's consent in order to:

- Engage in any business not related to present business.
- Create any mortgage, lien, or other security other than pending security on the property securing the loan.
- Create any mortgage, lien, or other encumbrance, including conditional sales agreements, other title-retention agreements, or lease-purchase agreements on any property of the company or its subsidiaries (unless excepted).
- Incur any new indebtedness except for trade credit or renewals, extensions, or refunding of any current indebtedness. The company's right to incur indebtedness may be conditional upon compliance with a specified ratio (actual or pro forma) of pretax income to interest expense for a designated period.
- Enter into leases of real or personal property (as lessee) in excess of a specified aggregate amount. The company's right to make leases may be conditional upon compliance with a specified ratio (actual or pro forma) of pretax income to fixed charges for a designated period.
- Purchase, redeem, or otherwise acquire or retire for cash any of the company's capital stock (with stated exceptions) such as from post-tax earnings in excess of a specified amount or for regular sinking fund requirements on preferred stock.
- Pay any cash dividends (with stated exceptions) such as from post-tax earnings earned subsequent to a specified date or in excess of a specified amount.
- Become a guarantor (except as to negotiable instruments endorsed for collection in ordinary course).
- Make loans or advances to or investments in any person or entity other than its subsidiaries.
- Merge or consolidate with any other corporation or sell or lease substantially all or the entirety of its assets. There may be exceptions where a company is the surviving corporation.
- Permit net worth or current assets to fall below a specified level.
- Permit capital expenditure to exceed a specified amount (which may be on an annual basis, with or without right to cumulate).

- Permit officers' and directors' remuneration to exceed a specified level.

- Sell or dispose all of the stock of a subsidiary (subject to permitted exceptions) or permit subsidiaries to incur debt (other than trade debt).

Note that covenants may be serious impediments to the ability of the company to grow and prosper over the long run. Covenants should also be carefully reviewed for consistency in relation to other corporate documents, such as the company's bylaws and shareholders' agreements. You should note, however, that under the rapidly changing area of lender liability law, some commercial bankers are backing away from the level of control that has traditionally been imposed on the borrower's company.

PREPAYMENT RIGHTS   Prepayment rights should be negotiated regardless of the actual term of the loan; that is, the borrower should have the right to prepay the principal of the loan without penalty or special repayment charges. Many commercial lenders seek to attach prepayment charges that have a fixed rate of interest in order to ensure a minimum rate of return over the projected life of the loan.

HIDDEN COSTS AND FEES   These include closing costs, processing fees, filing fees, late charges, attorneys' fees, out-of-pocket expense reimbursement (couriers, travel, photocopying, etc.), court costs, and auditing or inspection fees in connection with the debt financing. Another way that commercial lenders will earn ancillary revenue on a loan is to impose certain depository restrictions on the company as a condition of closing on the loan, such as a restrictive covenant to maintain a certain deposit balance in the company's operating account or the use of the bank as a depository.

Understanding the Legal Documents

Loan Agreement

The *loan agreement* sets forth all of the terms and conditions of the transaction between the lender and the borrowing company. The key provisions include amount, term, repayment schedules and procedures, special fees, insurance requirements, conditions precedent, restrictive covenants, the company's representations and warranties (with respect to status, capacity, ability to repay, title to properties, litigation, etc.), events of default, and remedies of the lender in the event of default. The provisions of the loan agreement and the implications of the covenants should be reviewed carefully by an experienced attorney and a knowledgeable accountant. The long-term legal and financial impact of the restrictive covenants should also be analyzed. The company should negotiate to establish a timetable under which certain covenants will be removed or modified as the company's ability to repay is clearly demonstrated. Do not rely on any oral assurances made by the loan officer that a waiver of a default on a payment or a covenant will subsequently be available.

Security Agreement

The *security agreement* identifies the collateral to be pledged in order to secure the loan, usually referencing terms of the loan agreement as well as the promissory note (especially with respect to the restrictions on the use of the collateral and the procedures upon default of the debt obligation). The remedies available to the lender in the event of default range from selling the collateral at a public auction to taking possession of the collateral and using it for an income-producing activity. The proceeds of any alternative chosen by the lender will be principally for repaying the outstanding balance of the loan.

Financing Statement

The *financing statement* records the interests of the lender in the collateral and is filed with the state and local corporate and land records management authorities. It is designed to give notice to other potential creditors of the company that a senior security interest has been granted in the collateral specified in the financing statement. Specific rules regarding this document and the priority of competing creditors can be found in the applicable state's version of the Uniform Commercial Code (UCC).

Promissory Note

The *promissory note* serves as evidence of the obligation of the company to the lender. Many of its terms are included in the more comprehensive loan agreement (such as interest rate, length of the term, repayment schedule, the ability of the company to prepay without penalty, conditions under which the lender may declare an event of default, and rights and remedies available to the lender upon such default).

Guaranty

The *guaranty* serves as further security in order to mitigate the risk of the transaction to the lender and is personally executed by the guarantor. The terms of the guaranty should be carefully reviewed and negotiated, especially with respect to its term, its scope, rights of the lender in the event of default, and type of guaranty provided. For example, under certain circumstances the lender can be forced to exhaust all possible remedies against the company before being able to proceed against the guarantor or may be limited to proceeding against certain assets of the guarantor. Similarly, the extent of the guaranty could be negotiated so that it is reduced on an annual basis as the company grows stronger and its ability to independently service the debt becomes more evident.

Periodic Assessment of Banking Relationships

Recognizing the value and importance of growing businesses in today's economy, many commercial lenders have recently begun to compete fiercely for the business of smaller companies. In general, this has resulted in greater access to debt capital for growth companies as well as more variety in services being offered by the banks. It's wise to periodically assess a banking relationship to ensure that the best rates and services currently available to businesses of your size and within your industry are being received. This does not mean that a long-standing and harmonious banking relationship should be discarded over a difference of 1 percentage point in an interest rate, but it does mean that you shouldn't remain loyal to a bank that does not offer a full range of services meeting the needs of your company "just because the company has banked there for years."

In periodically assessing the relationship, the following questions should be asked:

- When was the last time you heard from your designated loan officer?

- What was the bank's reaction to your most recent request for another term loan or an increase in the company's operating line of credit?

- How well does the bank know and understand your industry?

- How strict has the bank been in enforcing loan covenants, restrictions, or late charges?

- What support services has the bank offered your company?

- How do interest rates and loan terms offered by the bank compare with those offered by other local commercial lenders?

- What is the bank's general reputation in the business community? What has it done lately to enhance or damage its reputation?

- Is the bank itself basically operating on a solid financial foundation (especially given the recent wave of bank failures)?

- Is the bank large enough to grow with the financial needs of the company as the business expands and additional amounts of capital are required? (This should be considered early on in the company's development so that the relationship is not outgrown just at the time when you need it the most.)

• Does this bank *really* want your company as a customer? What has it done for you lately to demonstrate this?

For the growing company with a steady projected cash flow, debt financing offers an attractive alternative for capital formation. Among its benefits are lower transactional costs, the power of leveraging, tax deductions, and an avoidance of dilution of ownership. However, these benefits come with certain high costs: restrictive covenants and high risk in the event of an inability to meet debt-service obligations. When seeking debt financing, you should be armed with an experienced management team that will be able to assist in the presentation to the lender, structure a sensible debt-to-equity mix, and negotiate an affordable loan. An understanding of the lender's perspective, the loan proposal package, and the related legal documentation will go a long way in obtaining the most favorable financing.

Protecting Intellectual Property

A growing company's development and continued success depend on its ability to invent and exploit new products and services; open up new distribution channels; foster new production and training techniques; implement new promotional and marketing campaigns; establish new pricing methods; and adapt to changes in competition, consumers' preferences, or demographic trends. Your ability to identify, develop, and protect intellectual property rights is critical. This protection can help your company do the following:

- Improve overall value and rate of growth by increasing intangible assets

- Create competitive advantages for itself and barriers for competitors trying to enter the marketplace

- Understand the intellectual property rights of other firms

- Create licensing opportunities and additional revenue sources

- Build consumer goodwill and brand loyalty

- Maximize control over the development and ownership of the ideas and inventions of employees

The development and protection of intellectual property play a key role in building a foundation for fostering your company's growth. In today's services-driven economy, a wide variety of software companies, franchisers, Internet service providers, and consulting firms have built substantial revenues and profits with nothing more than some well-protected and well-promoted intangible assets. For example, Microsoft, perhaps the most successful company of the last two decades, has grown primarily based on a series of algorithms protected by copyright law and a series of brand names protected by trademark law. Many clients that I have worked with over the years have followed this same model as a foundation for building a successful company. To fully understand your basic rights, you must first understand the different types of intellectual property and how each type is protected.

Patents

Let's start with patents. A patent grants an inventor the right to exclude others from making, using, selling (or offering to sell) or importing his or her invention throughout the United States for a limited period of time. To obtain a patent, the inventor would submit an application with the U.S. Patent and Trademark Office (USPTO). There are three categories of patents:

1. *Utility patents* (granted most commonly) are issued for the protection of new, useful, nonobvious, and adequately specified processes, machines, compositions of matter, and articles of manufacture (or any new and useful genuine improvements thereof) for a period of 17 years from the date the patent is actually issued by the USPTO. Utility patents can be issued for very complex technological developments, such as the inner workings of a telephone or a computer, or for something basic, such as the portable, rolling bag that so many airline staff and business people can be seen carting around airports.

2. *Design patents* are issued for new, original, ornamental, and nonobvious designs for articles of manufacture for a period of 14 years from the date of issuance. For example, to the extent

that the outer shell or casing of a computer or other piece of equipment was novel, yet nonfunctional, the ornamental design features might qualify for design patent protection.

3. *Plant patents* (used less frequently) are issued for certain new varieties of plants that have been asexually reproduced, for a term of 17 years.

Preliminary Steps in Patenting

The first step in determining whether to protect a new product or invention with a patent is to *understand the costs and benefits of patent protection.* The patent application and registration process generally lasts three to five years and often involves costly legal and consulting fees. As a result, it is crucial that you first determine whether the benefits of being able to exclude others from manufacturing, distributing, or exploiting the subject matter outweigh the high costs of prosecuting and protecting the patent. You should also consider whether there are adequate alternatives for protecting the invention. Is adequate protection available under state trade secret laws? To what extent does the business plan exploit technology before the patent is issued? For example, in an average patent infringement civil suit attorneys' fees alone could easily cost hundreds of thousands of dollars. When conducting this cost-benefit analysis, you should strongly consider the following questions:

- What is the projected commercial value of the invention? What are the projected out-of-pocket expenses for registering the patent? In addition to legal fees, what advertising, marketing, or engineering expenses will be incurred? If you are concerned that the targeted market for the invention may be limited, a patent may not be worth the cost of prosecution and subsequent protection.

- With regard to both infringement and commercial development, how close is the subject matter of the invention to existing patented and nonpatented technology? If the subject matter of the patent is too close to existing technologies, then the claims allowed by the USPTO will be very narrow and difficult to commercialize and protect.

- Can the subject matter of the invention be exploited within the time frame granted by the federal statute? Will the market value of the technology or invention be lost during the three to five years that it will take to obtain a patent? Timing is always an issue. If the subject matter of the patent is in a field in which technology is developing quickly, you do not want to run the risk that the invention will be obsolete by the time the patent is finally issued.

The statutory requirement that the application must be filed within one year of the public use *or* publication of the invention significantly limits market research and testing.

If you do decide to pursue a patent, follow two more steps before obtaining a patent attorney.

Compile and maintain careful records relating to the research and testing of the product. These records must:

- Contain certain key dates, such as the date that the invention was conceived and the date that it was actually reduced to practice. (On the latter date, the invention is well beyond the conceptual phase and either has actually been developed and tested or is described so clearly in the application that a third party skilled in the particular art could understand and actually develop the technology.)
- Be able to demonstrate the company's diligence in the development and testing of the subject matter.
- Include the corroboration of independent witnesses who are capable of understanding the nature and scope of the invention and who can verify dates of conception and actual reduction to practice, and the continued diligence of the inventor.

Conduct a search at the USPTO Public Search Room located in Arlington, Virginia (this is usually done by an attorney) to determine what patents in your field have been already issued and how these patents will affect your application.

The Patent Registration Process

Registration is a complicated process. The actual patent application is made up of several distinct parts, such as the following:

- Clear, concise description of the company's declaration that it is the original and sole inventor.
- Written drawings (where necessary) of the invention.
- Filing fees.
- One or more of the company's "claims" of exclusivity. The claims define the actual boundaries of the exclusive rights that the inventor hopes to be granted during the term of the patent. If these claims are drafted too narrowly, imitators and competitors will be able to develop similar technologies or processes without worrying about infringement. If the claims are drafted too broadly, the inventor runs the risk that they will be rejected by the USPTO examiner or subsequently be declared invalid by the courts in litigation if the validity of the patent is challenged by a competitor.

The review and ultimate determination of the patentability of the invention will depend on the company's ability to demonstrate to the examiner that the following statutory requirements have been satisfied:

- The invention constitutes patentable *subject matter* (e.g., process, machine, composition of matter, article of manufacture, or some new and useful improvement thereof).
- The company is the *original inventor* or discoverer of the subject matter of the technology described in the application.
- The subject matter is *novel* or *new*. It is *not* patentable if: (1) it is already known or used by others (already covered by another patent); (2) it is merely a new use of an existing product or technology; or (3) the subject matter has already been described in a printed publication.
- The subject matter of the invention is *useful* and not merely of scientific or philosophical interest.

- The subject matter of the invention is *nonobvious* to others in that particular trade or industry. *The USPTO has broad discretion in deciding what may be considered nonobvious.* A patent will *not* be issued if there are only marginal differences between the subject matter for which a patent is sought and the current body of knowledge of those "skilled in the art."

Patent Protection

Once a patent has been issued, you must embark on an aggressive patent protection program. This entails the following:

- Use of proper notices and labeling of the registered patent for the product
- Monitoring developments in the industry
- Policing the activities of licensees, employees, and others who came into contact with the patented machine or technology
- Exploiting the marketplace that has been created by the patented product
- Aggressively pursuing known or suspected infringers of the patent

Although the costs of patent litigation may be high, the rewards of stopping an infringer are also very worthwhile. Damages and equitable remedies (such as an injunction or an accounting for profits) are available, and federal patent law allows a court to triple the damages for extraordinary cases (this is also known as "treble damages").

Trademarks

A "trademark," for the purposes of this chapter, is to any word, name, symbol, or device used to indicate the origin, quality, and ownership of products and services. To be afforded federal protection, the trademark must actually be used in interstate commerce, or you must have a bona fide intention to use it. Not all words and symbols are eligible for trademark protection. For example, a chain of stores that repair transmissions under the name "Transmission Repair Shop" could not get a service mark because its name is too generic. By contrast, AAMCO is a nationally known trademark for such services. A trademark that is properly selected, registered, and protected can be of great utility to a growing company fighting to establish, maintain, and expand its market share. There is perhaps no better way to maintain a strong position in the marketplace than to build goodwill and consumer recognition in the identity selected for products and services that can be protected under federal and state trademark laws. It is important to note that *state common-law protection and federal protection of marks, while similar, are independent and may be concurrent.*

Determining a Registerable Mark

One of the most important benefits to be gained from federal registration is that it serves as constructive notice to the rest of the country that the trademark belongs to the registrant. This becomes an important right if it is later discovered that a remote company in a different geographic market has decided to sell competing products under the registrant's marks, damaging goodwill and creating confusion when the registrant enters that local market. So long as a registration predates others' use of the mark, the registrant has the right to demand that they discontinue use, as well as the right to institute a civil action for damages and even lost profits.

Before registering a name, you should conduct a trademark search to determine whether a competitor has already secured rights to this trade name or any similar name for the same or a related type of product. Because common-law trademark rights are grounded in actual and prior use, even federal registration does not give a registrant a right to stop others who have used the same mark in their local markets *prior to* the registrant's application.

Trademarks are generally deemed protectable or not protectable on the basis of the following criteria:

- *Arbitrary, coined, or fanciful marks* are the strongest category of marks that can be protected. Such a trademark is either a coined word, such as XEROX, or a word in common usage that has no meaning when applied to the goods and services in question, such as SKIPPY (for peanut butter), DOVE (for dish detergent or body soap) or YOO-HOO (for a chocolate drink). These types of marks are distinctive for legal and registration purposes; however, as a result of the obscurity of the mark, the burden is on the manufacturer to establish goodwill.

- *Suggestive marks* are the next strongest category. Such a mark requires the consumer to use some degree of imagination in determining what product or service is identified by it. Owners of suggestive trademarks are usually not required to establish "secondary meaning" (see below). Examples of suggestive marks include CHIPS AHOY (for cookies), CHAMPS (for a chain of retail sporting goods stores), and SUN MAID (for raisins).

- *Descriptive trademarks* are a category that *cannot* be protected unless the manufacturer can establish distinctiveness. This requires the manufacturer or producer to demonstrate that the public associates a particular mark specifically with its goods (such an association is known as "secondary meaning"). This category would include names like HOLIDAY INN (for motels), REDDI WHIP (for instant whipped cream), and QUAKER OATS (for hot cereal), which are descriptive but are nevertheless registered because they are distinctive.

There are a host of marks that will be denied registration; however, a trademark will not be denied registration if the applicant can show that, through use in commerce, the mark has become so distinctive so that it now identifies to the public the applicant's products or services.

A trademark is the consumer's first impression of the nature and quality of a product or service offered by a company. Therefore, some companies will select a mark that is easily understood by the public and thus can serve as a compressed advertisement. While such a mark may please the advertising staff, it is difficult to register and protect because it is often descriptive in nature. Growth companies ready to launch a new product or service should generally resist the temptation to select a descriptive trademark merely because it is intended to intimate the nature or quality of the product. The costs of establishing that the mark has special or secondary meaning to the public regardless of its descriptive nature can be very high. On the other end of the spectrum, however, coined words such as KODAK, or arbitrary marks such as CAMEL for cigarettes, will mean nothing to a consumer until the manufacturer invests the promotional dollars to establish understanding and brand recognition.

Factors to consider in selecting a trademark include these:

- Nature of the product or service

- Purchasing habits of target consumers

- Difficulty of recognition and pronunciation (keep it short and easy to read if possible)

- Trademarks already used or registered by competitors and others

- Avoidance of misleading, egotistical, trendy, or laudatory claims

- Anticipated size of promotional budget

- Adaptability to various applications and media

The Trademark Registration Process

Before the passage of the Trademark Law Revision Act of 1988, you were not eligible to register a trademark if it had been actually used in interstate commerce. To entrepreneurs, this meant that a substantial amount of time and expense might be invested in a proposed trade identity for a new product or service, with virtually no assurance that the mark could ever be properly registered and protected. However, under the current law a company may file an application for registration of a trademark, based on actual use *or* upon a "bona fide intention" to use the mark in interstate commerce (the latter is known as an "intent-to-use" filing). This process allows the applicant to conduct some market research and further investigation, without the need to actually put the mark into the stream of commerce.

To file an "intent-to-use" application, you should do the following:

- File an application for registration that meets the basic requirements of the USPTO.

- If the application is approved by the examiner, a "notice of allowance" will be issued to the applicant.

- The applicant will then have *six months* to file a "statement of use," attaching actual examples of use, such as marketing materials, receipts, invoices, newspaper clippings, etc. (commonly referred to as "specimens"). After review of the statement of use and the specimens, the mark will be registered. An applicant may request extensions of time for filing the statement of use for up to four successive six-month periods. Failure to file by the deadline will result in an abandonment.

Regardless of whether the filing is made under the "actual use" or "intent-to-use" provisions, an application must be prepared and filed in the classification that is appropriate for the goods and services offered. A trademark examiner will then review the application to determine if it meets the statutory requirements and whether similar trademarks have already been registered in the same or similar lines of business. You or your attorney must respond to all of the concerns of the examiner (if any). This process continues until the application is either finally refused or recommended by the examiner for publication in the *Official Gazette* (which serves as notice to the general public).

Those who believe that they would be injured by a registration may file a "notice of opposition" within 30 days of the publication date. If the parties fail to resolve any differences, there will be a hearing before the Trademark Trail and Appeal Board (TTAB). The TTAB is also the appropriate body to which to appeal a final refusal by an examiner.

Registration is effective for 10 years but may be renewed for additional 10-year terms thereafter so long as it is still in actual use in interstate commerce. The registration may, however, be canceled after six years unless an affidavit of continued use is filed with the USPTO, demonstrating that the registrant has not abandoned the trademark.

Benefits of Trademark Registration

Once your trademark has been registered with the USPTO, you will enjoy several commercial and legal benefits. These include: (1) the right to prevent businesses from using your marks in the future; (2) the right to bring legal action in federal court for trademark infringement; (3) recovery of profits, damages, and costs in a federal court infringement action and the possibility of triple damages and attorneys' fees; (4) the right to deposit the registration with the U.S. Department of Customs in order to stop the importation of goods bearing an infringing mark; and (5) a basis for filing trademark applications in foreign countries.

The Supplemental Register

A trademark that is in actual use in commerce but does not qualify for registration on the Principal Register for one or more reasons (e.g., it is merely descriptive or a surname) may be registered with the USPTO on the Supplemental Register. Registration on the Supplemental Register does not give a trademark the same level of protection afforded by registration on the Principal Register, but it does give the registrant the following:

- Right to sue in federal court and obtain statutory remedies for infringement
- Possible right to foreign registration, in foreign countries whose laws require prior registration in the home country
- Protection against federal registration by another of the same mark or a confusingly similar mark
- Right to use the encircled "R" symbol (®) on goods

Registration on the Supplemental Register allows owners of trademarks to put the world on notice of their use of and rights to the mark. Further, registration of a descriptive trademark on the Supplemental Register may be advantageous for a period of time while the mark's use is increased to the point where it becomes so substantial as to acquire "secondary meaning." It is at this time that the mark may qualify for registration on the

Principal Register. It may be advantageous for a company just starting up to use the Supplemental Register, if registration is denied on the Principal Register, until its products or services are sold and the mark, through increased use, gains secondary meaning.

The Trademark Application

The trademark application consists of the following. Note that a separate application must be filed for each mark for which registration is requested.

- Written application.
- Drawing of the mark. The *drawing* is a black-and-white or typed rendition of the mark that is used in printing the mark in the *Official Gazette* and on the registration certificate.
- Required filing fee (as of this writing, $245) *only if the application is based on prior use of the mark in commerce.*
- Three examples showing actual use of the mark in connection with the goods or services. For example, trademarks may be placed on the goods, on the container for the goods, on displays associated with the goods, or on tags or labels attached to the goods. Those filing under intent-to-use provisions must make use of the mark in commerce before the examples are submitted to the USPTO (they are filed along with the statement of use within six months of filing the intent-to-use application).

Trademark Protection

When the battle with the USPTO is finally over, a new battle begins, against the rest of the world. Once the mark is registered, you must develop an active trademark protection program designed to educate the company's staff, consultants, distributors, and suppliers, and all others that may come into contact with the company's marks, as to proper usage and protection of the marks. As with laws governing trade secrets, the courts will usually help only those who have attempted to help themselves. A company that tolerates misuse of its marks by the public or fails to enforce quality control standards in any licensing of the mark may lose its trademark rights—and thereby lose one of its most valuable weapons in the war for market share.

A well-managed trademark protection program begins with a formal compliance manual drafted with the assistance of trademark counsel and the company's advertising agency. The compliance manual should contain detailed guidelines for proper trademark usage, grammar, and quality. For example, a trademark is correctly used only as a proper adjective, and therefore it should always be capitalized and should always modify a noun. An example of a commonly misused trademark in this context is Xerox®, which is often used improperly as a noun to refer to the end product instead of the source of the process, or even as a verb to refer to the process itself. The trademark should always be used in conjunction with the generic name of the class of products to which it belongs: For example, Kleenex® facial tissues or Sunkist® orange juice. Compliance guidelines should address the following:

- Proper display of the marks (use of the ®, ™, or sm symbol).

- All documents, correspondence, and other materials on which the licensee must display the trademarks and identify itself as a licensee.

- All authorized uses of the marks and prohibited uses (e.g., the mark may not be used as part of licensee's corporate name).

In addition to a compliance manual, strategies should be developed to monitor competitors and other third parties from improper usage or potential infringement of the mark. A staff member should be designated to read trade publications, the business press, marketing materials of competitors, and in-house production, labeling, and correspondence to ensure that the mark is properly used and is not stolen by competitors. If an infringing use is discovered by a clipping service, company field representative, trade association, or supplier, then the owner of the mark must be vigilant in protecting it. This will require working closely with trademark counsel to ensure that all potential infringers receive letters demanding that such practices be immediately discontinued and infringing materials destroyed. As much evidence as possible should be gathered on each potential infringer, and accurate files kept should be kept, in the event that trademark infringement litigation is necessary to settle the dispute. A registrant who is considering litigation should carefully weigh the costs and likely result of the suit against the potential loss of goodwill and market share. It may be wiser to allocate those funds for advertising rather than for legal fees, especially if the likelihood of winning is remote.

Trademark Infringement and Dilution

The principal reason for a trademark monitoring program is to guard against trademark infringement or dilution. Under the Lanham Act, infringement is a demonstration by the owner of a registered mark that some third party is using a reproduction or imitation of the registered mark in connection with the offer or sale of goods and services in such a way as to be likely to cause confusion, mistake, or deception from the perspective of the ordinary purchaser.

The exact definition of the "likelihood of confusion" standard has been a source of much debate over the years. The focus has always been on whether the ordinary purchaser of the product in question is likely to be confused as to source of origin or sponsorship. The courts have listed a variety of factors as criteria for determining whether a likelihood of confusion exists, such as the following:

- Degree of similarity and resemblance between the infringer's marks and the registered marks (in terms of visual appearance, pronunciation, interpretation, etc.)

- Strength of the registered mark in the relevant industry or territory

- Actual or constructive intent of the infringer

- Similarity of the goods or services offered by the infringer and the owner of the registered mark

- Overlap (if any) in the distribution and marketing channels of the infringer and the owner of the registered mark

- Extent to which the owner of the registered mark can demonstrate that consumers were actually confused (this is usually demonstrated with consumer surveys and affidavits)

In addition to a federal cause of action for trademark infringement, many state trademark statutes provide owners of registered marks with a remedy against dilution. This remedy is available when a third party is using a mark in a manner that has the effect of diluting the distinctive quality of a mark registered under the state statute or used under common law. The owner of the registered mark and the diluting party need not be in competition, nor must a likelihood of confusion be demonstrated. However, in order for the registrant to make a claim of dilution, the trademark must have a "distinctive quality," which means that it must enjoy very strong consumer loyalty, recognition, and goodwill.

Trademark rights are often the most valuable asset of an emerging growth company in today's competitive marketplace. The goodwill and consumer recognition that trademarks and service marks represent have tremendous economic value and are therefore usually worth the effort and expense to properly register and protect them. For example, in the Internet search engine industry, companies such as Netscape and Yahoo! have actively promoted and defended their trademark rights to become international powerhouses, recognizing that the underlying services that they offered were basically the same as other search engines, so the distinguishing feature was one *brand* and the consumer's perception of the brand, which was closely guarded and protected. This also requires a commitment by management to implement and support a strict trademark compliance program, which includes usage guidelines for all departments inside the company, as well as for suppliers, licensees, service providers, and distributors. Clipping services, semiannual trademark searches, media awareness programs, designation of in-house compliance officers, warning letters to infringers and diluters, and even litigation are all part of an aggressive trademark protection program.

❛opyrights

A copyright is a form of protection available to the author of original "literary, dramatic, musical, artistic, graphical, sculptural, architectural, and certain other intellectual works which are fixed in any tangible medium of expression." The owner of a copyright generally has the exclusive right to do or authorize others to do the following: *reproduce* the copyrighted work; *prepare derivative works; distribute and transmit* copies of the work; and *perform or display* the copyrighted work, typically for the life of the author, plus 50 years.

Congress has struggled to keep up with the many modes of authorship that were not contemplated when the original copyright laws were written in 1790. Computers, photography, television, phonograph records, motion pictures, videodisks, the Internet, and advanced telecommunications have presented new challenges to legislators as to how to protect the rights of innovators and pioneers. A wide variety of database management companies such as Westlaw and Lexis, as well as Internet access and content or services companies such as America Online and CompuServe, have built large and successful businesses based on a foundation of protectable copyrights, both from an original works and a compilation perspective. For more information on the legal issues surrounding cyberspace, see Chapter 14.

The latest major revision of the copyright laws was the 1976 Copyright Act. Under the new laws, a copyright is recognized and can be protected as soon as a literary or artistic work is created in any tangible medium of expression. This gives the copyright owner control over access to and publication of the work right from the start. Copyright protection is typically available only to the person whose labor created the work; however, it is also available for certain types of compilations (the assembly of preexisting materials) and derivative works (translations, re-creations, etc.).

Copyright and Work for Hire

The Copyright Act defines a "work for hire" as being either a work prepared by an employee within the scope of his or her employment or a work specially ordered or commissioned if the parties expressly agree in a signed written instrument that the work shall be owned, as a work for hire, by a party other than the author.

This is in contrast to the typical situation, in which the author of the work is the owner of the copyright.

Under the doctrine of "work made for hire," works developed by an employee are considered to be owned by the employer. However, under the ruling in a recent major Supreme Court case, this presumption does not necessarily apply to freelance workers or independent contractors *unless* there is a written agreement stating that it is the clear intent of the parties that the copyright to the work will belong to the "commissioning party" and not to the "creating party."

Notice of Copyright

The author of a work protectable by copyright should, whenever possible, use a notice of copyright, which puts the world on notice that the author claims the work as a copyright. The prescribed notice consists of: (1) © or the word "copyright"; (2) the year of first publication of the work; and (3) the name of the copyright owner. However, as explained in Box 8-1, the lack of a copyright notice does not necessarily mean that the author does not intend to protect the rights to the work.

Copyright Registration

Pursuant to the Copyright Act, copyright protection arises *as soon as the work is created and fixed in a tangible medium* of expression. The work need not be registered prior to its publication; however, registration is necessary if the author wants to take advantage of the many benefits and protections offered under the Copyright Act, which include the right to sue for infringement, the ability to obtain damages, and the ability to stop others from using the work. Materials are protected *without registration* provided that they contain the required statutory notice of copyright (as described above). Prior to registration, it is advisable to examine whether registration would compromise the confidentiality of any trade secrets that may be contained in the work. For example, the content of a new marketing brochure is a natural candidate for copyright registration; however, the content of a confidential operations manual should not be registered, because of its proprietary nature.

Infringement of Copyright

To be able to enforce rights in court for copyright infringement, the author must register and deposit copies of the work in the Library of Congress. The Copyright Office will then examine the application for accuracy and determine that the work submitted is copyrightable subject matter. The Copyright Office, unlike the Patent and Trademark Office, will not compare a work against works already registered, and it does not conduct interference or opposition proceedings. The copyright laws do provide remedies for private civil actions. Remedies for copyright infringement include injunctions against unauthorized use, attorneys' fees, damages for lost profits, and certain statutory damages.

A copyright generally is infringed by the unauthorized use or copying of the work. However, since it usually is difficult to prove copying, proof of "access" to the work and "substantial similarity" from the viewpoint of a reasonable person is used instead. This shifts to the alleged infringer the burden of proving that the work has been independently created. There are several limitations on the exclusive rights of a copyright owner, and there are several acts that are permissible without triggering an actionable remedy for infringement (such as use of the basic idea expressed in the work, independent creation of an identical work without copying, and "fair use" of the work for purposes of criticism, comment, news reporting, teaching, scholarship, or research).

There are many different types of copyright problems that might arise for owners and managers of small and growing businesses. One common problem arises when independent contractors are hired to develop a key intangible asset that will be critical to the future success of the business, such as a critical software program, the design of a new line of jewelry or toys, an operators' manual, or a trademark design or slogan that will be the heart of the company's brand-promotion strategy. Issues of ownership and the possibility of joint ownership must be addressed early on in the relationship and then clarified in writing. Failure to do so could subject the small business to a loss of the asset and exposure to damages for copyright infringement.

The federal copyright laws make willful copyright infringement for commercial profit a crime. The court is required to order a fine of not more than $10,000, or imprisonment not exceeding one year, or both, as well as seizure, forfeiture, and destruction or other disposition of all infringing reproductions and all equipment used in their manufacture. The following civil remedies are among those also available to the holder of any exclusive rights in the copyrighted work under the federal law:

- Injunction against future infringement
- Actual damages suffered by the copyright owner
- Any additional profits of the infringer
- Full costs, including a reasonable attorneys' fee

Trade Secrets

A trade secret may consist of any type of information, including a formula, pattern, compilation, program, device, method, technique, or process, that derives independent economic value from not being generally known to other persons who could obtain economic value from its disclosure or use. A company uses its trade secrets to provide it with an advantage over competitors, and therefore such a secret must be treated by its owner as confidential and proprietary. The scope of protection available for trade secrets may be defined by a particular contract or fiduciary relationship as well as by state statutes and court decisions. Trade secrets are unlike other forms of intellectual property in that there are no federal civil statutes protecting trade secrets. Trade secrets are protected by state law.

Owners of small and growing companies whose success is due in part to the competitive advantage they enjoy by virtue of some confidential formula, method, or design—or some other

B O X 8 - 1

Some Quick Tips to Remember About the Ever-Changing World of Copyright Law

1. Remember that copyright protection can extend to computer programs, as a set of statements or instructions to be provided to a computer in order to achieve a specific result.

2. To be protectable, a work must be fixed in a tangible medium of expression. Copyright protects the *expression* of ideas, but *not* ideas, procedures, facts, or principles on a stand-alone basis.

3. Copyright law issues permeate the legal issues surrounding the Internet. Don't put on the World Wide Web what you don't intend others to use without adequate notice. Some courts have interpreted the ability of a "web surfer" to view or browse through your "work" as an "implied license" to use your work. (See Chapter 14 for more on the Internet.)

4. The purchase of copyrighted work does not necessarily mean that you own the underlying copyright. The object of the copyright can be separated under the law from the intangible copyright interest. The actual copyright interest can be only transferred by a signed agreement or by operation of law. For example, if you buy a sculpture, you have the right to display it in your home or office, but without an actual agreement of the copyright you do not have the right to sell pictures of it, nor may you operate a mold to reproduce it for distribution.

5. As explained in the section on "work for hire," independent contractors and freelance workers—not the company that pays for it—normally own the copyright in what they create, unless a written agreement specifies otherwise.

6. The absence of a formal copyright notice does not mean that the given work may be duplicated without the permission of the creator. The amendments to the Copyright Act of 1976 allow an author more flexibility, and it is not safe to assume that something is in the public domain merely because it lacks a formal copyright notice.

type of proprietary know-how—generally understand the importance of protecting trade secrets against unauthorized disclosure or use by a current or former employee, licensee, supplier, or competitor. It could be the formula for making Coca-Cola, the ingredients for the special sauce on the Big Mac, the recipe for Mrs. Field's cookies, the coveted customer list of a growing business, or a more technical process for delivering services in the telecommunications industry. Disclosure can cause severe and irreparable damage, especially to a smaller company whose trade secrets may be its single most valuable asset.

Criteria for Protection of Trade Secrets

Courts have generally set forth three requirements for information to qualify for trade secret protection: (1) the information must have some commercial value; (2) the information must not be generally known or readily ascertainable by others; and (3) the owner of the information must take all steps that are reasonable under the circumstances to maintain its confidentiality and secrecy. Examples of trade secrets include business and strategic plans, research and testing data, customer lists, manufacturing processes, pricing methods, and marketing and distribution techniques. In order to maintain the status of a trade secret, a company must follow a reasonable and consistent program for ensuring that the confidentiality of the information is maintained.

However, there are many factors in addition to those discussed above that courts have considered in deciding the extent to which protection should be afforded for trade secrets. Among the other factors most often cited are these:

- Extent to which the information is known by others outside the company
- Value of the information, including the resources expended to develop it
- Amount of effort that would be required by others to duplicate the information or reverse-engineer the technology
- Nature of the relationships between the alleged infringer and the owner of the trade secret

Unlike many large corporations, smaller companies cannot generally afford a complicated security system to protect their trade secrets. Given the mobile nature of today's workforce, turnover caused by promotion within, and the chaotic nature of most growing businesses, it is practically impossible to prevent a determined employee from gaining access relatively easily to the company's proprietary information. Unfortunately, therefore, it is easier to simply ignore the problem and do nothing at all about it. However, there are some fundamental, affordable, and practical measures (discussed below) that a company can readily adopt to protect the data that are at the core of its competitive advantage.

Implementing a Protection Program

Even in an effort to protect trade secrets, there is such a thing as overkill. In fact, the situation is like the story of the boy who cried wolf. If an emerging growth business tries to protect every aspect of its operation by classifying everything in sight as a trade secret, it is likely that virtually nothing at all will be afforded protection when put to the test. Genuine trade secrets may be diluted if the owners (and their managers) try to protect too much.

The process of establishing a protection and compliance program for trade secrets should start with a "trade secret audit" to identify which information is *genuinely* confidential and proprietary. Each type of business will have its own priorities; however, all companies should consider financial, technical, structural, marketing, engineering, and distribution documents as candidates for protection. The owner should next classify and develop security measures for protecting these documents. A separate office manual should be drafted for employees, written in basic terms, to inform them of procedures for protecting trade secrets. The importance of following the procedures in the manual could then be supported with timely interoffice memorandums, employee seminars, and incentive programs. Protection of trade secrets must be a part of the orientation program for newly hired employees, and departing employees should be fully briefed on their continuing duty and legal obligation to protect the secrets of their former employer. Periodic reviews of the technical and creative staffs are also recommended to identify new and existing trade secrets and reiterate the duty of nondisclosure.

The central components of such a compliance program are as follows:

- Ensure that adequate building security measures are taken, such as restricted access to highly sensitive areas, fences or gates to protect the premises, visitor control and log-in procedures, alarm systems, and locked desks, files, and vaults for proprietary documents. Post signs and notices in all appropriate places.

- Purchase stamps to be placed on documents that are trade secrets in order to give notice to users of their proprietary status and restrict the photocopying of these documents to limited circumstances.

- Designate a "trade secret compliance officer" who will be in charge of all aspects relating to the proper care and monitoring of trade secrets.

- Restrict employees' access to trade secrets. Ask: Do they really "need to know" this information to do their jobs properly?

- Carefully review advertising and promotional materials and press releases to protect trade secrets. Restrict access for interviews by reporters and other members of the media. Everyone has a horror story about a "wandering reporter" who brought a camera along for the ride, or about a company that was so proud of its new product that it inadvertently disclosed the proprietary features of the discovery in its promotional materials.

- Ensure that *all* key employees, marketing representatives, service providers, licensees, prospective investors or joint venturers, customers, or suppliers—or anyone else who has access to the company's trade secrets—has signed a carefully prepared confidentiality and nondisclosure agreement.

- Police the activities of former employees, suppliers, and licensees. Include post-term obligations in agreements, imposing on former employees a duty to keep you aware of their whereabouts.

- If trade secrets are contained on computers, use passwords and data encryption to restrict access to terminals and telephone access through modems.

- Establish controlled routing procedures for the distribution and circulation of certain documents.

- Purchase a paper shredder and use it as appropriate.

- Restrict photocopying of documents. Use legends and maintain logbooks on the whereabouts of originals.

- Monitor the trade press and business journals for any news indicating a possible compromise or exploitation of your trade secrets by others.

- Employees must be provided with guidelines on the care and use of confidential documents. These data should never be left unattended in offices, cars, airplanes, or hotel rooms, or at trade shows, conventions, meetings, or conferences.

- Conduct exit interviews with all employees who have had access to the company's trade secrets. Remind them of their obligations not to use or disclose confidential and proprietary data owned by the company, and of the costs and penalties for doing so. Notify the future employer in writing of these obligations, especially if it is directly or indirectly competitive. Conversely, in order to avoid litigation as a defendant, remind new employees of the company's policies regarding trade secrets, and remind them that they are being hired for their skills and expertise, *not* for their knowledge of a former employer's trade secrets.

Misappropriation

Misappropriation is the wrongful taking of your trade secrets by those who had a duty not to take this information for their own competitive advantage. Therefore, in order to be able to bring an action for misappropriation, you must establish a legal duty owed by those who come into contact with the information not to disclose or use the information. The simplest way to create this duty is by agreement. The owner of a small or growing business should have a written employment agreement with each employee who may have access to the employer's trade secrets. As discussed in Chapter 2, the employment agreement should contain provisions regarding the nondisclosure of proprietary information as well as covenants of nonexploitation and noncompetition applicable both during and after the term of employment. These covenants will be upheld and enforced by a court if they are reasonable, consistent with industry norms, and not overly restrictive. In the event of any subsequent litigation, such an agreement will go a long way toward proving to a court that the owner intended to take, and in fact took, reasonable steps to protect the trade secrets. The agreement should be only the beginning, however; it should be part of an ongoing program to make employees mindful of their continuing duty to protect the trade secrets of the employer. In some states, the unauthorized removal or use of trade secrets may also be a felony under criminal statutes.

Employment is not the only context in which the duty of nondisclosure might arise. An entrepreneur submitting proposals or business plans to prospective investors, lenders, licensees, franchisees, joint venturers, lawyers, accountants, or other consultants should take steps to ensure confidentiality at the commencement of any such relationship where trade secrets may be disclosed in presentations, meetings and documents.

PROTECTING AGAINST MISAPPROPRIATION   In order to bring a lawsuit against another party for trade secret misappropriation, the plaintiff must demonstrate four essential elements:

1. *Existence:* a trade secret existed.
2. *Communication:* the secret was communicated to the defendant.
3. Defendant was in a *position of trust or confidence* (had some duty not to disclose).
4. Information constituting the trade secrets was *used* by defendant to the *injury of the plaintiff.*

In analyzing whether these essential elements are present, the court will consider the following factors:

a. Was there any *relationship of trust and confidence,* either by express agreement or implied, that was breached?

b. How much time, value, money, or labor has been expended in developing the trade secret?

c. Had the trade secret reached the public domain? If so, through what channels?

d. Has the company made a conscious and continuing effort to maintain secrecy (agreements of nondisclosure, security measures, etc.)?

e. What were the mitigating circumstances (if any) surrounding the alleged breach or misappropriation?

f. What is the value of the secret to the company?

REMEDIES FOR MISAPPROPRIATION The most important and most immediate remedy available in any case of misappropriation of a trade secret is the temporary restraining order and preliminary injunction. This remedy immediately restrains the unauthorized user from continuing to use or practice the trade secret, pending a hearing on the owner's charge of misappropriation. Prompt action is necessary to protect the trade secret from further unauthorized disclosure. If the case ever goes to trial, the court's decision will address the terms of the injunction and may award damages and profits resulting from the wrongful misappropriation of the trade secret.

However, you should be aware that there are certain risks to evaluate before instituting a trade secret suit. The company may face the risk that the trade secret at issue, or collateral trade secrets, may be disclosed during the course of the litigation—although certain federal and state rules of civil procedure and laws of evidence will protect against this risk to a limited extent. The prospective plaintiff should also consider that the law covering trade secrets is very unsettled and often turns on the facts of each case. Establishing the "paper trail" needed to prove all of the elements of misappropriation may be virtually impossible in some cases. Also, lengthy litigation is likely to be prohibitively expensive for the average small business owner. For all these reasons, preventive and protective measures are a far more attractive alternative than litigation.

Trade Secrets and Departing Employees

Growing companies must be aware of their rights and obligations when attempting to protect intellectual property in connection with a departing employer. For example, if an employee has threatened to leave the company if certain plans were not implemented, can the employee leave and take the intellectual property with him or her? No employer can prevent an enterprising employee from using his or her personal skills and experience in the launching of a new venture or in a new job. The law does not mandate, nor will it enforce, an agreement requiring employees to "clean their mental slate" upon departure. There is a fine line between what knowledge belongs to the employee and what belongs to the former employer. Courts have attempted, relatively unsuccessfully, to develop some objective standard for what an employee in such a position would have learned regardless of where he or she might have been employed. Growing companies should note, however, that a few states (such as Pennsylvania) have determined that an employee *may use* trade secrets that he or she created while still in the employ of the former employer. About a dozen states severely limit or even prohibit the nature and scope of noncompetition agreements.

In analyzing a claim against an employee were he or she to leave, the company should consider the following factors: what information the employee was exposed to that truly constituted a trade secret; the terms of any employment or noncompetition agreements; steps taken by the company to protect the secret; the extent to which this secret could have been discovered through "reverse engineering"; the extent to which the employee used any company assets or resources to form his or her own business; the extent to which the employee acquired this knowledge independent of the company; the extent to which the employee contracted current vendors or customers of the company during or after his or her employment with the company; the similarity of the product or service to be offered; and the proximity of the new business to the former employer. Overall, the courts will be hesitant to stifle competition and the entrepreneurial spirit of the employee, absent some express agreement or foul play. However, clear breach of an agreement, a breach of a noncompetition clause, or misappropriation of a customer list or proprietary data should be pursued.

Trade Dress

Trade dress is a combination or arrangement of elements making up the interior or exterior design (or both) of a business. This concept usually arises in the context of a retail or restaurant business. For example, trade dress can be symbols, designs, product packaging, labels and wrappers, exterior building features, interior designs, greeting cards, uniforms, etc., used to build brand awareness and loyalty among consumers. Trade dress is protected by federal and state trademark laws if it distinguishes the goods or services of one company from those of its competitors. Protectable trade dress consists of three elements: (1) a *combination* of features (used in the presentation, packaging, or "dress" of goods or services); (2) which is *nonfunctional;* and (3) whose *distinctiveness* reveals to consumers the source of goods or services.

For example, in *Taco Cabana International, Inc. v. Two Pesos,* the jury found the following combination of restaurant decor features to be protectable:

Interior and patio dining areas decorated with artifacts, bright colors, paintings, and murals

Overhead garage doors sealing off the interior from the patio areas

Festive exterior paintings having a color scheme using top border paint and neon stripes

Bright awnings and umbrellas

A food-ordering counter set at an oblique angle to the exterior wall and communicating electronically with the food preparation and pickup areas

An exposed food preparation area accented by cooking and preparation equipment visible to the consumer

A condiment stand in the interior dining area proximate to the food pickup stand

Following are suggestions for enhancing the strength of trade dress:

- Adopt a combination of several features.

- Ensure that several of the features are unique.

- Avoid using features that are arguably functional.

- Use the features consistently and continuously.

- Include as many of the features as possible in advertising.

- Refer to trade dress features in advertising and promotional literature.

- Advertise as extensively as possible.

- Carry the "theme" of the trade dress throughout the entire business.

- Keep competitors from adopting similar combinations of features and from using features that are unique to your trade dress.

- Where possible, federally register the trade dress or its components.

- Do not advertise utilitarian advantages of any trade dress you wish to protect.

- Keep detailed records of instances of possible confusion among consumers between your trade dress and a competitor's subsequently adopted trade dress.

The best way to avoid claims of infringement of trade dress is *prevention*. To prevent such claims, avoid copying competitors' trade dress, investigate competitors' potential trade dress rights, and consult a skilled trademark attorney. Also, it may also be advisable to use disclaimers and to be more cautious when there is a potentially aggressive opponent.

Show-how and Know-how

Certain types of intellectual property are treated as such primarily because some third party is willing to buy or license them from a company or individual with particular expertise. In such cases, *show-how* consists of training, technical support, and related educational services, whereas *know-how* usually takes the form of information that has been reduced to written rather than spoken form. The concepts of know-how and show-how usually arise in the context of a licensing agreement where the licensee is requesting support services in addition to the tangible technology or patent that is the central subject matter of the agreement. To the extent that know-how or show-how is confidential and proprietary, it will generally be governed by the law of trade secrets unless otherwise covered by a patent. To the extent that know-how or show-how is nonproprietary and constitutes common knowledge, it will be governed by the term and conditions of the agreement between the parties.

Ideas and Concepts

As a general rule, an idea or concept as such does not qualify for patent, copyright, trade secret, or trademark protection. The right to the exclusive use of an idea is lost by voluntary disclosure unless the following three elements are present: (1) the idea is in a concrete form; (2) the idea is original and useful; and (3) the idea is disclosed in a situation where compensation is contemplated. If this test is satisfied, the idea may qualify as a "property right" and may be protected under theories of implied contract, unjust enrichment, misappropriation, breach of a fiduciary relationship, or passing off. Recovery under these circumstances usually will depend on the relationship between the submitter and the receiver of the idea, as well as by the facts surrounding the disclosure.

As a general rule, the law of intellectual property seeks to protect and reward creative firms, innovators, and entrepreneurs for their efforts by prohibiting misappropriation or infringement by competitors. It is therefore crucial that the legal considerations for protecting these "crown jewels" are incorporated into the strategic marketing plan of any emerging business. If proper steps are not taken to protect these new products, services, and operational techniques, then it will be extremely difficult to maintain and expand the company's share of the market, because others will be free to copy an idea as or concept as if it were their own.

The proper protection and, where possible, registration of intellectual property is essential to building and sustaining a company's growth. The procedures and expenses necessary to protect these valuable *intangible assets* are crucial to the continued well-being of the company and its ability to survive in a competitive marketplace.

CHAPTER 9

Growth Strategies for Emerging Businesses

The various challenges and problems associated with build-ing a company beyond the start-up phase have certainly taken a toll on the many entrepreneurs who began new businesses recently. Growth has traditionally been regarded by academics as the stage of the business life cycle that follows market entry. Many small companies that were founded during the "decade of the entrepreneur" never made it to this stage, usually due to stagnation or failure. To advance to the growth stage (and stay there), all of the challenges and changes caused by sustained growth must be well-managed, which is no easy task.

Growth causes a variety of changes, all of which present different managerial, legal, and financial challenges. Growth means that new employees will be hired who will be looking to the top management of the company for leadership. Growth means that the company's management will become less and less centralized, and this may raise the levels of internal politics, protectionism, and dissension over what goals and projects the company should pursue. Growth means that market share will expand, calling for new strategies for dealing with larger competitors. Growth also means that additional capital will be required, creating new responsibilities to shareholders, investors, and institutional lenders. Thus, growth brings with it a variety of changes in the company's structure, needs, and objectives.

179

The plans and strategies developed by management in order to cope with the changes caused by rapid growth cannot be made in a vacuum. The legal implications, costs, benefits, and risks of each proposed decision, transaction, plan, or strategy must be understood. An understanding of the legal issues raised by the inevitable changes caused by business growth is a necessary prerequisite to effectively managing the organization and to ensuring the long-term success and continued profitability of the company.

Business growth is truly a two-edged sword. When it is controlled and well managed, it has the potential of providing tremendous rewards to the managers and shareholders of the company. When it is poorly planned and uncontrolled, it often leads to financial distress and failure. For many companies, rapid growth is the only way to survive in highly competitive industries. These companies are faced with a choice of either acting quickly to capture additional market share or sitting on the sidelines and watching others play the game. Do these competitive conditions justify unplanned and unbridled growth, where sound management and legal and accounting principles are disregarded? Certainly not. But what these conditions do mean is that the need of the organization to grow must be tempered by the need to understand that meaningful, long-term, profitable growth is a by-product of effective management and planning. A strategy that focuses on sensible, logical growth dictates a balance between the need for a controlled, well-managed expansion plan and the need for organizational flexibility to quickly seize upon market opportunities, adapt to changes in the marketplace, and develop creative solutions for problems. Failure to achieve this balance will result in vulnerability to attack by competitors, creditors, hostile employees, and creative takeover specialists.

A commitment to properly growing the company will invariably trigger a need for management to undertake greater risks. These risks must be managed from a legal, financial, and strategic perspective, as must the changes that the organization will experience as a result of the growth. Accelerated growth means that these risks and changes will occur more frequently and will have more serious implications. The legal requirements and restrictions that affect most business objectives and transactions will typically retard the rate at which a company can grow. Since the law is not likely to go away any time soon, prudent owners and managers of growing companies should take the time to learn the fundamental legal issues governing their plans and strategies.

An emerging growth business is likely to experience a wide variety of changes in its structure, its products and services, its markets, and its capital requirements. Each change will raise a host of legal issues that must be considered before the implementation of a particular strategy for achieving the company's growth objectives. Naturally, the specific *legal* requirements of a growing company will depend on the following:

- Market segments and industry sectors in which the business operates
- Exact stage of the company's development
- Current and projected capital needs of the business
- Barriers that the company must overcome to achieve its objectives

Franchising

Over the last two decades, franchising has emerged as a popular expansion strategy for a variety of product and service companies, especially for smaller businesses that cannot afford to finance internal growth. According to recent statistics from the Department of Commerce, retail sales from franchised outlets make up nearly 45% of all retail sales in the United States, are estimated at over $800 billion, and employed some 8 million people in 1996. Notwithstanding these impressive figures, and despite the favorable media attention franchising has received over the past few years, franchising as a method of marketing and distributing products and services is really appropriate only for certain kinds of companies. *This strategy is not for everyone.* That is because a host of legal and business prerequisites must be satisfied before any company can seriously consider franchising as a method for rapid expansion. If franchising turns out not to be a viable route for your company, then, you may want to explore the alternatives to franchising discussed later in this chapter.

Many companies prematurely select franchising as a growth alternative and then haphazardly assemble and launch a franchising program. Some other companies are urged to franchise by unqualified consultants or advisers who may be more interested in professional fees than in the long-term success of the franchising program. This has caused financial distress and failure for both the growing company and its franchises, usually resulting in litigation. Current and future members of the franchising community must be urged to take a responsible view of the creation and development of their franchising programs.

Reasons for Franchising

Successful growing companies cite a variety of reasons why franchising has been selected as a method of growth and distribution. These reasons include the following:

- To obtain operating efficiencies and economies of scale
- To achieve more rapid market penetration at a lower capital cost
- To reach targeted consumers more effectively through cooperative advertising and promotion
- To sell products and services to a dedicated distributor network
- To replace internal personnel with motivated owner-operators
- To shift the primary responsibility for site selection, employee training, personnel management, local advertising, and other administrative concerns to the franchisee, licensee, or joint venture partner, with the guidance or assistance of the growing company

In the typical franchising relationship, the franchisees share the risk of expanding the market share of the growing company by committing their capital and resources to the development of satellite locations modeled after the proprietary business format of the company. The growing company's risk of business failure is further reduced by improvement in competitive position, by reduced vulnerability to cyclical fluctuations, by the existence of a captive market for its proprietary products and services (due to the network of franchisees), and by reduced administrative and overhead costs.

The Foundation for Franchising

Responsible franchising is the *only* way that growing companies and franchisees will be able to harmoniously co-exist in the 21st century. Responsible franchising means that there must be a secure foundation from which the franchising program is launched. Any company considering franchising as a method of growth and distribution or any individual considering franchising as a method of getting into business must understand the components of this foundation. The *key components of this foundation* are as follows:

- A *proven prototype* location (or chain of stores) which will serve as a basis for the franchising program. The store or stores must have been tested, refined and operated successfully and be consistently profitable. The success of the prototype should not be too dependent on the physical presence or specific expertise of the founders of the system;

- A *strong management team* made up of internal officers and directors (as well as qualified consultants) who understand both the particular industry in which the company operates as well as the legal and business aspects of franchising as a method of expansion;

- *Sufficient capitalization* to launch and sustain the franchising program to ensure that capital is available for the growing company to provide both initial as well as ongoing support and assistance to franchisees (a lack of a well-prepared business plan and adequate capital structure is often the principal cause of demise of many early-stage franchisors);

- A *distinctive and protected trade identity*, which includes federal and state registered trademarks as well as a uniform trade appearance, signage, slogans, trade dress, and overall image;

- Proprietary and proven *methods of operation and management* that can be reduced to writing in a comprehensive operations manual, not be too easily duplicated by competitors, be able to maintain its value to the franchisees over an extended period of time and be enforced through clearly drafted and objective quality control standards;

- *Comprehensive training* program for franchisees—both at the company's headquarters and on-site at the franchisee's proposed location at the outset of the relationship and on an ongoing basis;

- *Field support staff* who are skilled trainers and communicators who must be available to visit, inspect and periodically assist franchisees, as well as monitor quality control standards;

- A set of comprehensive *legal documents* that reflect the company's business strategies and operating policies. Offering documents must be prepared in accordance with applicable federal and state disclosure laws and franchise agreements should strike a delicate balance between the rights and obligations of growing company and franchisee;

- A demonstrated *market demand* for the products and services developed by the growing company that will be distributed through the franchisees. The growing company's products and services should meet certain minimum quality standards, not be subject to rapid shifts in consumer preferences (i.e., fads) and be proprietary in nature. Market research and analysis should be sensitive to trends in the economy and specific industry, the plans of direct and indirect competitors, and shifts in consumer preferences;

- A set of carefully developed set of uniform *site selection criteria and architectural standards* that can be readily and affordably secured in today's competitive real estate market;

- *A genuine understanding of the competition* (both direct and indirect) that the growing company will face in marketing and selling franchises to prospective franchisees as well as that franchisee will face when marketing products and services;

- *Relationships* with suppliers, lenders, real estate, developers, and related key resources as part of the operations manual and system;

- Each growing company should develop a *franchisee profile and screening system* in order to identify the minimum financial qualifications, business acumen and understanding of the industry that will be required to be a successful franchisee;

- An effective system of *reporting and record keeping* to maintain the performance of the franchisees and ensure that royalties are reported accurately and paid promptly;

- *Research and development* capabilities for the introduction of new products and services on an ongoing basis to consumers through the franchised network;

- A *communication system* that facilitates a continuing and open dialogue with the franchisees, and as a result reduces the chances for conflict and litigation with the franchise network; and

- National, regional and local *advertising, marketing and public relations programs* designed to recruit prospective franchisees as well as consumers to the sites operated by franchisees.

Many successful franchisers have built companies that have created wealth not only for their shareholders but also for the franchisees, by incorporating all the elements of the foundation described above as well as by being genuinely committed to the success of their franchisees. These companies include franchisers in a wide variety of industries, such as RE/MAX (real estate), General Nutrition Centers (retail health food and vitamins), Jani-King (janitorial services), and McDonald's (fast food).

Regulatory Issues

The offer and sale of a franchise is regulated at both the federal and the state level. At the federal level, in 1979 the Federal Trade Commission (FTC) adopted its trade regulation rule 436 (the FTC Rule), which specifies the minimum amount of disclosure that must be made to a prospective franchisee in any of the 50 states. In addition to the FTC Rule, over a dozen states, known as the "registration states," have adopted their own rules and regulations for the offer and sale of franchises within their borders. These states generally follow a more detailed disclosure format, known as the Uniform Franchise Offering Circular (UFOC).

Each of the registration states has slightly different procedures and requirements for a growing company before offers and sales are authorized. In all cases, however, a package of disclosure documents is assembled, consisting of a UFOC, a franchise agreement, supplemental agreements, financial statements, a franchise roster, an acknowledgment-of-receipt form, and the special disclosures required by the state, such as corporation verification statements, salesperson disclosure forms, and documents for consent to service of process. The specific requirements of a state should be checked carefully by the growing company and its counsel.

Structuring and Preparing Franchise Agreements

The *franchise agreement* is the principal document that sets forth the binding rights and obligations of each party to the franchise relationship. A franchise agreement contains the various provisions that will be binding on the parties for the life of their relationship and therefore must maintain a delicate balance of power. The franchisor must maintain enough control through the franchise agreement, to enforce uniformity and consistency throughout the system, yet at the same time must be flexible enough to anticipate changes in the marketplace and modifications to the franchise system and to meet the special considerations or demands of the franchisee's local market conditions.

The franchise agreement can and should reflect the business philosophy of the franchisor and set the tenor of the relationship. If well drafted, it will reflect a culmination of literally thousands of business decisions and hundreds of hours of market research and testing. Length, term, and complexity will (and should) vary from franchisor to franchisor and from industry to industry. Many start-up franchisors make the serious mistake of "borrowing" terms from a competitor's franchise agreement. Such a practice can be detrimental to the franchisor and the franchisee, since the resulting agreement will not accurately reflect the actual dynamics of the relationship. Early-stage franchisors should resist the temptation to copy from a competitor or to accept a "standard form and boilerplate" from an inexperienced attorney or consultant. The relationship between franchisor and franchisee is far too complex to accept such compromise in the preparation of such a critical document.

Regardless of the size, stage of growth, industry dynamics, or specific trends in the marketplace, all basic franchise agreements should address the following key topics:

RECITALS   The recitals—or "introduction to the purpose of the agreement"—essentially set the stage for the discussion of the contractual relationship. This section provides background information regarding the development and ownership of the proprietary rights of the franchisor that are being licensed to the franchisee. The recitals should always contain at least one provision specifying the obligation of the franchisee to operate the business format in strict conformity with the operations manual and quality control standards provided by the franchisor.

GRANT, TERM, AND RENEWAL   The typical initial section of the franchise agreement is the grant of a franchise for a specified term. The length of the term is influenced by a number of factors, including market conditions, the franchisor's need to periodically change certain material terms of the agreement, cost of the franchise, franchisee's expectations in relation to start-up costs, length of related agreements necessary to the franchisee's operations (such as leases and bank loans), and anticipated consumer demand for the franchised goods and services. Renewal rights granted to a franchisee, if included at all, will usually be conditional upon the franchisee's being in good standing (i.e., no material defaults by franchisee) under the agreement. Other issues that must be addressed in any provision regarding renewal include renewal fees, obligations to execute the "then current" form of the franchise agreement, and any obligations of the franchisee to upgrade its facilities to the "latest" standards and design. The franchisor's right to relocate the franchisee, adjust the size of any exclusive territory granted, or change the fee structure should also be addressed.

TERRITORY   The size of the geographic area granted to the franchisee by the franchisor must be specifically discussed in conjunction with what exclusive rights, if any, will be granted to the franchisee with respect to this territory. These provisions address whether the size of the territory is a specific radius, city, or county and whether the franchisor will have a right to operate company-owned locations or grant additional franchises within the territory. After conducting market research, some franchisors will designate a specific territory that could be successful without market oversaturation and then will sell that exact number of franchises, without regard to specific location selected within the geographic area. Any rights of first refusal for additional locations, restrictions on advertising, performance quotas relating to territory, and policies of the franchisor with regard to territory are addressed in this part of the agreement.

SITE SELECTION The responsibility for finding the specific site for the operation of the franchised business will rest with either the franchisor or the franchisee. If the franchisee is free to choose its own site, then the franchise agreement will usually provide that the decision is subject to the approval of the franchisor. Some franchisors provide significant assistance in site selection—conducting marketing and demographic studies and lease negotiations, and securing local permits and licenses—especially if a "turnkey" franchise is offered. Site selection, however, can be the most difficult aspect of being a successful franchisee, and therefore, most franchisors are reluctant to take on full responsibility for this task contractually. For additional protection and control, some franchisors will insist on becoming the franchisee's landlord through a mandatory sublease arrangement once an acceptable site has been selected. A somewhat less burdensome method of securing similar protection is to provide for an automatic assignment of the lease to the franchisor upon termination of the franchise.

SERVICES TO BE PROVIDED BY THE FRANCHISOR The franchise agreement should clearly delineate which products and services will be provided to the franchisee by the franchisor or its affiliates, in terms of both the initial establishment of the franchised business ("pre-opening obligations") and any continuing assistance or support services provided throughout the term of the relationship ("post-opening services"). The pre-opening obligations will generally include a trade secret and copyright license for the use of the confidential operations manual, recruitment and training of personnel, standard accounting and bookkeeping systems, inventory and equipment specifications and volume discounts, standard construction, building and interior design plans, and assistance with grand opening promotion and advertising. The quality and extent of the training program are important; this is clearly the most crucial pre-opening service provided by the franchisor, and it should include classroom as well as on-site instruction. Post-opening services provided to the franchisee on a continuing basis generally include field support and troubleshooting, research and development for new products and services, development of national advertising and promotional campaigns, group purchasing programs, and volume discounts.

FRANCHISE, ROYALTY, AND RELATED FEES PAYABLE TO THE FRANCHISOR; REPORTING   The franchise agreement should clearly set forth the nature and amount of fees that will be payable to the franchisor by the franchisee, both initially and on a continuing basis.

The initial franchise fee is usually a nonrefundable lump-sum payment due upon execution of the franchise agreement. Essentially, this fee is compensation for the grant of the franchise, the trademark and trade secret license, pre-opening training and assistance, and the initial opening supply of materials, if any, to be provided by the franchisor to the franchisee.

A second category of fees is the continuing fee, usually in the form of a specific royalty on gross sales. This percentage can be fixed or can be based on a sliding scale for different ranges of sales achieved at a given location. Often, a minimum royalty payment will be required, regardless of the franchisee's actual performance. These recurring fees should be payable either weekly or monthly and submitted to the franchisor together with some standardized reporting form for internal control and monitoring. A weekly or monthly payment schedule will generally allow the franchisee to budget for this payment from the perspective of cash flow, as well as provide the franchisor with an early warning system if there is a problem and allow the franchisor to react before past-due royalties accrue to a virtually uncollectible sum.

A third category of fees—also recurring—is usually in the form of a fund for national cooperative advertising and promotion. The promotional fund may be managed by the franchisor, by an independent advertising agency, or even by a franchisee association. In any case, the franchisor must build into the franchise agreement a certain amount of control over the fund, in order to protect the company's trademarks and ensure consistency in marketing efforts.

Other categories of fees payable to the franchisor may include the sale of proprietary goods and services to the franchisee, and fees for consulting, audits and inspections, lease management (where the franchisor is to serve as sublessor), and renewals or transfers.

The obligations of the franchisee to provide periodic weekly, monthly, quarterly, and annual financial and sales reports to the franchisor should also be addressed in the franchise agreement.

QUALITY CONTROL   A well drafted franchise agreement will always include a variety of provisions designed to ensure quality control and consistency throughout the franchise system. Such provisions often take the form of restrictions on the franchisee's sources of products, ingredients, supplies, and materials, as well as strict guidelines and specifications for operating procedures. These operating procedures will usually specify standards of service, requirements for trade dress and uniforms, condition and appearance of the facility, hours of business, minimum insurance requirements, guidelines for trademark usage, advertising and promotional materials, accounting systems, and credit practices. Any restrictions on the ability of the franchisee to buy goods and services, or requirements to purchase from a specific source, should be carefully drafted within the parameters of applicable antitrust laws. If the franchisor is to serve as the sole supplier or manufacturer of one or more products to be used by the franchisee in the day-to-day operation of the business, then such exclusivity must be justified by a product that is truly proprietary or unique (such as the eleven special herbs and spices protected for many decades by KFC).

INSURANCE, RECORD KEEPING, AND OTHER RELATED OBLIGATIONS OF THE FRANCHISEE   The minimum amounts and types of insurance that must be carried by the franchisee in connection with its operation of the franchised businesses should also be discussed. Typically, the franchisor is named as an additional insured under these policies. Other, related obligations of the franchisee that must be set forth in the franchise agreement include: keeping proper financial records (which must be made available for inspection by the franchisor upon request); maintaining and enforcing quality control standards with its employees and vendors; complying with all applicable employment laws, health and safety standards, and related local ordinances; upgrading and maintaining the franchisee's facilities and equipment; promoting the products and services of the franchisor; reasonably processing requests by patrons for franchising information; refraining from producing goods and services that do not meet the franchisor's quality control specifications or that may be unapproved for offer at the franchisee's premises (such as video games at a fast-food restaurant or X-rated material at a bookstore); not soliciting customers outside its designated territory; personally participating in the day-to-day operation of the franchised business (this required by many, though not all, franchisors); and generally refraining from any activity that may reflect adversely on the reputation of the franchise system.

PROTECTION OF INTELLECTUAL PROPERTY AND COVENANTS AGAINST COMPETITION   The franchise agreement should always contain a separate section on the obligations of the franchisee and its employees to protect the trademarks and trade secrets being licensed against misuse or disclosure. The franchisor should provide a clause clearly setting forth that the trademarks and trade names being licensed are the exclusive property of the franchisor and that any goodwill established is to inure to the sole benefit of the franchisor. It should also be made clear that the confidential operations manual is "on loan" to the franchisee under a limited-use license, and that the franchisee or its agents are prohibited from the unauthorized use of the trade secrets both during and after the term of the agreement. To the extent that such provisions are enforceable in local jurisdictions, the franchise agreement should contain covenants against competition by a franchisee—both during the term of the agreement and following termination or cancellation.

TERMINATION OF THE FRANCHISE AGREEMENT   One of the most important sections is that which discusses how a franchisee may lose its rights to operate the franchised business. The various "events of default" should be carefully defined and tailored to meet the needs of the specific type of business being franchised. Grounds for termination can range from the bankruptcy of a franchisee to failure to meet specified performance quotas or strictly abide by quality control standards. Certain types of defaults will be grounds for immediate termination, while other types of default will provide the franchisee with an opportunity to fix its mistakes within a certain time period before termination. This section should address the procedures under which the franchisor will provide notice to the franchisee of a default and should clearly explain how much time the franchisee will have to rectify the problem, as well as the alternative actions that the franchisor may pursue to enforce its rights to terminate the franchise agreement. Such clauses must be drafted in light of certain state regulations limiting franchise terminations to "good cause," and these clauses must state minimum procedural requirements to be followed. The obligations of the franchisee upon default and notice of termination must also be clearly spelled out, such as the duty to return all copies of the operations manuals, pay all past-due royalty fees, and immediately cease use of the franchisor's trademarks.

MISCELLANEOUS PROVISIONS   As with any well prepared business agreement, the franchise agreement should include a notice provision, a governing law clause, severability provisions, an integration clause, and a provision discussing the relationship of the parties. Some franchisors may want to add an arbitration clause, a "hold harmless" and indemnification provision, a reservation of the right to injunctions and other forms of equitable relief, specific representations and warranties of the franchisee, attorney's fees for the prevailing party in the event of dispute, and even a contractual provision acknowledging that the franchisee has reviewed the agreement with counsel, has conducted an independent investigation of the franchise, and is not relying on any representations other than those expressly set forth in the agreement.

Licensing

Licensing is a contractual method of developing and exploiting intellectual property by transferring rights of use to third parties *without* a transfer of ownership. Virtually any proprietary product or service may be the subject of a license agreement, ranging from the licensing of the Mickey Mouse character by Walt Disney Studios in the 1930s to modern-day licensing of computer software and high technology. From a legal perspective, licensing involves complex issues of contract, tax, antitrust, international, tort, and intellectual property law. From a business perspective, licensing involves weighing the economic and strategic advantages of licensing against other methods of bringing the product or service to the marketplace, such as direct sales, distributorships, and franchises.

Many of the *benefits* of licensing for a growing company closely parallel the advantages of franchising:

- Spreading the risk and cost of development and distribution
- Achieving more rapid market penetration
- Earning initial license fees and ongoing royalty income
- Enhancing consumers' loyalty and goodwill
- Preserving capital that would otherwise be required for internal growth and expansion
- Testing new applications for existing and proved technology and
- Avoiding or settling litigation regarding a dispute over ownership of the technology

The *disadvantages* of licensing are also similar in nature to the risks inherent in franchising. Disadvantages include the following:

- Somewhat diminished ability to enforce quality control standards and specifications
- Greater risk that another party will infringe upon the licensor's intellectual property

- Dependence on the skills, abilities, and resources of the licensee as a source of revenue

- Difficulty in recruiting, motivating, and retaining qualified and competent licensees

- Risk that the licensor's reputation and goodwill may be damaged or destroyed by the act or omission of a single licensee

- Administrative burden of monitoring and supporting the operations of a network of licensees

Failure to consider all of the costs and benefits of licensing could easily result in a regrettable strategic decision or in being stuck with the terms of a license agreement that is unprofitable because it either underestimates the licensee's need for technical assistance and support or overestimates the market demand for the licensor's products and services. In order to avoid such problems, a certain amount of due diligence should be conducted by the licensor before any serious negotiations with a prospective licensee. This preliminary investigation will generally include market research, legal steps to fully protect intellectual property, and an internal financial analysis of the technology with respect to pricing, profit margins, and costs of production and distribution. It will also include a more specific analysis of the prospective licensee with respect to its financial strength, research and manufacturing capabilities, and reputation in the industry. Once the decision to enter into more formal negotiations has been made, the terms and conditions of the license agreement should be discussed. Naturally, these provisions will vary, depending on whether the license is for merchandising an entertainment property, exploiting a specific technology, or distributing a particular product to an original equipment manufacturer or value-added reseller.

There are two principal types of licensing: (1) *technology licensing,* in which the strategy is to find a licensee for exploitation of industrial and technological developments; and (2) *merchandise and character licensing,* in which the strategy is to license a recognized trademark or copyright to a manufacturer of consumer goods in markets not currently served by the licensor.

Technology Licensing

The principal purpose behind technology transfer and licensing agreements is a marriage between the technology proprietor, as licensor, and the organization that possesses the resources to properly develop and market the technology, as licensee. This marriage is made between companies and inventors of all shapes and sizes, but the context is often an entrepreneur that has the technology but lacks the resources to adequately penetrate a marketplace, as licensor; and a larger company, which has sufficient research and development, production, human resources, and marketing capability to make the best use of the technology, as licensee. The industrial and technological revolution has a history of very successful entrepreneurs who have relied on the resources of larger organizations to bring their products to market, such as Chester Carlson (xerography), Edwin Land (Polaroid cameras), Robert Goddard (rockets), and Willis Carrier (air-conditioning). As the base for technological development becomes broader, large companies look not only to entrepreneurs and small businesses for new ideas and technologies, but also to each other, foreign countries, universities, and federal and state governments to serve as licensors of technology.

In the typical licensing arrangement, a proprietor of intellectual property rights (patents, trade secrets, trademarks, and know-how) permits a third party to make use of these rights pursuant to a set of specified conditions and circumstances, which are set forth in a license agreement. Licensing agreements can be limited to a very narrow component of the proprietor's intellectual property rights, such as one specific application of a single patent, or can be much broader in context—as in a classic "technology transfer" agreement, where an entire bundle of intellectual property rights are transferred to the licensee in exchange for initial fees and royalties. The classic technology transfer arrangement is actually closer to a "sale" of the intellectual property rights, with a right by the licensor to get the intellectual property back if the licensee fails to meet its obligations under the agreement. An example of this type of transaction might be bundling a proprietary environmental cleanup system together with technical support and training services to a master overseas licensee with reversionary rights in the event of a breach of the agreement or the failure to meet a set of performance standards.

Merchandise and Character Licensing Agreements

The use of commonly recognized trademarks, brand names, sports teams, athletes, universities, television and film characters, musicians, and designers to foster the sales of specific products and services is at the heart of today's merchandise and character licensing. Manufacturers and distributors of a wide range of products and services license words, images, and symbols—ranging from clothing to housewares to toys and posters. Certain brand names and characters have withstood the test of time while others have fallen prey to fads, shifts in consumers, and stiff competition.

The trademark and copyright owners of these properties and character images are motivated to license for a variety of reasons. Aside from the obvious desire to earn royalty fees and profits, many manufacturers view this licensing strategy as a form of merchandising *to promote the underlying product or service.* The licensing of a trademark for application on a line of clothing helps to establish and reinforce brand awareness at the consumer level. For example, when R. J. Reynolds Tobacco Company licenses a leisure apparel manufacturer to produce a line of Camel wear, the hope is to sell more cigarettes, appeal to the lifestyle of targeted consumers, maintain consumer awareness, and enjoy the royalty income from the sale of the clothing line. Similar strategies have been adopted by manufacturers in order to revive a mature brand or failing product. In certain instances, the spin-off product that has been licensed was almost as financially successful as the underlying product it was intended to promote.

Brand-name owners, celebrities, and academic institutions must be very careful not to grant too many licenses too quickly. The financial rewards of a flow of royalty income from hundreds of different manufacturers can be quite seductive but must be weighed against the possible loss of quality control and dilution of the name, logo, or character. The loyalty of the licensee network is also threatened when too many licenses are granted in closely competing products. Retailers will also become cautious when purchasing licensed goods from a licensee if there is a fear that quality control has suffered or that the popularity of the licensed character, celebrity, or image will be short-lived. This may result in smaller orders and an overall unwillingness to carry inventory. This is especially true in the toy industry, where purchasing decisions are being made by (or at least influenced by) the whims of five-year-old children who may strongly identify with a character image one week and then turn their attention to a totally different character image the next week. It is incumbent on manufacturers and licensees to develop advertising and media campaigns to hold the consumer's attention for an extended period of time. Only then will the retailer be convinced of the potential longevity of the product line. This will require the character licensing agreement to balance risks and rewards between licensor and licensee in the areas of compensation to the licensor, advertising expenditures by the licensee, scope of the exclusivity, and quality control standards and specifications.

In merchandise licensing, the name, logo, symbol, or character is typically referred to as the "property" and the specific product or product line (e.g., T-shirts, mugs, posters) is referred to as the "licensed product." This area of licensing offers opportunities and benefits to both the owners of the properties and the manufacturers of the licensed products. For the owner of the property, brand recognition, goodwill, and royalty income are strengthened and expanded. For the manufacturer of the licensed products, there is an opportunity to leverage the goodwill of the property to improve sales of the licensed products. The manufacturer has an opportunity to "hit the ground running" in the sale of merchandise by gaining access to and use of an already established brand name or character image.

Naturally, each party should conduct due diligence on the other. From the perspective of the owner of the property, the manufacturer of the licensed product should demonstrate an ability to meet and maintain quality control standards, should be financially stable, and should offer an aggressive, well-planned marketing and promotional strategy. From the perspective of the manufacturer of the licensed product, the owner of the property should demonstrate a certain level of integrity and commitment to quality, should disclose its plans for the future promotion of the property, and should be willing to participate and assist in the overall marketing of the licensed product. For example, if a star basketball player was unwilling to appear for promotional events designed to sell his own specially licensed line of basketball shoes (or even had a particularly poor season), this would present a major problem and would probably lead to a premature termination of the licensing relationship.

As a general rule, any well-drafted license agreement should address the following topics.

Scope of the Grant   The exact scope and subject matter of the license must be initially addressed and carefully defined in the license agreement. Any restrictions on geographic scope, rights of use, permissible channels of trade, restrictions on sublicensing, limitations on assignability, or exclusion of improvements to the technology covered by the agreement should be clearly set forth in this section.

Term and Renewal   Commencement date, duration, renewals and extensions, conditions of renewal, procedures for providing notice of intent to renew, grounds for termination, obligations upon termination, and licensor's reversionary rights in the technology should all be included in this section.

Performance Standards and Quotas   To the extent that the licensor's consideration will be dependent on royalty income calculated from the licensee's gross or net revenues, the licensor may want to impose certain minimum levels of performance in terms of sales, advertising and promotional expenditures, and human resources to be devoted to the exploitation of the technology. Naturally, the licensee will argue for a "best efforts" provision that is free from performance standards and quotas. In such cases, the licensor may want to insist on a minimum royalty level that will be paid regardless of the licensee's actual performance.

PAYMENTS TO THE LICENSOR   Virtually every type of license agreement will include some form of initial payment and ongoing royalty to the licensor. Royalty formulas vary widely, however, and may be based upon gross sales, net sales, net profits, fixed sum per product sold, or a minimum payment to be made to the licensor over a given period of time; or they may include a sliding scale in order to provide some incentive to the licensee as a reward for performance.

QUALITY CONTROL ASSURANCE AND PROTECTION   Quality control standards and specifications for the production, marketing, and distribution of the products and services covered by the license must be set forth by the licensor. In addition, the agreement should include procedures allowing the licensor to *enforce* these standards and specifications, such as a right to inspect the licensee's premises; a right to review, approve, or reject samples produced by the licensee; and a right to review and approve any packaging, labeling, or advertising materials to be used in connection with the exploitation of the products and services that are within the scope of the license.

INSURANCE AND INDEMNIFICATION   The licensor should take all necessary and reasonable steps to ensure that the licensee has an obligation to protect and indemnify the licensor against any claims or liabilities resulting from the licensee's exploitation of the products and services covered by the license.

ACCOUNTING, REPORTS, AND AUDITS   The licensor must impose on the licensee certain reporting and record-keeping procedures in order to ensure an accurate accounting for periodic royalty payments. Further, the licensor should reserve the right to audit the records of the licensor in the event of a dispute or discrepancy, along with provisions as to who will be responsible for the cost of the audit in the event of an understatement.

DUTIES TO PRESERVE AND PROTECT INTELLECTUAL PROPERTY   The agreement must carefully define the obligations of the licensee, its agents, and its employees to preserve and protect the confidential nature and acknowledge the ownership of the intellectual property being disclosed in connection with the license agreement. This section also describes any required notices or legends that must be included on products or materials distributed in connection with the license agreement (such as the status of the relationship or actual owner of the intellectual property).

TECHNICAL ASSISTANCE, TRAINING, AND SUPPORT   Any obligation of the licensor to assist the licensee in the development or exploitation of the subject matter being licensed are included in this section of the agreement. The assistance may take the form of personal services or documents and records. Either way, any fees due to the licensor for such support services which are over and above the initial license and ongoing royalty fee must also be addressed.

WARRANTIES OF THE LICENSOR   A prospective licensee may demand that the licensor provide certain representations and warranties in the license agreement. These may include warranties regarding the ownership of the technology (such as absence of any known infringements of the technology or restrictions on the ability to license the technology) or statements that the technology has the features, capabilities, and characteristics previously represented in the negotiations.

INFRINGEMENTS   The license agreement should contain procedures under which the licensee must notify the licensor of any known or suspected direct or indirect infringements of the subject matter being licensed. The responsibilities for the cost of protecting and defending the technology should also be specified in this section.

Distributorships and Dealerships

Many growing product-oriented companies choose to bring their wares to the marketplace through independent third-party distributors and dealerships. This type of arrangement is commonly used by manufacturers of electronic and stereo equipment, computer hardware and software, sporting goods, medical equipment, and automobile parts and accessories. These dealers are generally more difficult to control than a licensee or franchisee; as a result, the agreement between the manufacturer and the distributor will be much more informal than a franchise or license agreement.

Although a distributorship network offers a viable alternative to franchising, it is not a panacea. As just noted, the management and control of the distributors may be even more difficult than that involved in franchising (especially without the benefit of a comprehensive franchise agreement), and the termination of these relationships is regulated by many state and antitermination statutes.

Drafting Distributorship and Dealership Agreements

In developing distributorship and dealership agreements, growing companies must be careful to avoid being included within the broad definition of a "franchise" under the Federal Trade Commission Trade regulation rule 436, which would require the preparation of a disclosure document. To avoid such a classification, the agreement must impose minimal controls over the dealer, the sale of products must be at bona fide wholesale prices without any form of initiation fee and minimal assistance in the marketing or management of the dealer's business must be provided.

A well-drafted distributorship or dealership agreement should address the following key issues:

- What is the scope of the appointment? Which products is the dealer authorized to distribute and under what conditions? What is the scope, if any, of the exclusive territory to be granted to the distributor? To what extent will product, vendor, customer, or geographic restrictions be applicable?

- What activities will the distributor be expected to perform with regard to manufacturing, sales, marketing, display, billing, market research, maintenance of books and records, storage, training, installation, support, and servicing?

- What obligations will the distributor have to preserve and protect the intellectual property of the manufacturer?

- What right, if any, will the distributor have to modify or enhance the manufacturer's warranties, terms of sale, credit policies, or refund procedures?

- What advertising literature, technical and marketing support, training seminars, or special promotions will be provided by the manufacturer to enhance the performance of the distributor?

- What sales or performance quotas will be imposed on the dealer as a condition to its right to continue to distribute the manufacturer's products or services? What are the rights and remedies of the manufacturer if the dealer fails to meet these performance standards?

- What is the term of the agreement, and under what conditions can it be terminated? How will post-termination transactions be handled?

Differences Between Distributors and Sales Representatives

Distributors are often confused with sales representatives. There are many critical differences, which must be understood. Typically, a distributor buys the product from the manufacturer, at wholesale prices, with the intent to resell to a retailer or directly to customers. There is usually no actual fee paid by the distributor for the grant of the distributorship, and the distributor will typically be permitted to carry competitive products. The distributor is expected to maintain some retail location or showroom where the manufacturer's products are displayed. The distributor must maintain its own inventory storage and warehousing capabilities. The distributor looks to the manufacturer for technical support; advertising contributions; supportive repair, maintenance, and service policies; new-product training; volume discounts; favorable payment and return policies; and brand name recognition. The manufacturer looks to the distributor for in-store and local promotion, adequate inventory controls, financial stability, preferred display and stocking, prompt payment, and qualified sales personnel.

The sales representative or sales agent, by contrast, is an independent marketing resource for the manufacturer. A sales representative, unlike a distributor, does not typically actually purchase the merchandise for resale, nor is a sales representative typically required to maintain inventories or retail locations or engage in any special price promotions other than those instigated by the manufacturer.

Multilevel Marketing

Multilevel marketing (MLM) is a method of direct sale of products or services whereby distributors or sales representatives sell products to the consumer outside a retail store context, and often in a one-to-one context. In some cases, the distributor purchases the manufacturer's products at wholesale and profits by selling them to the consumer at retail prices. In other instances, distributors sponsor other sales representatives or distributors and receive commissions on the sales made by the sponsored representative or any further representative sponsored in a continuous "down-line" sales organization. Leaing merchandisers who use this form of marketing include Shaklee Corporation, Amway Corporation, and Mary Kay Cosmetics.

Regulation of MLM

MLM companies are regulated by a variety of overlapping laws, which vary from state to state. MLM programs are affected by a combination of pyramid statutes, business opportunity statues, multilevel distribution laws, franchise and securities laws, various state lottery laws, referral sales laws, federal postal laws, and Section 5 of the Federal Trade Commission Act. Recently, many MLM plans have been targeted for prosecution and litigation pursuant to these various laws. To date, enforcement of statutes and regulations has been rather selective and arbitrary, and many regulatory officials have developed a negative attitude toward the legality of any one MLM program. Therefore, from a legal standpoint, MLM is uncertain and speculative, and there is no assurance that even the most legitimate MLM program will be immune from some type of regulatory challenge.

Some states have laws specifically regulating companies that adopt multilevel marketing programs. Typically, any MLM company operating in any of these states must file an annual registration statement giving notice of its operations in that state and must appoint the state's secretary of state as its agent for service of process. In a typical state where MLM is regulated, a multilevel marketing company is defined as an entity that "sells, distributes, or supplies, for valuable consideration, goods or services, through independent agents or distributors at different levels, in which participants may recruit other participants, and in which commissions or bonuses are paid as a result of the sale of the goods or services or the recruitment of additional participants."

In addition annual registration, several states have imposed additional regulations on the activities of the MLM companies, such as these:

- Requiring MLM companies to let independent representatives or distributors cancel their agreements with the company. Upon such cancellation, the company must repurchase unsold products at a price not less than 90% of the distributor's original net cost.

- Prohibiting MLM companies from representing that distributors have earned or will earn stated dollar amounts.

- Prohibiting MLM companies from requiring distributors to purchase certain minimum initial inventories (except in reasonable quantities).

- Prohibiting compensation to be paid solely for the recruiting of other participants.

Pyramid Laws and MLM

Consumers often confuse legitimate multilevel marketing programs, which are generally valid methods for distributing products and services to the public, with *pyramid schemes*— which are generally unlawful arrangements and are subject to criminal prosecution in many states. Numerous laws and regulations have been enacted in the United States to prohibit pyramid schemes. For example, some state laws declare unlawful "pyramid sales schemes," "chain distributions," "referral selling," "endless chains," and the like. Pyramid distribution plans have also been declared unlawful as lotteries, as unregistered securities, as violations of mail fraud laws, or as violations of the Federal Trade Commission Act.

Broadly speaking, a pyramid distribution plan is a means of distributing a company's products or services to consumers. Pyramid schemes generally consist of several distribution levels through which the products or services are resold until they reach the ultimate consumer. A pyramid differs from a valid multilevel marketing company in that in its elemental form it is merely a variation on a chain letter and will almost always involve large numbers of people at the lowest level who pay money to a few people at the upper levels. New participants pay a sum of money merely for the chance to join the program and advance to the top level, where they will profit from the initial payments made by later participants.

There are several ways to distinguish a legitimate multilevel marketing program from unlawful pyramid schemes:

- *Initial payment.* Typically, the initial payment required of a distributor of products and services of a multilevel marketing program is minimal—often, the distributor is required to buy only a sales kit, which is sold at cost. Because pyramid plans are supported by the payments made by the new recruits, participants in a pyramid plan are often required to pay substantial sum of money just to participate in the scheme.

- *Inventory loading.* Pyramid schemes typically require participants to purchase large amounts of nonrefundable inventory in order to participate in the program. Legitimate multilevel marketing companies will usually repurchase any such inventory if the distributor decides to leave the business. Many state laws require the company to repurchase any resaleable goods for at least 90% of the original cost.

- *Head-hunting.* Pyramid plans generally make more money by head-hunting—that is, recruiting new prospects—than by actually selling the products. Multilevel marketing programs, on the other hand, make money by the sale of legitimate and bona fide products to consumers.

More than 25 states have laws prohibiting pyramid schemes, whether as "endless chains," "chain distribution schemes," or "pyramids." Programs that have the following three elements are prohibited:

1. Entry fee or investment that must be paid by the participant in order to join

2. Ongoing recruitment of new prospects

3. Payment of bonuses, commissions, or some other valuable to participants who recruit new participants

Generally, the purchase by a participant of a sales kit (at cost) is not deemed to be an entry fee or investment.

Cooperatives

Cooperatives have been formed as associations of member companies in the same or similar industries in order to achieve operating, advertising, and purchasing efficiencies and economies of scale. Typically, a cooperative is owned and controlled by its members. Cooperatives have been especially effective in certain inventory-intense industries, such as hardware, automobile parts and accessories, pharmacies, and grocery stores. There is typically a common trade identity that each independent business may use in its advertising and promotion; however, ownership of the actual trademarks vests with the cooperative itself. The organization and ongoing operation of the cooperative should be periodically reviewed by counsel in order to ensure that certain federal and state antitrust and unfair competition laws are not violated.

Consulting and Training Services

Many veterans of a particular industry choose to share their expertise with others by charging fixed or hourly fees for consulting or training services. In some cases, building your business as a consultant in lieu of licensing your proprietary information may be a viable strategy. Under this strategy, proprietary information is essentially sold to the client or seminar attendee at a fixed price. If support is needed by the client, then additional increments of your time and expertise may be purchased. This alternative, however, creates competitors without the benefit of an ongoing royalty fee and should be considered only if the expertise to be conveyed falls short of what would be needed in a business format franchise or even in a licensing situation.

Employee Ownership and Profit Sharing

Many growing companies initially turn to franchising as an expansion alternative because of the need to develop motivated district or store managers at each site. The theory is that this owner-operator has a better feel for the local market and, as an owner, will be more motivated to promote the franchisor's products and services. But there are many ways to motivate managers and make them feel like owners, such as employee stock ownership plans, executive stock option arrangements, and profit-sharing plans. As an alternative to franchising, each unit could be separately incorporated, with a minority stock interest granted to the key individuals responsible for the operations of that particular store or region. Such an arrangement could be done on a "per store" or regional basis. Although this results in some dilution of the ownership and control of each corporation, the managers would be expected to execute a shareholders' agreement that would place certain stock transfer restrictions as well as predetermined buyout arrangements on the ownership of the stock. Naturally, the terms of these stock ownership and profit-sharing arrangements should be structured with the assistance of a tax accountant and securities law counsel.

C H A P T E R

Growth Through Acquisitions:
Strategies for Buyers (and Insights for Sellers)

The frenzy for mergers and acquisitions over the last few years has affected owners and managers of businesses of all types and sizes. Even though the days of hostile takeovers may be over for now, mergers or purchases of privately held companies are still ways for a small business to grow rapidly. This chapter will focus on how you should conduct due diligence, value the company, and structure the transaction when buying another company. The chapter is written primarily from the perspective of an emerging company considering the purchase of another business of similar size as a method of strategic growth or diversification. But even though the focus of this chapter will be on the buyer's perspective, it should also be helpful if the sale of a business is being considered, by providing insight into the buyer's strategies and areas of concern.

Objectives and Criteria for Analysis

Mergers and acquisitions often play a key role in the ongoing process of planning for growth. It may be more efficient to acquire assets and resources from outside rather than expand internally. The process begins with an acquisition plan that identifies the specific objectives of the transaction and the criteria to be applied in analyzing a potential target company.

Although the reasons for considering growth through acquisition will vary from industry to industry and from company to company, the most common strategic advantages from your perspective as a buyer include these:

- Operating and financial synergies and economics of scale can be achieved with respect to production and manufacturing, research and development, management, marketing, and distribution.

- The target company may own proprietary rights to products or services that are not being developed to their full potential. Your company may provide the capital needed to move projects forward.

- The target company may stand to lose its management team because of insufficient opportunities for career growth unless it is acquired by a business that can offer higher salaries, increased employee benefits, and greater opportunity for advancement. Conversely, you may have a surplus of strong managers who are likely to leave unless your company acquires other businesses, which these managers can operate and develop.

- A growing company may wish to stabilize its earnings stream and mitigate its risk of business failure by diversifying its products and services through acquisition rather than internal development.

- The growing company may need to deploy excess cash into a tax-efficient project (since both distributions of dividends and stock redemptions are generally taxable transactions to its shareholders).

- The growing company may want to achieve certain production and distribution economies of scale through vertical integration, which would involve the acquisition of a key supplier or customer.

- The target company's management team may be ready for retirement, or a key manager may have recently died (leaving

B O X   1 0 - 1

Steps Involved in an Acquisition

1. Development of acquisition objectives
2. Analysis of projected economic and financial gains to be achieved by the acquisition
3. Assembly of an acquisition team (typically managers, attorneys, accountants, and investment bankers)
4. Search for acquisition candidates
5. Performance of due diligence analysis of prime candidates
6. Conducting initial negotiations and valuation of the selected target
7. Selecting the structure of the transaction
8. Identifying sources of financing for the transaction
9. Detailed bidding and negotiations
10. Obtaining all shareholder and third-party consents and approvals
11. Structuring the legal documents
12. Preparation for the closing
13. The closing
14. Post-closing tasks and responsibilities
15. Implementation of the strategic integration of the buyer and the target

the business with residual assets that can be utilized by your company).

- You may wish to increase your market power by acquiring competitors (which may be a less costly alternative for growth than internal expansion).

- You may be weak in certain key business areas, such as research and development or marketing (and it may be more efficient to fill these gaps through an acquisition rather than attempting to build these departments internally).

- A growing company may have superior products and services but may lack the consumer loyalty or protected trademarks needed to gain recognition in the marketplace, and the acquisition of an older, more established firm becomes a more efficient method of establishing goodwill.

- A growing company may wish to penetrate new geographic markets and may find that it is cheaper to acquire firms already doing business in those areas, rather than attempt to establish market diversification from scratch.

- The target company may lack the technical expertise or capital needed to grow to the next likely stage in its development (unless it is acquired by a firm with such resources already in place).

In developing and defining a set of objectives, it is crucial to avoid certain myths. For example, do not rely too heavily on the previous year's earnings or a "multiple of sales" formula to determine the valuation of a target. Rather, you should look closely at the underlying foundation of the target's business, such as economic and technological trends affecting its outlook, the quality of its assets and management team, its dependency on a particular key supplier or customer, and the extent to which intellectual property has been protected. In addition, other financial data about the target should be examined, beyond its sales figures, such as cash flow, management of accounts receivable, credit ratings, and cost of goods sold. Probe beyond the data contained in the financial statements and remember that financial statements provided by a prospective target can be incomplete or very misleading—especially because most target companies have spent years trying to understate their financial performance in order to avoid excessive tax liability or percentage to lessors and licensors, and now for the first time are seeking to overstate their performance. In addition, certain steps can be taken by a target's management in order to make the financial statements more attractive in anticipation of a sale, such as capitalizing items that are normally taken as a direct expense, overstating the value of assets, and understating the extent of liabilities.

A second common misperception is that diversification significantly reduces the risk of business failure. Although a diversified line of products and services does tend to stabilize a company's earnings stream, it can also be a very dangerous and expensive acquisition strategy. For example, the negotiation and structure of the transaction will often be driven by an awareness of the special issues affecting the industry in which the target operates. You will be at an extreme disadvantage, *both during the negotiations and beyond the closing,* if you misunderstand or lack knowledge about the particular industry. It is therefore imperative for your acquisition team to conduct meaningful due diligence (as a result of their background and prior experience with a business similar or related to the target). An alternative is to structure part of the purchase price in the form of a post-closing long-term consulting contract so that the benefits of the target's expertise are preserved. That way the target's knowledge is transferred to the employees who will be responsible for managing the company once the target finally departs.

A third myth to avoid when developing acquisition objectives is the assumption that the best opportunities are found in "turnaround" situations. While a financially distressed target may be available at a lower price than a healthy firm, the difference in price may not be worth the drain on resources that would be necessary in order to rehabilitate the target. For example, a target company that has been grossly mismanaged may be put back on its feet by new, talented management. On the other hand, some companies that are available for acquisition may represent spin-offs of divisions of larger companies that have been a drain for the parent since inception or should have never been started. In such cases, it will be especially difficult (if not impossible) for you to apply enough talent, expertise, and capital to achieve a turnaround. The most effective way to distinguish between a target that has truly kinetic energy and salvageable assets and one that either has too many skeletons in the closet or will always be the "walking dead" is through effective due diligence and analysis.

The Search: Analysis of Target Companies

Once you have identified your objectives for an acquisition and developed the criteria for analyzing a target company, a logical next step is to narrow the field of candidates. The transaction should achieve one or more of your developed objectives, and the target should meet many (if not all) of the criteria identified. A candidate under serious consideration should have most or all of the following characteristics:

- Operating in an industry that demonstrates potential for growth.
- Protection of any proprietary aspects of its products and services.
- Development of a well-defined and established market position.
- Involvement in little or no litigation (especially litigation with a key customer or supplier).
- Positioned to readily obtain key third-party consents from lessors, bankers, creditors, suppliers, and customers. Failure to obtain necessary consents to the assignment of key contracts will be a substantial impediment to the completion of the transaction.
- Positioned for a sale (except in hostile takeover situations) so that negotiations focus on the terms of the sale, *not* on whether to sell in the first place.
- Principal place of business located within an hour (via plane) of your company's headquarters or satellite offices (unless, of course, your primary objective is to enter into new geographic markets).

Once the field of candidates has been narrowed, it is time to select the finalists. Effective analysis and rating of the finalists will involve two phases: (1) *pre-acquisition review;* and (2) detailed legal and business *due diligence.*

Pre-Acquisition Review

The *pre-acquisition review* is the preliminary analysis that is conducted on the two or three finalists that most closely meet your objectives. In all likelihood, these prospective targets will have different strengths and weaknesses, making the selection of the winner that much more difficult. Thus the central goal of the pre-acquisition review is to collect data that will be useful in determining the value of the finalists for negotiation and bidding purposes.

The key areas of inquiry at this stage in the transaction include these:

- Target's management team
- Financial performance (to-date and projected)
- Areas of potential liability to a successor company
- Identification of any legal or business impediments to the transaction
- Confirmation of any facts underlying the terms of the proposed valuation and bid
- Extent to which the intellectual property of the company has been protected

This information can be obtained from meetings and requests for information from the target's management team or from external sources such as trade associations, the target's customers and suppliers, industry publications, chambers of commerce, securities law filings, or private data sources such as Dun & Bradstreet, Standard & Poor's, and Moody's.

Once you have the data for the finalists, the pre-acquisition team should be assembled to analyze the information and to structure the terms of the offering. The end result of the analysis should be a letter of intent or preliminary agreement with the target selected.

Often, the buyer and seller execute a letter of intent as an agreement in principle to consummate the transaction. The parties should be very clear as to whether the letter of intent is a binding preliminary contract or merely a memorandum from which the formal legal documents can be drafted once due diligence is completed. The letter of intent has many advantages to both parties, which include the following:

- Psychological commitment to the transaction
- Expedition of the formal negotiations
- Overview of matters requiring further discussion

One difficult issue in drafting a letter of intent is whether or not to include a price. From the buyer's perspective, the price at which the target should be purchased should not be set until due diligence has been completed. However, the seller may be hesitant to proceed without a price commitment. Therefore, a range should generally be established, with a clause stating the factors that will influence the final price. As the buyer, you should always reserve the right to change the price and terms in case information is discovered during due diligence that will offset the target's value (or to draft "holdback" clauses to allow for any unforeseen liabilities or events).

Finally, it is not unusual for a seller to request that a buyer execute a confidentiality agreement before conducting extensive due diligence. Negotiate the narrowest possible scope in connection with such agreements, especially if you are in the same industry as the target, or a similar industry.

Conducting Due Diligence

Once a preliminary agreement has been reached, you and your acquisition team should immediately embark on the extensive legal and business due diligence that must occur before closing the transaction. *Legal due diligence* focuses on potential legal issues and problems that may be impediments to the transaction and may shed light on how the documents should be structured. *Business due diligence* focuses on the strategic issues surrounding the transaction, such as integration of the human and financial resources of the two companies; confirmation of the operating, production, and distribution synergies and economies of scale to be achieved by the acquisition; and the gathering of information necessary for financing the transaction.

Overall, the due diligence process can be tedious, frustrating, time-consuming, and expensive. Yet it is a necessary prerequisite to a well planned acquisition and can be quite informative and revealing in analyzing the target company and in measuring the costs and risks associated with the transaction. Expect sellers to become defensive, evasive, and impatient during the due diligence phase of the transaction. This behavior occurs because most managers really do not enjoy having their business policies and decisions under the microscope (especially for an extended period of time and by a party searching for skeletons in the closet). Eventually, the target is likely to give an ultimatum to the prospective buyer: Finish the due diligence soon, or the deal is off. In my experience, when negotiations have reached this point, it's probably best to end the examination process. Avoid "due diligence overkill" by keeping in mind that due diligence is *not* a perfect process. Information will slip through the cracks—and that is precisely why broad representations, warranties, and indemnification provisions should be structured into the final purchase agreement in order to protect you, as the buyer. The nature and scope of these provisions are likely to be hotly contested in the negotiations. One way to expedite the due diligence process and ensure that virtually no stone remains unturned is through effective preparation and planning.

Legal Due Diligence

In analyzing the target company, work closely with your attorney to gather and review the legal documents (which may be relevant to the structure and pricing of the transaction, to your potential legal risks and liabilities following the closing, and to the identification of all the concerns and approvals that must be obtained from third parties and government agencies). For a list of the legal documents, see Box 10-2.

In reviewing the legal documents and business records, the acquisition team, along with your attorney, should gather data necessary to answer the following types of preliminary legal questions relevant to the transaction:

- What legal steps will need to be taken to effectuate the transaction (e.g., approval by directors and stockholders, share transfer restrictions, restrictive covenants in loan documentation)?
- What antitrust problems (if any) are raised by the transaction? Will filing be necessary under the pre-merger notification provisions of the Hart-Scott-Rodino Act?

- Will the transaction be exempt from registration under applicable federal and state securities loans under the "sale of business" doctrine?

- What potential adverse tax consequences to the buyer, the seller, and their respective stockholders may be triggered by the transaction?

- What are the potential post-closing risks and obligations of the buyer? To what extent should the seller be held liable for such potential liability? What steps (if any) can be taken to reduce these potential risks or liabilities? What will it cost to implement these steps?

- What are the impediments to the ability to sell key tangible and intangible assets of the target company that are desired by the buyer (such as real estate, intellectual property, favorable contracts or leases, human resources, or plant and equipment)?

- What are the obligations and responsibilities of the buyer and seller under applicable environmental and hazardous waste laws, such as the Comprehensive Environmental Response Compensation and Liability Act (CERCLA)?

- What are the obligations and responsibilities of the buyer and seller to the creditors of the target (e.g., bulk transfer laws under Article 6 of the applicable state's commercial code)?

- What are the obligations and responsibilities of the buyer and seller under applicable federal and state labor and employment laws (e.g., will the buyer be subject to successor liability under federal labor laws and, as a result, be obligated to recognize the presence of organized labor and therefore be obligated to negotiate existing collective bargaining agreements)?

- To what extent will employment, consulting, confidentiality, or noncompetition agreements need to be created or modified in connection with the proposed transaction?

Finally, the acquisition team and legal counsel should carefully review the documents and records received from the target in order to determine how the information gathered will affect the structure or the proposed financing of the transaction.

Legal Documents to Gather During Due Diligence

A. Corporate matters

1. Corporate records
   a. Certificate of incorporation and all amendments
   b. Bylaws as amended
   c. Minute books, including resolutions and minutes of all director and shareholder meetings
   d. Current list of shareholders (certified by the corporate secretary) and stock transfer books
   e. List of all states, countries, and other jurisdictions in which the target transacts business or is qualified to do business
   f. Applications or other filings in each state listed in (e) for qualification as foreign corporation and evidence of qualification

2. Agreements among the shareholders

3. All contracts restricting the sale or transfer of shares of the company, such as buy-sell agreements subscription agreements, offeree questionnaire, or contractual rights of first refusal, as well as all agreements for the right to purchase shares, such as stock options or warrants

B. Financial matters

1. List of and copies of management and similar reports or memoranda relating to the material aspects of the business operations or products, such as a recent analysis of the company's inventory turnover problems, or a recent market research report that may affect the future growth of the seller

2. Letters of counsel in response to auditors' requests for the preceding five years

3. Reports of independent accountants to the board of directors for the preceding five years

4. Revolving credit and term-loan agreements, indentures, and other debt instruments, including all documents relating to shareholder loans

5. Correspondence with principal lenders to the target

(Box continued on next page)

6. Personal guarantees of target's indebtedness by its shareholders or other parties

7. Agreements by the target where it has served as a guarantor for the obligations of third parties

8. Federal, state, and local tax returns and correspondence with federal, state, and local tax officials.

9. Federal filings regarding subchapter S status (where applicable)

10. Any private placement memorandum prepared and used (as well as any document used in lieu of a private placement memorandum, such as an investment profile or a business plan)

11. Financial statements for the past five years, including:
    a. Audited annual balance sheets
    b. Monthly (or other available) balance sheets
    c. Audited annual and monthly (or other available) earnings statements
    d. Audited annual and monthly (or other available) statements of shareholders' equity and changes in financial position
    e. Any recently prepared projections for the target
    f. Footnotes or management's analysis of the financial reports

12. Any information or documentation relating to tax assessments, deficiency notices, investigations, audits, or settlement proposals

13. Informal schedule of key management compensation (this should include a list of at least the 10 most highly compensated management employees or consultants)

14. Projected budgets, accounts receivable reports, and related information

C. Management and employment matters

1. All employment agreements

2. Agreements relating to consulting, management, financial advisory services, and other professional engagements

3. Copies of all union contracts and collective bargaining agreements

4. Equal Employment Opportunity Commission (EEOC) and any state equivalent compliance files

5. Occupational Safety and Health Administration (OSHA) files and records

6. Employee benefit plans, including the following:
    a. Pension and retirement plans (including union plans)

(Box continued on next page)

      b. Annual reports for pension plans, if any

      c. Profit-sharing plans

      d. Stock option plans (including information concerning all options, stock appreciation rights, and other stock-related benefits granted by the company)

      e. Medical and dental plans

      f. All memos describing benefit plans that were distributed to employees

      g. Insurance plans and policies, including the following:

         (1) Errors and omissions policies

         (2) Directors' and officers' liability insurance policies

      h. Any employee stock ownership plan (ESOP) and trust agreement

      i. Severance pay plans or programs

      j. All other benefit or incentive plans or arrangements not covered by the foregoing (including welfare benefit plans)

7. All current contract agreements with or pertaining to the target to which directors, officers, or shareholders are parties, and any documents relating to any other transactions between the target and any director, officer, or shareholders (including receivables from or payables to directors, officers or shareholders)

8. All policy and procedures manuals of the target concerning personnel, business operations, sales, etc.

9. Name, address and phone number of any officer who has left within the past two years

D. Tangible and intangible assets

1. List of all commitments for rented or leased real and personal property (including location and address, description, terms, options, and annual costs)

2. List of all real property owned (including location and address, description of general character, and encumbrances)

3. List of all material tangible assets

4. List of all liens on all real properties and material tangible assets

5. Mortgages, deeds, title insurance policies, leases, and other agreements relating to the properties of the target

6. Real estate tax bills for the target

7. List of patents (including those pending), trademarks, trade names, copyrights, licenses, and all other intangible assets (including regis-

(Box continued on next page)

tration numbers, expiration dates, and copies of all correspondence relating to this intellectual property)

8. Copies of any survey, appraisal, engineering, or other reports as to the properties of the target

E. Material contracts and obligations

1. Material purchase, supply, and sale agreements currently outstanding or projected to come to fruition within 12 months, including the following:

    a. List of all contracts relating to the purchase of products, equipment, fixtures, tools, dies, supplies, industrial supplies, or other materials having a price under any such contract in excess of $5,000

    b. List of all unperformed sales contracts

2. Documents incidental to any planned expansion of the facilities

3. Consignment agreements

4. Research agreements

5. Licensing, distribution, and agency agreements

6. Joint venture agreements

7. Agreements for the payment of receipt of license fees or royalties and royalty-free licenses

8. Documentation relating to all property, liability, and casualty insurance policies owned, including for each policy a summary description of:

    a. Coverage

    b. Policy type and number

    c. Insurer

    d. Premium

    e. Expiration date

    f. Deductible

    g. Any material changes in any of the foregoing since the inception of the target and

    h. Claims made under such policies

9. Agreements restricting the right to compete in any business

10. Agreements for the target's current purchase of services, including, without limitation, consulting and management

11. Contracts for the purchase, sale, or removal of electricity, gas, water, telephone, sewage, power, or any other utility service

(Box continued on next page)

12. List of waste dumps, disposal, treatment, and storage sites

13. Agreements with any railroad, trucking, or any other transportation company or courier service

14. Letters of credit

15. Copies of licenses, permits, and governmental approvals applied for or issued to the target that are required in order to operate the business (such as zoning, operating permits, or health and safety certificates)

F. Litigation and claims

1. Opinion letter from each lawyer or law firm prosecuting or defending significant litigation to which the target is a party, describing such litigation

2. List of material litigation or claims for more than $5,000 against the target (asserted or threatened) with respect to the quality of the products or services sold to customers, including pending or threatened claims

3. List of settlement agreements, releases, decrees, orders, or arbitration awards

4. Description of labor relations history

5. Documentation regarding correspondence or proceeding with federal, state, or local regulatory agencies

Business and Strategic Due Diligence

At the same time that the attorneys are performing their share of the investigation of the target, a management team should be assembled to conduct business and strategic due diligence. The following general topic areas and specific questions will provide a starting point for their analysis from a management, marketing, and financial perspective.

THE MANAGEMENT TEAM   Has the organizational chart been carefully reviewed? How are management functions and responsibilities delegated and implemented? Are job descriptions and employment manuals (among other things) current and available? What is the general assessment of morale at the lower echelons of the corporate ladder? To what extent are these rank-and-file employees critical to the long-term health of the target? What are the prospects for future growth of the principal labor markets from which the target depends on to attract key employees? Are employees with the skills necessary to operate and manage the target generally available? How are the employees recruited, evaluated, trained, and rewarded? What is the background and experience of the key management team? What is the reputation of this management team within the industry? Has there been a high turnover rate among top management? Why or why not? Who are the key professional advisers and outside consultants? What are the basic management styles, practices and strategies of the current team? What are the strengths and weaknesses of the management team? To what extent has the current management engaged in long-term strategic planning, developed internal controls, or structured management and marketing information systems?

OPERATIONS   What are the methods of production and distribution? To what extent are these methods and systems protected either by contract or by proprietary rights? To what extent is the target operating at its maximum capacity? Why? What significant risk factors (e.g., dependence on raw materials or key suppliers and customers) affect production capacity and ability to expand? What are the significant costs of producing the goods and services? To what extent do production and output depend on economic cycles or seasonal factors? Are plant, equipment, supplies, and machinery in good working order? When will these assets need to be replaced? What are the annual maintenance and service costs for these key assets? At what levels are the inventories? What are the breakeven production efficiency and inventory turnover rates, and how do these compare with industry norms? Does the target maintain production plans, schedules, and reports? Have copies been obtained and analyzed by the buyer? What are the manufacturing and production obligations pursuant to long-term contracts or other arrangements?

SALES AND MARKETING STRATEGIES   What are the primary and secondary markets? What is the size of these markets, and what is the market share within each market? What strategies are in place to expand this market share? What are the current trends affecting either the growth or the shrinkage of these particular markets? How are these markets segmented and reached? Who are the direct and indirect competitors? What are the respective strengths and weaknesses of each competitor? In what principal ways do companies within the industry compete (e.g., price, quality, or service)? For each material competitor, the buyer should seek to obtain data on the competitor's products and services, geographic location, channel of distribution, market share, financial health, pricing, policies, and reputation within the industry. Who are the typical customers? What are their purchasing capabilities and patterns? Where are these customers principally located? What political, economic, social or technological trends or changes are likely to affect the demographic makeup of the customer base over the next three to five years? What key factors influence the demand for the goods and services? What sales, advertising, public relations, and promotional campaigns and programs are currently in place? To what extent have these programs been effectively monitored and evaluated?

FINANCIAL MANAGEMENT   On the basis of the financial statements and reports collected, what key sales, income, and earnings trends have been identified? What effect will the proposed transaction have on these aspects of the financial performance? What are the various costs incurred in connection with bringing the products and services to the marketplace? In what ways can these costs be reduced or eliminated? What are the billing and collection procedures? How current are the accounts receivable? What steps have been (or can be) taken to expedite the collection procedures and systems? How credible is the existing accounting and financial control system? What is the capital structure? What are the key financial liabilities and debt obligations? How do the target's leverage ratios compare with industry norms? What are the monthly debt-service payments? How strong is the target's relationship with creditors, lenders, and investors?

In conducting due diligence from a business perspective, you are likely to encounter a wide variety of financial problems and areas of risk. These typically include undervaluation of inventories, overdue tax liabilities, inadequate management information systems, incomplete financial documentation or incomplete information about customers, related-party transactions (especially in small closely held companies), an unhealthy reliance on a few key customers or suppliers, aging accounts receivable, unrecorded liabilities (e.g., warranty claims, vacation pay, sales returns and allowances), and immediate need for significant expenditures as a result of obsolete equipment, inventory, or computer systems. Each of these problems can pose different risks and costs, which you weigh against the benefits to be gained from the transaction.

Valuation, Pricing, and Sources of Financing

Following the completion of well planned and well executed due diligence (but before the structuring and drafting of the actual formal legal documentation), the acquisition team should reach certain conclusions regarding valuation, pricing, and source of financing for the proposed transaction.

One of the key members of the acquisition team should always be a qualified business appraiser who understands the special issues raised in assessing the value of a closely held company. By determining the valuation parameters of the target, the appraiser plays an important role in determining the proposed structure, pricing, and source of financing for the acquisition. Most of the information that an appraiser will need to analyze the value of the target can be gathered as part of the ordinary due diligence process. The appraiser's job is to answer the following types of questions:

- How will the value of the target be affected by the loss of its current management (if applicable)?

- How should the goodwill of the target be valued? What are the various components that make up the target's goodwill?

- How and to what extent should the target's intangible assets (such as lists of customers, intellectual property, license and distributorship agreements, regulatory approvals, leasehold interests, and employment contracts) be assigned some relative tangible value?

- If less than complete ownership of the target is being acquired, what effect do the remaining minority shareholders have on the target's overall value?

- If the transaction is structured as an acquisition of stock rather than assets, what effect do the unknown contingent liabilities have on overall value? This assumes that there is no comprehensive indemnification provision.

- What effect should the target's accounting methods, credit ratings, business plans or projections, or income tax returns have on the overall value of its business?

Although a comprehensive discussion of the various methods of valuation is beyond the scope of this chapter, it is crucial for the acquisition team to understand how the appraiser will arrive at the range of values for the target company. Most methods of valuation fall into one of three general categories: (1) *comparable worth;* (2) *asset valuation;* (3) *financial performance.* Which method or methods should be used by the appraiser will depend on the individual facts and circumstances surrounding each target company. There are very few prescribed formulas or rules of thumb.

Assuming that the appraiser is able to gain the full support and cooperation of the target—which will be needed to gather necessary data—a formal valuation report will be issued. It is then up to the acquisition team to determine the effect of the formal report on the pricing of the transaction. There is often only an indirect relationship between reported value and actual purchase price. For example, if the range of values established by the appraiser is between $3.2 million and $3.6 million, your willingness to pay a price equal to or greater than the valuation ceiling will depend on the extent to which operating synergies and long-term economies of scale will be achieved as a result of the transaction.

On the other hand, if you seek only to buy certain key assets owned by the target (known as "cherry-picking" or picking the "crown jewels"), then you are likely to be far less concerned with long-term synergies and more concerned with paying the lowest possible price for the particular assets. Similarly, if you plan to structure the transaction as a leveraged buyout (LBO) in which the purchase price will be financed primarily by borrowing against the assets and cash flow of the target, then the operating synergies will be less important than the need to acquire the assets necessary to serve as collateral for the transaction. Ultimately, issues of pricing will be decided by the negotiations between you and the target as well as the type of financing you select.

Financing the Acquisition

Many smaller-scale acquisitions are financed primarily with the buyer's excess cash or retained earnings. Under such circumstances, little to no external debt on equity financing is required and the only key issues become pricing the stock or assets to be purchased and establishing the terms of payment. However, if you lack the excess cash required to finance the transaction, you have essentially two choices: (1) Offer the shareholders of the target some form of consideration other than cash; for example, equity securities, promissory notes, or a share of the post-closing earnings ("earn-outs"); or (2) identify an external source of capital to finance the purchase of the target company.

When identifying external sources of financing for the transaction, coordinating the timing of the "closing" of both transactions is critical. I have seen many companies successfully use private placements, commercial lenders, venture capitalists, and even public offerings of their securities to finance the growth of their business. Depending on the size and complexity of the transaction, the acquisition team may want to retain the services of an investment banker. Most investment banking firms have acquisition and merger specialists who can assist in arranging and negotiating the necessary financing for the transaction, usually in exchange for a consulting fee and a percentage of the capital raised. The investment bankers may also be available to assist in the preparation of the proposal necessary to present to the potential sources of capital, in the structuring of the transaction, and in the valuation of the target. These services may also be available from accountants, attorneys, business brokers, and merchant bankers for smaller-scale transactions.

Structuring the Deal

Once the decision has been made to acquire the target company, strategies must be developed regarding the structural alternatives for the transaction.

There are virtually an infinite number of ways in which a corporate acquisition may be structured. A variety of corporate, tax, and securities law issues will affect the final decision about the structure of any given transaction. Each issue must be carefully considered from a legal perspective and an accounting perspective. However, at the heart of each alternative are the following basic issues:

- Will you be acquiring the *stock* or the *assets*?
- What form of payment will be made (e.g., cash, notes, securities)?
- Will the purchase price be fixed, contingent, or payable over time on an installment basis?
- What are the tax consequences of the proposed structure for the acquisition?

Perhaps the most fundamental issue in structuring the acquisition of a target company is whether the transaction will take the form of an *asset* or *stock* purchase. Each form has advantages and disadvantages, depending on the facts and circumstances surrounding each transaction. The acquisition team should consider the following factors in determining the ultimate form of the transaction.

Acquisition of Stock

The *advantages* of a stock purchase are:
- Business identity, licenses, and permits can usually be preserved.

- Continuity of corporate identity, contracts, and structure can be maintained.

The *disadvantages* of a stock purchase are:
- There is less flexibility to cherry-pick key assets of the seller.
- Buyer may be liable for unknown, undisclosed, or contingent liabilities (unless adequately protected in the purchase agreement).
- Buyer will be forced to contend with the seller's minority shareholders unless all shares of company are purchased.
- Offer and sale of the securities may need to be registered under federal or state securities laws.

Acquisition of Assets

The *advantages* of acquiring assets are:
- Buyer can be selective as to which assets of target will be purchased.
- Buyer is generally not liable for the seller's liabilities unless specifically assumed under contract.

The *disadvantages* of acquiring assets are:
- Bill of sale must be comprehensive enough to ensure that no key assets are overlooked and as a result not transferred to the buyer.
- Various third-party consents will typically be required to transfer key tangible and intangible assets to the purchaser.
- Seller will be responsible for the liquidation of the remaining corporate "shell" and distributing the proceeds of the sale of assets to its shareholders, which may result in double taxation unless a special tax election is made.
- Acquisition of assets requires compliance with applicable state bulk sales statutes, as well as state and local sales and transfer taxes.

Preparation of the Definitive Legal Documents

Once due diligence has been completed, valuations and appraisals have been conducted, initial terms and price have been negotiated, and financing has been arranged, the acquisition team must work carefully with the attorneys to structure and begin the preparation of the definitive legal documentation that will memorialize the transaction. Drafting and negotiating these documents will usually focus on the following:

- Nature and scope of the seller's representations and warranties

- Terms of the seller's indemnification to the buyer

- Conditions for closing the transaction

- Responsibilities of the parties during the time between execution of the purchase agreement and the actual closing

- Terms of payment of the purchase price

- Scope of post-closing covenants of competition

- Predetermined remedies (if any) for breach of the covenants, representations, or warranties

Following the execution of a letter of intent or memorandum of understanding, one of the first responsibilities of your attorney is to prepare a comprehensive *schedule of activities* ("schedule"). This should be accomplished well before beginning the due diligence process. The primary purpose of the schedule is to outline all of the events that must occur and documents that must be prepared before the closing date and beyond. In this regard, your attorney acts as an orchestra leader, assigning primary areas of responsibility to various members of the acquisition team as well as to the target company and its counsel. Once all tasks have been identified and assigned (and a realistic timetable for completion has been established), a closing time and date can be tentatively determined.

Naturally, the exact list of legal documents that must be prepared and the specific tasks to be outlined in the schedule will vary from transaction to transaction, usually depending on the specific facts and circumstances of each deal, such as: (1) whether the transaction is a purchase of stock or assets; (2) form and terms of the purchase price; (3) nature of the target's business; (4) nature and extent of the assets being purchased or the liabilities being assumed; and (5) the sophistication of the parties and their respective attorneys.

A comprehensive discussion of the preparation and negotiation of all of the documents that must be developed in connection with the transaction is beyond the scope of this chapter. However, it is important for the acquisition team to understand the key points to be negotiated in the primary documents in the transaction. The primary documents include the purchase agreement, noncompetition agreements, and opinion of the target's counsel.

Asset Purchase Agreement

At the heart of any acquisition is the asset or stock purchase agreement, from which *all* other documents in the transaction will flow. The purchase agreement includes several key components and issues:

1. *Indemnification.* One of the most contested areas is indemnification provisions that subsequently give rise to some claim or liability. Usually, you will want to be reimbursed for any transaction or occurrence that took place before closing. The target, on the other hand, will want to make a "clean break" from the business, including any responsibility for events that arose before closing.

2. *Representations and warranties.* The target will be expected to make a wide range of written and binding representations and warranties to you in connection with the acquisition. These provisions will include (a) that the sale is not in breach of any other agreement or obligation of the target; (b) that the assets are free and clear of all liens and encumbrances; (c) that the assets are in good operating condition; (d) that all material facts have been disclosed; and so forth. Naturally, you will want the scope of these representations and warranties to be as broad and comprehensive as possible, primarily because these clauses

serve as your insurance policy. It will be incumbent on the target and its counsel to negotiate limitations on the scope of these provisions where necessary.

3. *Conditions for closing.* This section is essentially a checklist of events that must occur as a condition of closing the transaction. Both parties will have their share of items that must be accomplished and documents or consents that must be signed. The nature and scope of these conditions must be carefully considered, since failure to satisfy them will give the opposing party the right to walk away from the transaction.

4. *Conduct of business prior to closing.* The target must have a contractual obligation to preserve the goodwill of the business and the condition of the assets during the time between execution of the purchase agreement and the closing of the transaction. The parties should negotiate all affirmative and negative covenants that will be imposed on the conduct of the target during this period, as well as the penalties for noncompliance (e.g., reduction of purchase price, or your ability to walk away from the deal).

Noncompetition Agreements

Covenants against competition and disclosure of confidential information are commonly a key part of any business acquisition. You will naturally want to include covenants that are broad in terms of the scope of subject matter, duration, and geographic territory. Although these agreements will be carefully scrutinized by the courts as potential restraints of trade, agreements prohibiting sellers from competing against buyers in a business purchase transaction are given considerably more latitude than in other agreements such as employment or consulting agreements.

Opinion of Target's Counsel

An often hotly contested area is the scope of the representations that will be made in the opinion letter to be prepared by the target's attorney for your and your attorney's benefit and review. Naturally, the target and its counsel will seek to narrow and dilute the scope of the representations, and you should insist on a comprehensive and thorough opinion letter.

Post-Closing Matters

A wide variety of legal and administrative tasks must be accomplished following the closing; these are necessary to complete the transaction. The nature and extent of these tasks will vary depending on the size (as well as on the type) of financing that you select. The parties to any acquisition must be careful to ensure that the jubilation of closing does not cause any post-closing matters to be overlooked.

In an *asset acquisition,* post-closing tasks might include a final verification that all assets acquired are free of liens and encumbrances; the recordation of financing statements and transfer tax returns; the recordation of any assignments of intellectual property with the Library of Congress or United States Patent and Trademark Office; notification of the sale to employees, customers, distributors, and suppliers; and adjustments to bank accounts and insurance policies.

In a *stock acquisition* (or merger), post-closing matters may entail all of the above, in addition to filing articles of amendment to the corporate charter or articles of merger; completion of the transfer of all stock certificates; amendments to the corporate bylaws; and the preparation of all appropriate post-closing minutes and resolutions.

Miscellaneous Tips for Buyers

Before you embark on the acquisition trail, here are a few tips for you to keep in mind:

- Don't accept anything less than a "known and should have known" standard in the representations and warranties.
- Don't skimp on due diligence.

- Negotiate an adequate holdback for unforeseen liabilities.

- Assemble a truly dynamic acquisition team that understands all the legal, strategic, and financial issues.

- Try to persuade the target to take a portion of the purchase price in an "earn-out" or installment basis.

- Be certain that all post-closing synergies (and challenges) have been identified.

- Before getting too close to closing, be certain that all necessary acquisition capital is available and in your possession. *TIMING IS EVERYTHING.*

Growth by external acquisition should be at the heart of the strategic planning of any rapidly expanding company. Economies of scale and operating synergies may be more efficiently obtained through an acquisition than through growth that must be internally financed and developed. In addition, internal expansion may be a much longer process, which may cause the loss of certain short-term market opportunities and may cause oversaturation of a market because it adds to the total capacity of the industry rather than consolidating fragmented operations more efficiently under one roof.

C H A P T E R 11

Managing Business Conflicts

As a company grows, the number of vendors, customers, employees, consultants, investors, and competitors that it comes into contact with will also grow. This increase in the number of relationships also increases the chances that business conflicts will arise. Most owners would prefer to engage in battle in the marketplace or in the boardroom rather than in the courtroom. Nevertheless, there will be situations where "reasonable people differ" and an amicable settlement or resolution of the conflict will seem impossible. If a business dispute cannot be quickly settled, and as a result matures into a courtroom battle, then you must understand the basic rules of litigation and the mechanisms for "alternative dispute resolution" (ADR).

Reducing the Risk of Litigation

Most disputes and conflicts among companies result from a misunderstanding over the rights and obligations of the parties to a particular agreement or in a particular situation. Failure to provide acceptable products or services, to pay the bills of a trade creditor on time, to meet the expectations of an investor, to comply with covenants imposed by a lender, to compensate an employee or consultant adequately, to complete a proposed transaction or investment, or to consider the antitrust laws in dealing with competitors—these are *all* situations that are likely to lead to litigation. Naturally, an understanding of the issues discussed in this book, a good working relationship with legal counsel, and a well-managed legal compliance program will contribute to reducing the risk of litigation. Methods that may be adopted in order to stay out of the courtroom include the following.

Management, Management, Management

A well-managed company is far less likely to get entangled in a legal dispute with an employee, an investor, a creditor, or a competitor than is a company that is managed haphazardly. This is generally because a well-managed company is far more likely to:

• Meet its contractual obligations on time

• Deal fairly with its employees, shareholders, and competitors

• Apply quality control standards to the production of goods and services

• Communicate regularly with legal counsel to identify risks and solve problems well before they mature into a formal dispute

Avoiding Undercapitalization

Undercapitalization is the kiss of death. When a growing company is undercapitalized, it is much more likely to experience financial problems that lead to litigation. Lack of capital translates into:

• Cutting the quality of products and services

• Paying bills late

• Not preparing legal documents and not following the appropriate procedures in connection with the issuance of securities

• Breaking covenants with lenders and investors

These acts of desperation, caused by financial distress, will lead to serious conflicts and problems—which will be discussed in greater detail in Chapter 13.

Getting It In Writing and Getting It Right

Many business disputes leading to litigation are a direct result of having no written agreement; or they arise when there is a written document, but the rights and obligations are unclear or ambiguous or the document failed to anticipate the facts that the parties are now disputing. Therefore, owners of growing companies who wish to avoid the time and expense involved in litigation should take steps to ensure that each significant transaction is evidenced by an agreement or series of agreements and, further, that these documents, taken as a whole, clearly reflect *both* the spirit and the intent of the transaction and the respective rights and obligations of each party. In addition, be certain that an arbitration or mediation clause is included in the contract. Such alternatives are a lot less expensive than arguing in court. Also, include a clause stating that the losing party pays the other party's legal fees: this forces someone to think before either breaching a contract or commencing litigation.

Understanding the "Big Picture"

In negotiating a contract, hiring an employee, or dealing with a competitor, it is very easy to get too caught up in the narrow objective of the given transaction. When this happens, an owner fails to see the "big picture"; as a result, legal risks or warning signals are overlooked or ignored. Each contemplated transaction must be analyzed with more than tunnel vision. The broader risks and potential problems, both short-term and long-term, must be taken into account and discussed with legal counsel, well before the documents are executed.

Being Skeptical

It's cheaper to be a skeptic than a plaintiff. As a company grows, it will take a wide variety of risks and seize opportunities, each with its respective share of costs and benefits. The financial intermediary that you may have hired to raise an unlimited amount of capital within 30 days and the sales representative who promises to deliver more customers than the company can handle are both a dime a dozen. That same dime probably represents a fair price for the value of such extravagant claims. Rather than trying to build a company on shallow representations, and then spending valuable time and money in court trying to enforce these worthless promises, it is far better to be skeptical at the outset. Either force the party on the other side of the table to document such claims, or forgo the opportunity.

Establishing a Legal Compliance Program

Employees at all levels within a growing company must be made aware of the legal risks of their actions. It is important to develop legal compliance programs with the assistance of legal counsel. These programs should include:

1. Periodic legal audits

2. Legal compliance manuals and employee seminars

3. Form letters and checklists for routine transactions

4. Established procedures for record keeping and file management

The bottom line is that the core of virtually every commercial lawsuit is *misunderstanding* and *miscommunication*. Simply talking openly and creatively with the opposing party can be the most effective way to resolve a dispute before it blooms into full-blown litigation.

Litigation: Planning and Strategy

Basic Considerations

If and when you determine that litigation is the most sensible and efficient way to resolve a business dispute, or if a suit is brought against your company, you must develop plans and strategies. Keep in mind the following principles:

- You must *develop goals and objectives* and communicate them to your attorney. Well before the litigation is initiated, counsel must be made aware of any specific business objectives, budgetary limitations, or time constraints that affect the company.

- You must *gather all documents* relevant to the dispute and organize them, in advance of the time that the opponent serves the first discovery request.

- You should *explore alternative methods* of resolving the dispute, clearly define parameters for settlement, and communicate them to your attorney.

- You should discuss with legal counsel the risks, costs, and benefits of entering into litigation

- You should review with counsel the terms of payment of legal fees (as well as the fees of any experts needed)

- You should review the terms of insurance policies with your risk management team to determine whether there is insurance coverage for defense costs or any judgment rendered against the company.

- You should develop a litigation management system for monitoring and controlling costs.

- You should *maintain clear lines of communication* with legal counsel throughout all phases of the litigation and should appoint a responsible individual to serve as a liaison with counsel.

Regardless of the subject matter, there are certain factors you must consider before you decide to litigate; see Box 11-1 for checklists.

The decision to resolve a dispute through litigation must be based upon a genuine understanding of the specific legal rights, remedies, and defenses available in a particular case. For example, suppose that a supplier is shipping goods of a lower quality than was originally anticipated by the purchaser. Upon the purchaser's review of the contract, the quality control specifications seem to be clear; however, a material difference of opinion has developed. Before filing a complaint for breach of contract, the purchaser should carefully review the following:

- Alternative methods for resolving the dispute
- Elements of a legal breach of contract in the jurisdiction that governs the agreement

- Various defenses available to the supplier

- Direct and indirect costs of litigation

- Range of damages that may be recovered if a breach is successfully established

Formal action should be pursued only after the purchaser is satisfied that the answers to these questions indicate that litigation is a viable alternative. Similarly, if the company is sued by a creditor or landlord, it should attempt to resolve these disputes before giving a formal answer.

Alternatives to Litigation

A wide range of methods and procedures are available that can generally expedite the resolution of disputes without the need for litigation. These are broadly referred to as "alternative dispute resolutions" (ADR). ADR methods are also more attractive than litigation to business owners because proprietary information, trade secrets, and the like can be protected—whereas in a proceeding in the judicial system, the commercial information can result in intense efforts by competitors to misappropriate and use the information through the right of access by the general public and news media.

The most common ADR method is arbitration. In arbitration, a neutral third party is selected by the disputants to hear the case and render an opinion, which may or may not be binding on the parties, depending on the terms of the arbitration clause or agreement. In addition to arbitration, various forms of mediation, private judging, small-claims courts, and moderated settlement conferences are available to companies that are unable to independently resolve their disputes but want to avoid the expense and delay of a trial.

Each method offers certain advantages and disadvantages, which may make one process far more appropriate for resolving a particular dispute than another. Therefore, the procedures,

B O X   1 1 - 1

Checklists for Deciding When to Litigate

Questions to Ask When Deciding to Litigate

1. What are the costs of the litigation?
   - What are the legal fees and costs?
   - What are the costs in hidden downtime?
   - What are the capital costs (disclosure of pending litigation)?
   - What are the costs of alternatives to litigation?
   - What are the costs of not litigating?
2. What public relations issues are involved in the litigation?
   - What aspects of the litigation might interest the media?
   - What aspects of the litigation might produce strong emotions in a jury?
   - What aspects of this case are critical to be kept confidential?
3. What legal precedents are relevant to this litigation?
4. What factors affect the possibility of settlement?
   - Who is the opposing attorney or law firm?
   - What is their track record and approach?
   - How complex are the legal issues?
   - What are the weak points of our opponent?
   - Are there any counterclaims?
5. What company policies are relevant to this litigation?
6. What are the chances of getting help from other members of the trade in this litigation?

Questions to Ask to Determine Total Legal Costs of Proposed Litigation

1. What is the hourly rate for the lawyer or lawyers involved?
2. How much assistance will the lawyer or lawyers need, and what are the hourly rates for those who will be assisting?
3. What types of expert witnesses will be needed, and how much will it cost to have them prepare and testify?

(Box continued on next page)

4. What types of fees will be involved? (Examples: filing fees, fees for reproduction of depositions and trial transcripts, and costs of travel involved in discovery.)

Questions to Ask About Proposed Collections Litigation

1. What amount of money is at issue in this dispute?
2. What is the financial condition of the debtor?
3. Where is the debtor located? Is the debtor in our state or in another state? (If the debtor is in a different state, costs of collecting the debt are likely to rise considerably.)
4. What reputation as creditors do we wish to maintain?

Questions to Ask About Proposed Regulatory Litigation

1. What publicity is this action likely to attract? What will the public's perception of the issues probably be?
2. Would a consent decree be in our best interests in this case?
3. What is our ongoing relationship with this regulator? What relationship do we wish to have? How will this action affect our relationship?
4. Does this action involve a new regulation? Is the agency likely to be using it as a test case?
5. Are other companies involved or likely to be involved in this action? If so, might they help us in the suit?
6. What is the nature of the regulatory environment involved in this action? How is the current environment likely to affect our case?

---

costs, and benefits of each ADR method should be carefully reviewed with experienced legal counsel.

Benefits of ADR include the following:

- *Faster resolution of disputes.* Reducing delays was one of the driving forces behind the ADR movement. As the number of civil filings continues to increase every year, it is clear that the courts cannot expeditiously accommodate the influx unless parties seek alternatives to such filings.
- *Cost savings.* In a study by the accounting firm Deloitte & Touche, 60% of all ADR users and 78% of those characterized as

extensive users reported that they had saved money by using ADR. The amount saved ranged from 11% to 50% of the cost of litigation.

- *Preserving relationships.* ADR offers the opportunity for parties to resolve a dispute without destroying a relationship, whether business or personal.

- *Preserving privacy and confidentiality.* Traditional litigation often results in public disclosure of proprietary information, particularly in business disputes. ADR procedures allow the parties to structure a dispute resolution process while protecting confidential information.

- *Flexibility.* ADR allows the parties to tailor a dispute resolution process that is uniquely suited to the matter at hand. Parties can select the mechanism, determine the amount of information that needs to be exchanged, choose their own neutral party, and agree on a format for the procedure—all in a way that makes sense for the issue at hand.

- *Durability of the result.* Resolutions achieved by consensus of the disputants are less likely to be challenged than resolutions imposed by third parties.

- *Better, more creative solutions.* By allowing litigants early and direct participation, ADR provides a better opportunity for achieving a resolution based on the parties' real interests. Such agreements often involve terms other than the distribution of dollars from one party to another and may well produce a solution that makes more sense for the parties than one imposed by a court.

ADR is likely to be *successful* in the following situations:

- *When an ADR contract clause is in place.* The most important indicator of possible success is the existence of an effective contract clause that provides for the use of ADR in the event of a future dispute.

- *In continuing relationships.* If a continuing relationship between the parties is possible (as with franchisors and franchisees or suppliers and customers), the chances of success are greatly increased. It makes more sense for the parties to continue making money from each other over the duration of

B O X   1 1 - 2

Things to Consider If You Are Being Sued

Questions to Ask When Assembling a Dispute Management Team

1. Who will be on the team?

- Who will act as our attorney? (In-house counsel? Regular outside firm? Special attorney?)
- Who will act as our public relations representative? (In-house person? Consultant?)
- Will the CEO be on the team? If not, who will represent the CEO?
- What technical expert or experts will be on the team?
- Will the director of public affairs be on the team?
- Will a consumer representative be on the team? If so, who will it be?
- Will a sales or marketing representative be on the team? If so, who will it be?

2. What tasks will the team perform?

- What public relations issues will the team need to handle? Which of these are short-term issues? Which are long-term?
- What internal investigation will the team need to conduct? How should it be conducted?
- What specific information should we give employees? What instructions should we give them for answering questions from family, friends, and the media?
- What legal strategy should be followed?
- What corrective action do we need to take?

Questions to Ask When Attempting a Settlement

1. Have we conducted an internal investigation to find out all relevant facts? (Remember that finger-pointing and written memos can later be discoverable as litigation progresses.)
2. Is the CEO involved in the negotiations? If so, has he or she been properly briefed?
3. If a settlement is not reached quickly, have we left the door open for possible future negotiations?

(Box continued on next page)

4. Are personality conflicts hindering negotiation? If so, has the possibility of hiring a mediator been explored?

5. Do our negotiators have a clear understanding of the costs, benefits, and goals of this litigation?

---

an agreement than for them to sever the relationship and suffer the cost and disruption of litigation.

- *In complex disputes.* If a case is based on, for example, highly complex technology, there is a substantial chance that a jury and even a judge may become confused. Under these circumstances, ADR may be the best option, particularly if the proceedings are conducted before a neutral person who is an expert in the subject matter of the dispute. In addition, the American Arbitration Association (AAA) has enacted rules specifically designed for use in complex cases.

- *When relatively little money is at stake.* If the amount of money in dispute is relatively small, the cost of litigation may approach or even exceed that amount.

- *When confidentiality is important.* The parties can maintain confidentiality more effectively in an ADR proceeding than in litigation. The need for confidentiality can prove to be more important than any other consideration in the dispute resolution process.

ADR is likely *not* to be successful in the following situations:

- *Skeptical and mistrusting adversary.* The adversary may see the overture to use ADR after a complaint as a ploy designed to get an edge in litigation.

- *Parties or counsel with harsh attitudes.* When the parties or counsel are particularly emotional, belligerent, and abusive, the chances for successful nonbinding ADR are significantly diminished.

- *One of many cases.* If the case at issue is just one of many that are expected to be filed, then it is highly unlikely that the defendant will be motivated to agree to ADR. In such a setting, there is little if any hope for the successful use of nonbinding ADR, at least at an early stage. This also may be one of those rare situations where full-blown litigation is actually more cost-effective, because of the efficiencies of consolidation.

- *Delays.* If a delay will benefit one of the parties, then the chances for the successful use of ADR are diminished.
- *Monetary imbalances.* If there is a monetary imbalance between the parties, and the wealthier party thinks it can wear down the other party through traditional litigation, then it probably will be difficult to get the wealthier party to agree to ADR.

Arbitration

There are many types of formal arbitration, but each involves a process for the parties in dispute to submit arguments and evidence to a neutral person or persons for the purpose of adjudicating the differences between the parties. The evidentiary and procedural rules are not nearly as formal as in litigation, and there tends to be far greater flexibility in the timing of the proceeding and the selection of the actual decision makers.

Arbitration may be a voluntary proceeding that the parties have selected before a dispute arises (as in a contract), or it may be a compulsory, court-annexed procedure that is a prerequisite to full-blown litigation. Owners and managers of growing companies who wish to avoid the cost and delay of litigation should consider adding arbitration clauses before entering into a contract. An arbitration clause should specify:

- That the parties agree to submit any controversy or claim arising from the agreement or contract to binding (or nonbinding) arbitration
- Choice of location for the arbitration
- Method for selecting the parties who will hear the dispute
- Any limitations on the award rendered by the arbitrator
- Which party shall be responsible for the costs of the proceeding
- Any special procedural rules that will govern the arbitration

However, owing to the increasing controversy over mandatory arbitration clauses in contracts, it is advisable not to include arbitration as a boilerplate provision in your key contracts. For example, in the August 1996 issue of the *ABA Journal*, it was reported that "Employment law has been one of the most significant sectors of ADR growth, as management lawyers have seized upon several Supreme Court decisions upholding mandatory arbitration clauses on statutory grounds." However, in the September 1996 issue it was reported that "consumer advocates are criticizing a U.S. Supreme Court decision invalidating a state law that required the prominent display of arbitration provisions in contracts." The following clause is recommended by the American Arbitration Association (AAA):

> Any controversy or claim arising out of or relating to this contract, or the breach thereof, shall be settled by arbitration in accordance with the Commercial Arbitration Rules of the American Arbitration Association, and decision rendered upon the award rendered by the arbitrator(s) may be entered in any court having jurisdiction thereof.

Because the arbitrator selected is usually an attorney whose expertise may be negotiating rather than adjudicating, arbitration often results in "splitting the baby down the middle," not providing a clear award for one party or the other. Additionally, because no jury is involved, the likelihood of recovering punitive or exemplary damages from an attorney or experienced arbitrator is less: the arbitrator is unlikely to be swayed by appeals to emotion.

A key factor is whether the decision of the arbitrator will be binding or nonbinding. If the parties agree that the award will be binding, then the parties must live with the results. Binding arbitration awards are usually enforceable by the local court, unless there has been a defect in the arbitration procedures. On the other hand, the opinion rendered in a nonbinding arbitration is advisory only. The parties may either accept the result or reject the award and proceed to litigation. In a court-annexed arbitration, the court will order the arbitration as a nonbinding proceeding that is intended to work out the differences between the parties without the need for litigation. A drawback of nonbinding arbitration is that after the award is made, the losing party often threatens litigation (a trial de novo, or new trial) unless the monetary award is adjusted. Thus, the party that wins the arbitration is often coerced into paying more or accepting less than was awarded simply to avoid a trial after arbitration.

There are many sources of arbitration rules if the parties do not have specific rules and procedures in mind that will govern the arbitration. The two best known sources in the United States are the American Arbitration Association (212-484-4000) and the International Chamber of Commerce (212-206-1150). Both offer copies of their rules at no cost; the fees for handling arbitration proceedings vary for these and other such organizations. Other sources include the U.N. Commission on International Trade Law Arbitration Rules and the Inter-American Commercial Arbitration Commission.

Whether or not arbitration will be faster and cheaper than litigation really hinges on the parties and their interests. Arbitration costs and the length of arbitration can escalate to rival those of litigation. For example, in *Advanced Micro Devices Inc. v. Intel Corp.*, the proceeding lasted seven years, cost about $100 million, and included several rounds of collateral litigation. Intel's vice president and general counsel describes the issue as a basic contract dispute; however, a pre-dispute arbitration clause routed it into arbitration. Ultimately, the arbitrator's ruling led the parties to settle in a mediation proceeding.

Mediation

Mediation differs substantially from arbitration. An arbitrator renders a decision that is often binding. In the mediation process, the parties decide how to resolve their dispute by discussing their differences with a mediator who only makes suggestions or recommendations. The mediation process typically consists of five stages:

1. Presentation of positions
2. Identification of interests
3. Generation and evaluation of options
4. Narrowing of options to resolve the dispute
5. Executing a written settlement agreement

Costs of mediation are minimal and generally include only payment on an hourly basis to the mediator for his or her services. However, because the mediator has no authority to render a binding decision, the mediation process will be effective only if both parties are committed to achieving a voluntary resolution. In the mediation process, the participants always have the ultimate authority, and they are free to reject any suggestion by the mediator and can ultimately pursue litigation.

The controversies surrounding mediation typically include how the mediator should resolve disputes and how to determine ethical standards of conduct for mediators. Some experts believe that mediation should facilitate the parties' own resolution of the problem by digging deep into the interests and feelings underlying the surface dispute. Others say that the proper purpose of mediation is to bring the parties into an amicable accord. Still others contend that mediators should provide expertise in the subject matter, acting essentially as sounding boards to help the parties evaluate the merits of the dispute or the proposed settlement. The American Bar Association (in its Section on Dispute Resolution), the Society of Professionals in Dispute Resolution, and the AAA, in an attempt to draft ethical standards of conduct, concluded that mediators should only try to facilitate the parties' own resolution and admonished professionals who serve as mediators (including lawyers) to "refrain from providing professional advice." Florida, New Jersey, and Hawaii are the only states that have adopted qualification requirements for mediators. Many states merely require completion of 40 hours of training, while in others a law license is enough. Florida is the only state that has taken the further step of implementing a disciplinary process for mediators.

Private Judging

In many communities, retired judges are available at an hourly fee (often as high as $250 per hour) to hear and resolve disputes. Parties may agree in advance whether the decision will be legally binding. The disadvantages of nonbinding arbitration also apply to nonbinding private judging. While the costs of private judging are substantially higher than those of court-annexed arbitration, private judging is considerably more flexible. A private judge may be retained without court intervention and without first instituting litigation. The parties are free to select a judge and a mutually convenient date for the hearing. The hearing itself tends to be informal, and the rules of evidence are not strictly applied. The private judge often uses a settlement conference approach, as opposed to a trial approach, to resolve the dispute.

Moderated Settlement Conferences

After litigation begins, a court may insist that the parties participate in settlement discussions before a judge. If the court does not schedule a settlement conference, the parties can usually request one, often with a particular judge.

The attorneys are often required to prepare settlement briefs to inform the judge of each party's contentions, theories, and claimed damages. Parties, as well as attorneys, attend so that the judge may explain his or her view of the case and obtain their consent to any proposed settlement. If a resolution is reached in the judge's chambers, the litigants often proceed to the courtroom so that the settlement (and the parties' consent to it) can be entered in the record, to eliminate any further disputes. Because moderated settlement conferences produce no out-of-pocket costs (other than attorneys' fees), and information obtained or revealed is for settlement purposes only, they provide an excellent "last-ditch effort" for resolving a dispute before trial.

Small-Claims Courts

Matters that involve a small amount of money (usually no greater than $2,500) are often best resolved in small-claims court. Generally, litigants represent themselves and describe the dispute in an informal manner to a judge, who renders a decision at the time of the hearing. Court filing fees are moderate, and a trial date usually is set for within two or three months. Often a bookkeeper or credit manager may represent the franchisor as long as he or she is knowledgeable about the dispute and has supporting documentation. Unfortunately, it is often difficult for a successful plaintiff to actually collect the judgment. Because of this, many courts have small-claims advisers who can assist litigants in collecting the money awarded.

Owners and managers of growing companies must be committed to developing programs and procedures within the organization that are specifically designed to avoid the time and expense of litigation. Business conflicts are inevitable, but lengthy trials are not if prompt steps are taken to resolve business conflicts and legal disputes. If disputes cannot be resolved amicably, then the costs and benefits of litigation and its alternatives must be understood well before the pleadings are filed. If litigation is, in fact, the only alternative available, then growing companies must work closely with counsel to establish specific strategies, objectives, and budgets for each conflict that matures into a formal legal dispute.

CHAPTER 12

Preparing for an Initial Public Offering

The market for initial public offerings (IPOs) is like a well-designed roller coaster—it will always have sharp peaks and deep valleys. The mid-1990s presented one of the wildest rides in history for the IPO market, as hundreds of new companies, at stages much earlier than ever before, brought their shares for sale to the public and then watched their prices and valuations soar to new heights. For the 19-month period from January 1, 1995, to August 1, 1996, investors and institutions poured over $60 billion into the treasuries of start-up companies, primarily in the fields of *computer software* (Internet access and service providers such as Netscape and Yahoo), *telecommunications* (such as Lucent Technologies, the AT&T spin-off, which netted $2.7 billion on its first day), *entertainment* (such as Pixar), *restaurants* (such as Planet Hollywood and Rainforest Cafe), *fashion designers* (such as Donna Karan International and Gucci), and *retailers* (such as Saks Fifth Avenue). The NASDAQ stock market set a record pace for initial public offerings in the first six months of 1997, with 325 public offerings raising a total of $13.8 billion, with the dollar value of trading volume for this period being 74.4 percent highter than the same period in 1996.

The wild ride of the mid-1990s, together with the advent of the Internet, even spurred the creation of the direct public offering (DPO), such as the offering by Spring Street Brewery, which used the newly revamped Regulation A guidelines (as discussed later in this chapter) to raise almost $5 million through the World Wide Web. This type of offering, pioneered by the former Wall Street corporate attorney Andy Klein of Spring Street, has been followed by many since early 1996, and it has the SEC excitedly scrambling to work out new regulations to deal with it (as of this chapter writing). Klein's DPO was so successful that he established Wit-Trade, a digital stock exchange, to provide a market for the more than 3,500 investors who bought Spring Street shares.

Many of these IPOs, especially those in the technology sector, were created and motivated by the rapid rise in venture capital investment in the early 1990s. Investments by institutional venture capital firms soared from $4 billion in 1992 to almost $8 billion in 1995. As discussed in Chapter 6, venture capital firms are not necessarily looking for a long-term marriage, and their preferred exit strategy is the IPO, where an initial investment of a few million can yield much more in a short period of time. Perhaps the most striking example was the $4 million investment in Xylan by Brentwood Associates, which reaped $390 million in profits on the day Xylan went public. The infamous Silicon Valley firm Kleiner Perkins, earned $250 million on Netscape's IPO's first day of trading in August 1995.

But although the ride appears to be slowing down to a more moderate pace, history teaches us that it will never actually stop. The speed may change, industry sectors will run hot and cold, and the valuations may range from highly aggressive to arch-conservative, but there will always be a market for high-quality growing companies to investors who want to get their hands on the next Microsoft.

Understanding the Costs and Benefits of the IPO

An IPO is a process whereby a company initially registers its securities with the Securities and Exchange Commission (SEC) for sale to the general investing public. Many entrepreneurs view the process of "going public" as the epitome of financial success and reward; however, the decision to go public requires considerable strategic planning and analysis from both a legal and a business perspective. The planning and analysis process involves: (1) weighing the costs and benefits; (2) understanding the process and costs; and (3) understanding the obligations of the company, its advisers, and its shareholders once it has successfully completed its public offering.

Benefits of IPOs

For a rapidly expanding privately held company, the process of going public represents a number of *benefits*, including the following:

- Significantly greater access to capital
- Increased liquidity for the shares
- Market prestige
- Enhancement of public image
- Flexibility for employee ownership and participation
- Improved opportunities for mergers, acquisitions, and further rounds of financing
- Immediate increase in the wealth of the founders

Business Costs of IPOs

The many benefits of going public are not without their corresponding costs, however, and the downside of being a public company must be strongly considered in the strategic planning process. Among the costs of IPOs are various obvious business costs:

- Dilution of the founders' control of the entity
- Pressure to meet the expectations of the market and shareholders regarding growth and dividends
- Changes in management styles and employees' expectations
- Compliance with complex federal and state securities laws

- Restrictions on stock resale for company insiders
- Vulnerability to shifts in the stock market
- Sharing the company's financial success with hundreds, even thousands, of other shareholders

Hidden Legal Costs of IPOs

In addition to some of the more obvious business costs, the most expensive aspect of registering securities is often the hidden costs imposed by federal and state securities laws. The rules and regulations imposed by the SEC make going public a time-consuming and expensive process, which in reality begins several years before the public offering and continues (through the SEC's periodic reporting process) for as long as the company remains public. From a legal perspective, the following costs and factors should be strongly considered.

PLANNING AND PREPARING THE BUSINESS FOR THE IPO From the day a company is formed, there are a host of legal and structural pitfalls that must be avoided if an IPO is in its future. Some of these pitfalls, if not avoided early on, will serve as a significant impediment to a successful IPO and will be expensive to remedy once the damage has been done. In addition, being a public company will require a more formal management style from a legal perspective, which normally entails holding more regular meetings of the board of directors and following all formalities imposed by state corporate laws. It is best to operate the company as if it were public right from the start.

DUE DILIGENCE AND HOUSECLEANING Many owners who take their companies public—and their managers—complain that they feel as though the company and their own personal lives are being conducted "in a fishbowl." Federal and state securities laws dictate that a prospective investor must have access to all material information about a company offering its securities to the public. As a result, well before you are ready to file a registration statement with the SEC, you must go through the due diligence process—to repeat, this takes place *before* any documents are filed. Corporate charters, bylaws, shareholder agreements, employment agreements, leases, licenses, accounting methods, and related documents and procedures may need to be formalized, amended, or even terminated before you are ready to operate in the public fishbowl.

THE REGISTRATION PROCESS The time, effort, and expense required to prepare the registration statement should not be underestimated. In fact, the 6- to 12-month time frame and the out-of-pocket expenses alone make this method of capital formation prohibitively costly for many growing businesses. While costs will vary depending on a number of factors, a company planning to offer its securities to the public should be prepared to spend anywhere from $200,000 to $500,000 in legal and accounting fees, appraisal costs, printing expenses, and consulting and filing fees. This amount does not include the underwriters' and brokers' commissions, which may run as high as 10% or more of the total offering. As discussed later in this chapter, the SEC has implemented new regulations for small-business owners that have brought decreases in legal and accounting fees. Still, you must remember that few, if any, of these costs will be contingent on the success of the offering; therefore, most or all must be paid regardless of how many or how few shares are actually sold.

In addition to the registration statement, exhibits and attachments documenting major business transactions (such as plans of acquisition, reorganization, and liquidation), customer and vendor arrangements, and financial statements must be filed *prior to* the offering. These required disclosures will result in a loss of confidentiality, which may be costly, especially since competitors, creditors, labor unions, suppliers, and others will have access to these documents once they become available to the public.

PERIODIC REPORTING AND ONGOING COMPLIANCE Most public companies are subject to the ongoing periodic reporting requirements imposed by the SEC, such as quarterly financial reporting (Forms 10-Q and 10-QSB), annual financial reporting (Forms 10-K and 10-KSB), reporting of current material events (Form 8-K), and related reporting requirements, including those for sale of control stock and tender offers. The ongoing costs of being a public company also include increased use of attorneys, accountants, and other advisers; dedication of staff time to meet with securities analysts and the financial press; implementation of a program for shareholder relations and media relations; and the significantly greater cost of annual reports, shareholders' meetings, and solicitations of proxies when shareholders' approval is needed for major corporate transactions.

Preparation for Due Diligence

As you learned in Chapter 10, the due diligence process means that the company's corporate records, personnel, products, agreements, and financial data will be viewed under a microscope (regardless of whether going public or some other financing strategy is ultimately adopted). You should begin preparing for the due diligence process well in advance, to avoid the significant expenses incurred by being unprepared. Observe all formalities imposed by applicable corporate laws, and maintain accurate and detailed minutes of corporate decisions. Be sure that the following documents are available when the due diligence team arrives:

- Articles of incorporation (and any amendments), bylaws, organizational resolutions, minutes of board meetings and shareholders' meetings, and any shareholder agreements or voting trusts

- Executed copies of all material supplier, distributor, and customer contracts (or other written evidence of such arrangements)

- Any business, marketing, or management plans, along with any pro forma financial projections and allocation of proceeds

- Completed copies of officers' and directors' questionnaire, containing information regarding possible conflicts of interest or insider transactions as well as information on each person's qualifications and experience

- All files pertaining to previous, current, or threatened litigation with creditors, customers, vendors, or employees

- All leases, title reports, or title insurance policies, deeds of trust, mortgages, invoices, and bills of sale for real estate and equipment

- All investment agreements, loan agreements, warrants, stock options, or any other documentation relating to the company's (or issuer's) capital structure, debt obligations, or duties to issue additional stock

- All insurance policies, government permits, and licenses and other documents or certificates of authority to operate the business

- Copies of any patents, copyrights, trademarks, and franchise or license agreements which the company may own or to which it may be a party.

Preparation for the IPO

In preparing for a public offering, you should immediately implement a more formalized management structure, which will include holding formal monthly or quarterly board meetings, maintaining complete and accurate corporate minutes and resolutions, and recruiting an experienced and independent board of directors who would be acceptable to the investing public.

The Three P's, and Some Problems

Of greatest interest to any prospective underwriter or investor analyzing a company will be the three P's of due diligence: *people, products,* and *profits*. From a legal perspective these key assets should have been adequately protected since the company's inception:

- *People.* Key employees should be carefully selected, since their background and role in the company will be subsequently disclosed in the prospectus. As discussed in Chapter 2, these employees should be subject to reasonable employment agreements, nondisclosure agreements, and incentive programs that ensure a long-term commitment to the company. Professional advisers (as discussed in Chapter 4) should have a strong background in corporate and securities law and should be capable of growing with the company as its requirements for professional services become more comprehensive and complex.

- *Products.* The products and services offered should be protected to the fullest extent possible under patent, trademark, and copyright laws (see Chapter 8). Any key vendor, licensee, customer, or distributor agreement that materially affects the production or distribution of these products and services should be negotiated and reduced to writing as formally as possible, with the eventual disclosure of these documents kept in mind.

- *Profits.* The company's capital structure and financial performance will be under the microscope of any potential underwriter. Although the wild market of the mid-1990s seemed to have little concern for actual profits (or, in the case of some high-tech companies, even for revenues), the more conservative financial markets of the late 1990s are more likely to require a solid financial track record demonstrating durable and steady cash flow and earnings.

Here are a few items that will have a *negative* effect on the company's valuation and the underwriter's willingness to take the company public:

- Inefficient management structure
- Overly restrictive shareholder agreements (which affect the company's control)
- Self-dealing among the board of directors and key stockholders
- Inadequate corporate records
- Capital structure with excessive debt
- Series of unaudited and uncertain financial statements
- Poor earnings history

Selecting an Underwriter

At the heart of the network established for the distribution and sale of securities is the managing or "lead" underwriter, whose selection and negotiation is a key ingredient in the success of the IPO. A significant amount of time should be devoted to interviewing and selecting the lead underwriter. Consider a variety of underwriters, ranging from small local firms (which may devote a considerable amount of time and attention to the transaction) to larger firms (which have a genuine "Wall Street" presence and reputation but entail a risk that the offering will be "lost" among bigger transactions or delegated to junior staff members).

There are many factors that should be considered in selecting the lead underwriter. The size and reputation of the underwriter that the company is able to attract will typically depend on (1) the strength of the company, (2) the amount of stock being offered, and (3) the company's future business plans. Underwriters typically offer a wide range of support services, such as management consulting services, business valuations, development of media and shareholder relations programs, assistance in developing an optimum capital structure or location, and analysis of candidates for merger or acquisition (which may or may not be needed when considering a public offering). Any company (regardless of size or industry) should closely examine the reputation, experience, distribution capability, market-making ability, research capabilities, and specific industry expertise of a potential underwriter.

Letter of Intent

Once selected, the lead underwriter will usually execute a *letter of intent.* The letter of intent states the terms and conditions of the proposed distribution of the securities and will typically also set a range for the price of the securities and hence the valuation of the company; however, the final decision on these issues will be determined by the *post-effective price amendment* (which may adjust the price on the basis of recent events affecting the company or any changes in market conditions). Since underwriters have many different methods of arriving at the preliminary valuation and pricing, be prepared to solicit competing bids if possible to ensure the best valuation for your company. The letter of intent will also govern the relationship throughout the preparation and registration process, because the final underwriting agreement is usually not signed until the day that the registration statement becomes effective following SEC approval. An understanding of the key terms of the letter of intent is crucial. These include the following.

TYPE OF UNDERWRITING   There are two basic variations of commitments by the lead underwriter: (1) the *firm* commitment, whereby the underwriter pledges to purchase all of the securities offered and then bears the responsibility for resale to the public; and (2) the *best efforts* commitment, whereby the lead underwriter merely promises to use its best efforts to offer and sell the securities. Under the best-efforts commitment, there is no assurance that the amount of capital required to meet the business objectives will be received, even though the company must still incur the extensive costs of the offering and the legal burden of being publicly held. One form of protection is the *all-or-nothing* or *go-no-go amount,* under which if a certain minimum number of shares are not sold, the entire offering will be withdrawn. An underwriter may also want to negotiate an *over-allotment option,* whereby the underwriter is granted an option to purchase a specific number of additional shares if the maximum number of shares to be sold is exceeded.

COMPENSATION OF THE UNDERWRITER   The compensation package usually comprises commission schedules, ongoing consulting fees, and any warrants to purchase shares (during a certain period of time and at a fixed price). The rate of commission, the amount of advance payment, the number of warrants to be issued, etc., will depend on the company's negotiating leverage, the risk of the offering, and the underwriter's projected internal time and effort to manage the distribution network.

OFFERING, SIZE, PRICE, AND SPECIAL CHARACTERISTICS This encompasses number of shares to be sold, type of security to be issued, price of the security per share, and any special characteristics or restrictions. Remember, however, that the final decisions regarding these factors may not be made until just prior to the actual offering (depending on market conditions and completion of due diligence). Under these circumstances, you and the underwriter should at least agree on price ranges, which will be subject to the terms of the final "pricing amendment" filed with the SEC just before the public offering.

RESPONSIBILITY FOR FEES AND EXPENSES Usually, you will be responsible for all of the company's costs as well as some portion of the underwriter's expenses. Expect that the lead underwriter will want to hold a series of parties and "dog and pony shows." To prevent excessive costs, a ceiling on these expenses should be established.

MISCELLANEOUS PROVISIONS Among the other key terms to be negotiated are the following:

- Rights of first refusal on future financing
- Responsibility for registration under state blue-sky laws (see Chapter 6)
- Selection of professional advisers
- Representations and warranties
- Restrictions on activities before and after the sale of the securities
- Accessibility of employee records for further due diligence

Co-Underwriters

Once an agreement has been signed, the lead underwriter will organize a group of co-underwriters to share in the risk of the offering and to establish the network of participating registered broker-dealer firms. The role of the broker-dealer firms is to sell the company's securities to their clientele. During this period of negotiations, the company's management team and operations will be closely reviewed and scrutinized by the members of the distribution network, commonly referred to as the "road show." This allows members of the syndicate to learn more about the company and the proposed offering as well as start building excitement about the impending offering. This process prepares you for the review and scrutiny by the SEC and then again by the general investing public.

Preparing the Registration Statement

The first step in preparing the registration statement is setting up an initial meeting of all key members of the registration team: attorneys, accountants, lead underwriter, chief executive officer, chief financial officer, etc. During this meeting, responsibility for preparation of each aspect of the registration statement is delegated, along with a timetable for completion of each task. Several preliminary tasks must be completed when preparing a registration statement, such as the following:

- Extensive due diligence.
- Meetings of the board of directors to authorize the offering.
- Preparation and completion of the confidential questionnaire for the officers and directors.
- Legal research as to compliance with applicable state blue-sky laws.
- NASD regulations. (The National Association of Securities Dealers, NASD, is a self-regulatory body that reviews the underwriting and distribution agreements prepared in connection with the public offering in order to ensure that the terms and conditions are consistent with industry practices.)
- Establishment of marketing and distribution strategies.

Components and Basic Forms

The registration statement itself consists of two distinct parts: (1) *offering prospectus,* which is used to assist underwriters and investors in analyzing the company and the securities being offered; and (2) *exhibits and additional information,* which are provided directly to the SEC as part of the disclosure and registration regulations. The registration statement is part of the public record and is available for public inspection.

There are a variety of alternative forms for the registration statement. The form chosen depends on the company's history, its size and the nature of the specific offering. The most common form used is Form S-1, which is required for all companies (unless an alternative form is available). The S-1, however, is complicated; has several requirements that must be fulfilled *before* going public; and requires a *description* of the company's business, its properties, material transactions between the company and its officers, pending legal proceedings, plans for distribution of the securities, and intended use of the proceeds from the IPO. Forms S-2 and S-3 (subject to certain requirements) are available for companies that are already subject to the reporting requirements of the Securities Exchange Act of 1934 (the Exchange Act). Form S-4 is limited to corporate combinations. Forms S-1 through S-4 are filed and processed at the SEC's headquarters office in Washington, D.C., by the Division of Corporate Finance.

The SEC's "Small Business Initiatives"

In 1992, the SEC implemented the "Small Business Initiatives" (SBIs), significantly modifying its special provisions for offerings by small businesses (Regulation S-B) that are not already subject to the reporting requirements of the Exchange Act. The SBIs were designed to streamline the federal registration process in connection with IPOs to encourage investment in small businesses. A "small-business issuer," as defined in Rule 405 of the Securities Act of 1933 (the Securities Act) is a company meeting all of the following criteria:

- Has revenue of less than $25 million
- Is a United States or Canadian issuer
- Is not an investment company
- If a majority-owned subsidiary, has a parent corporation that is also a small-business issuer.

Small-business issuers can use Form SB-1 or Form SB-2 to register with the SEC securities to be sold for cash.

Form SB-1 can be used *only* to register up to $10 million of securities (its predecessor, Form S-18, had a ceiling of $7.5 million). Also, the company must not have registered more than $10 million in any continuous 12-month period (including the transaction being registered). In addition, Form SB-1 allows for financial statements (which *must* be audited by an independent party) to be given in accordance with generally accepted accounting principles (GAAP), not the detailed requirements of the SEC.

Form SB-2 (its predecessor, Form S-1, was typically used by small businesses before 1992) allows small-business issuers to offer an unlimited dollar amount of securities; thus companies that meet the SEC's definition of a small business are allowed to sell more securities without having to undergo the same extensive disclosure process as larger companies. The advantages of Form SB-2 include: (1) repeated use; (2) location of answered forms in a central depository; (3) filing with either the SEC's regional office (which is located near to your company's principal location) or its headquarters office in Washington, D.C.; and (4) the benefits afforded by Form SB-1. These advantages translate into economic benefits. For example, the average cost of the legal and accounting fees for small businesses registering to make an IPO went from $200,000 to between $75,000 and $100,000. *Imagine—the government has actually created a program to save us money.*

The Key Elements

The key disclosure areas of the registration statement include the following:

- *Cover page and forepart.* The SEC has very specific requirements as to the information that *must* be stated on the cover page and forepart of the prospectus. These include summary information pertaining to the nature of the company's business, terms of the offering, determination of the offering price, dilution, plan of distribution, risk factors, and selected financial information.

- *Introduction to the company.* Overview of the company: its business, employees, financial performance, and principal offices.

- *Risk factors.* Description of the operating and financial risk factors affecting the company's business, with particular regard to the offering of the securities (such as depending on a single customer, supplier, or key personnel; lack of an operating history in the new areas of business the company wants to pursue; unproven market for the products and services offered; or lack of an earnings history).

- *Use of proceeds.* Discussion of the anticipated use of the proceeds raised by the offering.

- *Capitalization.* Description of the capital structure of debt obligations, the company's anticipated dividend policy, and dilution of purchaser's (investor's) equity.

- *Description of business and property.* Description of the key assets, principal lines of business, human resources, properties, marketing strategies, and competitive advantages of the company and any of its subsidiaries for the last five years.

- *Management and principal shareholders.* Discussion of the key management team and description of each member's background, education, compensation, and role in the company, as well as a table of all shareholders who hold a beneficial interest of 5% or more.

- *Litigation.* Statement of any material litigation (past, pending, or anticipated) affecting the company or any other adverse legal proceedings that would affect an investor's analysis of the securities being offered.

- *Financial information.* Summary of financial information, such as sales history, net income or losses from operations, long-term debt obligations, dividend patterns, capital structure, founder's equity, and shareholder loans.

- *Securities offered and underwriting arrangements.* Description of the underwriting arrangements, the distribution plan, and the key characteristics of the securities being offered.

- *Experts and other matters.* Brief statement regarding the identity of the attorneys, accountants, and other experts retained as well as the availability of additional information from the registration statement filed with the SEC (such as indemnification policies for the directors and officers, recent sales of unregistered securities, a breakdown of the expenses of the offering, and a wide variety of corporate documents and key agreements).

An Overview of the Registration Process

When the initial draft of the registration statement is ready for filing with the SEC, you have two choices: either file the document with the transmittal letter and required fees *or* schedule a pre-filing conference with an SEC staff member to discuss any anticipated questions or problems regarding the disclosure document or the accompanying financial statements.

The initial registration process is generally governed by the Securities Act, which is designed to ensure full and fair disclosure of material facts to prospective investors in connection with the offer and sale of securities. The Securities Act requires the company to file a registration statement with the SEC as well as a prospectus to prospective investors.

Once the registration statement is officially received by the SEC, it is then assigned to an examining group (usually composed of attorneys, accountants, and financial analysts, within a specific industry department of the Division of Corporate Finance). The length of time and depth of the review by the examining group will depend on the history of the company and the nature of the securities offered. For example, a company that operates in a troubled or turbulent industry and is publicly offering its securities for the first time should expect a detailed review by all members of the examining group.

Following the initial review, a deficiency or comment letter will be sent, suggesting changes to the registration statement. The modifications of the statement will focus on the quality of the disclosure (such as inadequate discussion of risk factors, or verbiage in management's discussion of the financial performance)—*not* on the quality of the company or the securities being offered. In most cases, the company will be required to file a material amendment in order to address the staff's concerns. This process continues until all concerns raised by the examining group have been addressed. The final pricing amendment is filed following the pricing meeting of the underwriters and the execution of the final underwriting agreement. The SEC has developed detailed regulations and restrictions on what information may be released to the public or the media during this period (the "quiet period"), and especially on communications that appear to be designed to influence the price of the shares. The registration statement then is declared effective, and the securities can be offered to the public. The registration statement is declared effective 20 days after the final amendment has been filed, unless the effective date is accelerated by the SEC. Most companies tend to seek an accelerated effective date, which is usually made available if the company has complied with the examining group's suggested modifications.

In addition to SEC regulations, a company offering its securities to the public must also meet the requirements of NASD and state securities laws. NASD will analyze all elements of the proposed corporate package for the underwriter in order to determine its fairness and reasonableness. The SEC will not deem a registration statement effective for public offering unless and until NASD has approved the underwriting arrangements as being fair and reasonable.

Section 18 of the Securities Act states that federal securities laws do not supersede compliance with any state securities laws; therefore, the requirements of each state's blue-sky laws must also be satisfied. Although various exemptions from formal registration are often available, the state securities laws must be checked very carefully with regard to filing fees, requirements for registered agents, disclosure obligations, and regulations covering underwriters or broker-dealers for each state in which the securities will be offered.

The Closing and Beyond

Once the final underwriting agreement is signed and the final pricing amendment is filed with the SEC, the registration statement will be declared effective and the selling process begins. Throughout the selling period, *wait patiently* and hope that any minimum sales quotas (such as those for "all-or-nothing" offerings) are met and that the offering is well received by the investing public.

To facilitate the mechanics of the offering process, you may want to consider retaining the services of a registrar and transfer agent who will be responsible for issuing stock certificates, maintaining stockholder ownership records, and processing the transfer of shares from one investor to another. These services are usually offered by commercial banks and trust companies (which also offer ongoing support services such as mailing annual reports and proxies, disbursing dividends, and maintaining custody of the authorized but unissued stock certificates). Once the offer and sale of the shares to the public have been completed, a closing must be scheduled to exchange documents, issue stock certificates, and disburse net proceeds.

In addition to the obligations discussed previously, you are usually required to file the SEC's Form SR. This is a report on the company's use of the proceeds raised from the sale of the securities. *The information should be substantially similar to the discussion contained in the prospectus provided to prospective investors.* Form SR must be filed initially within 90 days after the registration statement becomes effective, and then once every six months until the offering is complete and the proceeds are being applied toward their intended use.

●ngoing Reporting and Disclosure Requirements

The Exchange Act generally governs the ongoing disclosure and periodic reporting of publicly traded companies. Section 13 grants broad powers to the SEC to develop documents and reports that must be filed. The three primary reports required by Section 15 (d) are:

* *Form 10-K or 10-KSB (for small-business issuers)* is an *annual* report, which must be filed within 90 days after the close of the company's fiscal year covered by the report. It must also include a report of all significant activities of the company during its fourth quarter, an analysis and discussion of its financial condition, a description of the current officers and directors, and a schedule of certain exhibits. Form 10-K requires the issuer's

income statements for the prior three years and balance sheets for the prior two years. Form 10-KSB requires the income statement for the prior two years and the balance sheet for the prior year (which can be prepared in accordance with GAAP).

- *Form 10-Q or 10-QSB (for small-business issuers)* is a *quarterly* report, which must be filed no later than 45 days after the end of each of the first three fiscal quarters of each fiscal year. This quarterly filing includes copies of quarterly financial statements (accompanied by a discussion and analysis of the company's financial condition by its management) and a report of any litigation as well as any steps taken by the company that affect shareholder's rights or may require shareholder's approval. The difference between Form 10-Q and Form 10-QSB is the same as that between 10-K and 10-KSB. Form 10-Q requires an issuer's balance sheet from the previous year and a report of the most recent fiscal quarter; 10-QSB requires a report on the most recent quarter.

- *Form 8-K* is a *periodic* report, which is designed to ensure that *all material information* about significant events affecting the company is disclosed to the investing public as soon as it is available, but not later than 15 days after the occurrence of the event. (The event triggers the need to file the Form 8-K).

The duty to disclose "material information" to the general public (whether as part of a Form 8-K filing or otherwise) is an ongoing obligation that continues for as long as the company's securities are publicly traded. An ongoing compliance program must be established to ensure that all *material* corporate information is disclosed as fully and as promptly as possible. A fact is generally considered to be material if there is a substantial likelihood that a reasonable shareholder would consider it important in his or her investment decision (whether to buy, sell, or hold or how to vote on a particular proposed corporate action). The following kinds of information are examples of what is typically considered material for purposes of disclosure:

- Acquisitions and dispositions of other companies or properties
- Public or private sales of debt or equity securities
- Bankruptcy or receivership proceedings affecting the issuer

- Significant contract awards or terminations
- Changes in the key management team

Pursuant to Section 12(g), certain companies of publicly traded securities are subject to additional reporting and disclosure requirements. For example, if a company either elects to register its securities under 12(g) or has more than 500 shareholders and at least $5 million worth of total assets, then it will also be subject to the rules developed by the SEC for: (1) solicitation of proxies; (2) reporting of beneficial ownership; (3) liability for short-swing transactions; and (4) tender offers.

1. *Solicitation of proxies.* Because of the difficulty of assembling each and every shareholder of a corporation for matters requiring a vote by shareholders, voting by proxy is a fact of life for most publicly held corporations. When soliciting the proxies of shareholders for voting at annual or special meetings, special statutory rules must be carefully followed. The request for the proxy must be accompanied by a detailed proxy statement, which should specify the exact matters to be acted upon and any information that would be required by the shareholder in reaching a decision.

2. *Reporting of beneficial ownership.* Section 16(a) requires that all officers, directors, and 10% shareholders (if any) file a statement of beneficial ownership of securities. Filed on Form 3, the statement must reflect all holdings (direct and indirect). Section 16(a) also requires that whenever the officers and directors increase or decrease their holdings by purchase, by sale, by gift, or otherwise, the transaction must be reported on Form 4 no later than the tenth day of the month following the month in which the transaction occurred.

3. *Liability for short-swing transactions.* Section 16(b) requires that officers, directors, employees, or other insiders return to the company any profit they may have realized from any combination of sales and purchases, or purchases and sales, of securities made by them within any six-month period. Any acquisition of securities (regardless of form of payment) is considered to be a "purchase." The purpose of Section 16(b) is to discourage even the possibility that directors and officers will

take advantage of "inside information" by "speculating" in a company's stock. Liability occurs automatically if there is a sale and purchase within six months, even if the individual involved in the transaction did not actually take advantage of inside information.

4. *Rules and regulations for tender offers.* Sections 13 and 14 generally govern the rules for parties who wish to make a tender offer to purchase the securities of a publicly traded corporation. Any person acquiring (directly or indirectly) beneficial ownership of more than 5% of an equity security registered under Section 12 must report the transaction by filing Schedule 13D within 10 days from the date of acquisition. Schedule 13D requires disclosure of certain material information, such as the identity and background of the purchaser, the purpose of the acquisition, the source and amount of funds used to purchase the securities, and disclosure of the company. If the purchase is in connection with a tender offer, then the provisions of Section 14(d) also apply, pursuant to which the terms of the tender offer must be disclosed (as well as the plans of the offerer if it is successful and the terms of any special agreements between the offerer and the target company). Section 14(e) imposes a broad prohibition against the use of false, misleading, or incomplete statements in connection with a tender offer.

Rule 10b-5 and Insider Trading

A great deal of attention has been devoted by the business and financial press to the SEC's Rule 10b-5 and its application in the prosecution of insider trading cases. Here is the text of Rule 10b-5.

It shall be unlawful for any person, directly or indirectly, by the use of any means or instrumentality of interstate commerce, or of the mails or of any facility of any national securities exchange, to:

(a) employ any device, scheme, or artifice to defraud;

(b) make any untrue statement of a material fact or omit to state a material fact necessary in order to make the statements made, in light of the circumstances under which they were made, not misleading; or

(c) engage in any act, practice, or course of business which operates or would operate as a fraud or deceit upon any person, in connection with the purchase or sale of any security.

The most frequent use of Rule 10b-5 has been in insider trading cases, typically those in which an officer, director, or other person who has a fiduciary relationship with a corporation buys or sells the company's securities while in the possession of material, nonpublic information. However, Rule 10b-5 is also used in a variety of other situations, such as these:

- When a corporation issues misleading information to the public or keeps silent when it has a duty to disclose

- When an insider selectively discloses material, nonpublic information to another party, who then trades securities on the basis of the information (this is generally called "tipping")

- When a person mismanages a corporation in ways that are connected with the purchase or sale of securities

- When a securities firm or another person manipulates the market for a security traded in the over-the-counter market

- When a securities firm or a securities professional engages in certain other forms of conduct connected with the purchase or sale of securities

It is imperative for all officers, directors, employees, and shareholders of publicly traded companies (or companies considering being publicly traded) to be keenly aware of the broad scope of this antifraud rule in their transactions that involve the company.

Disposing of Restricted Securities

All shares of a public company held by its controlling persons (who typically include its officers, its directors, and 10% shareholders, if any) are deemed "restricted securities" under the Securities Act. The sale of restricted securities is generally governed by Rule 144, which requires the following as a condition of sale:

- The company must be current in its periodic reports to the SEC.
- The restricted securities must have been beneficially owned for at least one year preceding the sale.
- The amount of securities that may be sold in any three-month period must be limited to 1% of the outstanding class of securities *or* to the average weekly reported volume of trading in the securities on a registered national security exchange (if the securities are listed)—whichever figure is greater.
- The securities must be sold only in brokers' transactions, and the notice of the sale must be filed with the SEC concurrently with the placing of the sale order.
- If the sale involves 500 shares or $10,000, a report of the transaction on Form 144 must be filed.

It is imperative that you and your managers understand the planning and registration process before pursuing a public offering of the company's securities. Substantial time and expense can be saved if the process of planning begins early in the development of methods of operation and formulation of strategies for company's growth. As with any contemplated method of capital formation, going public has its costs and benefits, all of which should be carefully weighed and understood prior to selling the first share of stock to the public.

13

What to Do When Financial Problems Hit Your Company

The fable that turns into a nightmare often goes like this: A growing company begins to achieve and exceed its projected growth plans. The company moves into new offices, recruits new employees, increases managers' salaries and benefits, hires a team of outside advisers, and begins plans for acquisitions and eventually a public offering. The founding entrepreneurs have built a successful company but have also created a challenge beyond their experience and capabilities. Their ego and bull-headedness prevent them from accepting the fact that a professional management team needs to be appointed. A climate of "growth at any price" begins to build within the company. Most of the staff ride an emotional roller-coaster from excitement to fear to blind trust. Cash flow shortages are subtle at first, but with each new month of growth, expenses begin to exceed revenues at an increasing pace. The company is not paying attention to the bottom line; furthermore, it begins to get so caught up in its own growth that it is not paying sufficient attention to aggressive steps taken by its competitors or to changes in the marketplace that are affecting its industry. If this nightmare sounds a little too familiar, then pay close attention to this chapter.

As you can see from the story described above, growth for growth's sake is not acceptable in today's competitive marketplace. In addition to managing and adapting to the positive aspects of growth, you must also manage and adapt to problems:

- Anticipate financial problems.
- Manage the costs and risks associated with economic problems.
- Understand the methods and alternatives available for solving financial problems.

Risk Management and Control

Risk management, commonly used in the insurance industry, is the process of identifying and analyzing a company's exposure to risk, and then selecting alternatives for protecting against these risks. Certain types of economic and financial risks are predictable and can be managed once identified, while other types of risks are usually beyond the control of even the best management team. Similarly, certain types of risks can be mitigated with insurance, while others, such as hostile acts by suppliers or competitors, will not be insurable. The implementation of a risk management program begins with the answers to the following questions:

- What aspects of operations could directly or indirectly cause an economic loss?
- What is the likelihood that such a loss will actually occur?
- If an identified potential loss actually occurs, what are its tangible and intangible costs?
- To what extent are the potential losses insurable? Does the cost of the insurance policies outweigh the cost of potential conflict or loss?
- To what extent can internal financial controls be implemented in order to prevent or reduce the exposure to financial distress?

Effective risk management goes far beyond the installation of smoke detectors and a periodic safety check for all company-owned vehicles. From a *management perspective*, it means establishing internal financial and managerial controls, which are designed to ensure ongoing compliance with the company's strategies, policies, and procedures. From an *accounting perspective*, it means maintaining accurate, comprehensive financial records so that periodic financial statements are produced on a timely basis in accordance with GAAP. From a *legal perspective*, it means compliance with the following: corporate laws; labor and employment laws; antitrust and trade regulations; all necessary business licenses and permits; material contractual obligations (such as vendor agreements, leases, and loan documents); obligations to protect intellectual property; and any other laws and regulations applicable to the company's operation and management.

As discussed in Chapter 4, periodic legal audits are one effective method of ensuring that a company remains in compliance with its legal obligations, the nature and extent of which are likely to change as the company grows and develops.

Anticipating Financial Distress

The primary function of a system of risk management and control is to provide early warning signs of financial distress. Early detection of business problems is vital to a company's continued growth and to the management of situations that are likely to cause economic distress. Business problems rarely occur suddenly. Most problems develop over a long period of time and are caused by a series of financial, legal, operational, and strategic mistakes, or by miscalculations that went largely undetected by management. Some of the more obvious "symptoms" that a company is heading down the wrong course include these:

- Persistent operating losses
- Departure of several key employees

- Loss of more than 5% market share per quarter in two consecutive quarters
- Recurring cash flow shortages
- General loss of morale and enthusiasm among workers at all levels

Distressed companies often share common traits: inability to service debt, decline in profits and margins, and inefficiency in management structure or in delivery of services. Also, it is often difficult to convince management of the actual steps necessary to cure the problem or problems. In my experience, most entrepreneurs believe that "more is better" and as a result believe that problems can be solved by selling more or doing more.

Red Flags

To determine whether your company is on a course leading to disaster, see if you can spot any of the "red flags" described below.

LACK OF DEPTH IN THE MANAGEMENT TEAM   A company's risk of business failure is greatly increased when it depends on an overly centralized management team made up of the original founders. The long-term health of the company lies in the founders' ability to recruit and retain qualified personnel who are capable of taking and guiding it to its next phase of growth.

OPERATING IN AN INDUSTRY WITH RAPIDLY CHANGING TECHNOLOGY   When a company operates in a marketplace where rapidly changing technology could suddenly render its products and services obsolete, the chances of business failure are very high. As a result, management must stay abreast of technological developments, attempt to establish product diversification, and ensure adequate capitalization for ongoing research and modernization of equipment.

DEPENDENCE ON A KEY CUSTOMER, SUPPLIER, LENDER, OR CONTRACT   Many companies are built and continue to flourish as a result of a single critical customer, a single source of supply, or a special relationship with a lender or investor. But if you want to grow your business even more, you can't be a hostage to any third party who cannot be completely controlled. For example, if your company relies on a major customer for 35% to 60% of its revenues, and the customer is lost to a competitor, what will be the effect on your company? Worse yet, if the key customer is aware of your company's dependence on it, how many of its demands will you grant as a result of your need to preserve the account? Similarly, an excessive dependence on patents, licenses, concessions, and related contractual advantages that may be terminated or expire significantly increases the chance of business failure. The only way to help mitigate the risk of dependence on a third party is to diversify product lines, geographic trading areas, targeted markets, and distribution channels.

UNDERCAPITALIZATION FOR SPECIFIC PROJECTS It is easy for rapidly growing companies to charge ahead and seek to take advantage of market opportunities even if they lack the capital necessary to complete the components of the project. For example, manufacturing a product needed to remain competitive is a waste of time and resources if no capital is available for bringing the product to the market. Under such circumstances, it would often make more sense to sell or license the technology to another company and then use the proceeds or licensing royalties to exploit an existing product or service offered.

DEFECTIVE INFORMATION AND MONITORING SYSTEMS A growing company with an inadequate or defective management information system is likely to have difficulty monitoring its competition, internal costs and budgets, changes in the economic and political environment, inventory controls, management problems and internal conflicts, cash flow, and sales growth. If your company cannot obtain this information in an organized, timely, and accessible fashion, then it is likely to experience difficulty in making informed day-to-day decisions or engaging in meaningful long-term strategic planning.

RETAINING UNPRODUCTIVE DIVISIONS, ASSETS, AND PEOPLE FOR NO GOOD REASON In my experience, most companies that are growing quickly will inevitably have some unproductive operating division, asset, or person putting a strain on the overall profitability of the company. Get rid of the deadwood. Espcially dangerous are projects or people that remain for paternalistic or egotistical reasons. Chances are that such a division of assets is a hemorrhage, which is bleeding precious cash. Also, obsolete or idle equipment, unused real estate, and unnecessary employee benefits (e.g., a company car, boat, condominium, or plane) should all be candidates for disposal when cash is at a premium.

PROBLEMS WITH ACCOUNTS RECEIVABLE MANAGEMENT There is nothing more frustrating than to experience a tremendous increase in sales along with an equally tremendous problem in accounts receivable management. Customers must be carefully monitored, with no further goods or services provided when overdue accounts reach certain levels. As soon as a customer shows signs of difficulty paying, collateral should be obtained to secure the obligation. Collection agencies and attorneys should be used for larger problematic accounts. If cash flow becomes a real problem, consider discounting the accounts receivable at a commercial bank, obtaining the services of a factoring company, or obtaining credit insurance to protect against excessive bad-debt losses.

Costs of Financial Distress

Overall, the effects of financial distress are felt by employees, customers, stockholders, creditors, and suppliers. For example, customers and vendors will often attempt to avoid dealing with a troubled company, and this is likely to further damage its financial performance and its ability to raise capital. Vendors, to the extent that they are still willing to sell to a distressed firm at all, will usually demand unreasonable sales terms in order to protect their risk. Key employees, fearful about their jobs, will often flee to a more stable competitor, usually taking their enthusiasm, ideas, and expertise with them. This will cause the distressed company even more difficulty attracting and retaining skilled personnel, who may be desperately needed to keep the company alive. Stockholders will often seek to dispose of their securities, driving down the market price per share. Creditors of a troubled company will often seek to accelerate obligations in order to protect against the risk of default. During this difficult period, it is likely that inventory is becoming obsolete, buildings and machinery are deteriorating, and equipment is not being maintained because the company lacks the resources to commit to servicing or replacing worn parts. Finally, even competitors are likely to become more aggressive in order to take advantage of the window of opportunity created by the company's financial distress.

Understanding Bankruptcy and Its Alternatives

Even if you do get in a difficult financial situation, all hope is not lost. There may be ways of salvaging your company by considering bankruptcy and its alternatives.

Bankruptcy does not carry with it quite the same stigma that it had 20 years ago. In fact, reorganization under the federal bankruptcy laws has emerged as an integral part of the long-term strategic planning process and as a viable alternative for a troubled project, subsidiary, or entire company.

Nevertheless, bankruptcy is far from the only solution to problems caused by economic distress. It can be extremely time-consuming and disruptive to management's responsibilities and morale, and it often results in extensive negative publicity and loss of goodwill, involves substantial legal fees, and creates a significantly weakened bargaining position with creditors and competitors. A formal bankruptcy proceeding usually results in:

- Transfer of the company's control to creditors
- Termination of a large percentage of the company's workforce
- Significantly reduced ability to raise capital, and difficulty in attracting qualified employees and service providers

These costs and risks should be carefully weighed when considering bankruptcy.

A troubled company has several alternatives available, both under the federal bankruptcy laws and informally, in an arrangement with major creditors. Whether the principal cause of failure is temporary or permanent determines which alternative your company should follow. When the principal cause is temporary, creditors tend to favor formal or informal reorganization (known as a Chapter 11 filing). When the principal cause is permanent, creditors tend to favor liquidation of assets (known as a Chapter 7 filing), because the company is ultimately worth more to the stockholders dead than alive.

The troubled company should also weigh the viability of developing and implementing a formal *turnaround plan,* which usually involves a critical evaluation and assessment from an outside adviser* who can make recommendations for eliminating waste by downsizing and "trimming the fat." This assessment may include:

- Intensive data-gathering
- Listening carefully to key employees
- Tightening controls (including expenses and an extra-"slim" inventory)
- Developing strong internal reporting systems
- Negotiating for extended terms with suppliers
- Reviewing materials, labor, and engineering
- Studying administrative overhead

Many companies find that once the "bleeding" has stopped and internal attitudes have been repositioned, the company can once again start down the path of profitable operations.

---

* For more information on the development of a turnaround plan or to contact turnaround professionals, I highly recommend the Turnaround Management Association (TMA) 230 North Michigan Avenue, Suite 1310, Chicago, Illinois 60601 (312-857-7734). TMA publishes the *Journal of Corporate Renewal* six times a year.

Informal Alternatives to Bankruptcy

In my experience, many companies should initially explore the more informal alternatives before considering going through the process of a formal bankruptcy. These alternatives include:

INFORMAL NEGOTIATIONS WITH CREDITORS   In almost all cases, an *informal* "workout" with creditors is more efficient and less disruptive than a formal Chapter 11 proceeding. An informal workout may include:

1. Negotiating an extension

2. Restructuring overall costs or terms

3. Composing an agreement (under which all known creditors accept partial payment on a pro rata basis in full satisfaction of the obligation)

4. Transferring partial control of the company or even exchanging all or part of its debt for equity

If chosen, this route must have the cooperation of all known creditors, because there is usually no way to force dissenting creditors to become parties to a composition or settlement agreement. This would *not* be the case, however, in a formal Chapter 11 proceeding, where the judge has the power of the "cram down"—rules used to force a creditor to accept the terms of whatever the court deems to be a generally fair and equitable plan of reorganization.

INFORMAL REORGANIZATION   Also, seek to voluntarily reorganize or restructure the corporation in order to achieve more efficient and more profitable operations. For instance, your board of directors may choose to merge with or be acquired by another company that could make more effective use of your company's remaining assets. Alternatively, the company could separate one of its profitable divisions from an unprofitable division and create two different subsidiaries. Capital formation efforts could then be placed on the profitable subsidiary, with plans to rebuild the unprofitable subsidiary at a later date. Finally, you could simply "spin off" certain assets to third parties and then use the proceeds of the sale to repay debts and concentrate on the growth and development of the remaining operations. Each of these basic methods of informal reorganization usually can be implemented more quickly and inexpensively than a formal proceeding under Chapter 11, provided, however, that the principals of the company can obtain the cooperation and support of its stockholders and creditors.

The benefits of implementing an informal workout or reorganization plan as an alternative must not be underestimated. This is especially true for owners and managers of closely held companies, where the list of trade creditors and lenders is likely to be far shorter than in a larger, publicly traded corporation. Smaller companies are much more likely to be able to round up their creditors for the purposes of negotiating a composition agreement than a multinational corporation with thousands of creditors.

Chapter 11: Petition for Formal Reorganization

The troubled company may voluntarily petition for relief under Chapter 11 of the Bankruptcy Act, *or* be involuntarily forced into reorganization by at least three of its creditors (unless the company has fewer than 12 creditors, in which case even a single creditor can force a reorganization).

In a typical Chapter 11 proceeding, the debtor is essentially reclassified as a *debtor-in-possession*. It may be permitted to continue to operate and manage its business, subject to certain restrictions imposed by the court and the federal bankruptcy statues; *or* the court may determine that the company's management is so incompetent that a trustee or management committee must be appointed to full or partial control and will operate the company during the period that the plan of reorganization is being developed and approved. Once the company has been reclassified as a debtor-in-possession, it has a fiduciary duty to protect the assets of the business on behalf of its secured and unsecured creditors. There is also the possibility that the court will deem the current management incapable of running the company and will, in that case, appoint a "receiver" to manage the day-to-day affairs for the benefit of the creditors. Either way, restrictions will be placed on the company's ability to borrow and raise capital, enter into new contracts, hire new employees, implement management strategies, and conduct certain business operations. The direct and indirect costs of these restrictions are high, in terms of both professional fees and management resources. It is likely that the founding entrepreneurs will be spending so much time at court appearances, at meetings with creditors, and on the preparation of financial statements and schedules that they will have little time to actually operate and manage the business.

To be weighed against these costs, however, are the benefits to be enjoyed by the company both after the petition has been filed and once the formal plan of reorganization has been approved. Upon the filing of the petition for reorganization, all actions against the company and its assets are subject to an automatic stay, which has the effect of delaying almost all immediate obligations and proceedings until the formal plan has been approved. In fact, creditors who attempt to violate the automatic stay provisions may be held in contempt of court.

Once the statutory requirements of the formal plan have been met and all necessary consents obtained, the plan is ready to be confirmed by the presiding bankruptcy judge. The confirmation of the plan has the following legal ramifications:

- The plan has a binding effect on the troubled company and its creditors.
- All property of the bankruptcy estate is vested in the reorganized debtor, free and clear of all liens and encumbrances unless otherwise stated in the plan.
- All prior debts of the troubled company are discharged except as may be provided in the plan.
- The debtor company commences its operations pursuant to the terms of the plan.

The benefits to a troubled company from the development and approval of a formal plan of reorganization are significant. However, approval marks the beginning, not the end, of a successful turnaround. If the company has been reorganized properly, then it may emerge and prosper even more effectively than before the bankruptcy proceedings. Many emerging growth companies survive the bankruptcy process but are subsequently unable to flourish under the terms and conditions of the approved reorganization plan. The changes in control, management policies, and operational freedom that may be caused by the reorganization plan could result in an eventual collapse of the company, leading to another reorganization or even to liquidation proceedings under Chapter 7.

Chapter 7: When Things Are Not Getting Better

If the troubled company cannot be formally reorganized, or if the plan of reorganization proves to be unsuccessful, then a formal liquidation under Chapter 7 of the Bankruptcy Act must be considered. Proceedings under Chapter 7 begin with the filing of either a voluntary or an involuntary petition for liquidation. Upon filing of the petition, the court will issue to the petitioner an "order for relief," which triggers the automatic stay provisions. At the same time, a trustee will be appointed to manage the company's assets, referred to as the *bankruptcy estate*. Creditors must file a *proof of claim* within 90 days of the first meeting between the debtor, trustee, and creditors. The appointed trustee then gathers together all available assets into the bankruptcy estate for liquidation, sets aside any fraudulent transfers, reviews the validity of all proofs of claims submitted by creditors, separates the interests of secured and unsecured creditors, determines if any assets collected are exempt from liquidation, and arranges for the sale of the assets in the bankruptcy estate in a manner and on terms most advantageous to the creditors. Once the assets have been gathered, inventoried, appraised, and sold, the proceeds are distributed to the creditors according to the terms of the plan of liquidation by the trustee, and virtually all obligations of the debtor are discharged.

Owners and managers of growing companies must work closely with their accountants and attorneys to identify and manage those situations that are likely to lead to financial distress. The risks and costs of financial distress are very high, and in some cases are fatal. The formal and informal legal strategies available to companies experiencing financial distress must all be carefully analyzed and assessed, in hopes that the path selected and the lessons learned will ultimately lead to a successful turnaround and the company's continued growth.

14

Doing Business in Cyberspace and the Global Village:

Opportunities and Challenges in the Twenty-First Century

As we approach the year 2000, companies of all sizes in virtually all industries are facing the challenge of how to adapt to the "knowledge era" and how to use the many technological developments of the late twentieth century to enhance the performance and productivity of their businesses and organizations. In this new era, the speed of access to data and the quality of the information often determine the competitiveness of a business and ultimately its success or failure. Small and growing companies that are able to extract reliable information, transform it into knowledge, and efficiently meet customers' needs will grow and prosper while others will be left at the entrance ramp. Major changes in organizational structure and culture are affecting how and where we work, how and where we offer our products and services, and what types of legal, financial, and organizational issues entrepreneurs and growing companies will face in this new economy.

For many of these challenges, the more things change, the more they seem to stay the same. Owners of small and mid-sized businesses continue to worry about some of the same issues that plagued them at the turn of the last century, such as OSHA health and safety standards, minimum wage standards, personal injury and workers' compensation claims, and product liability litigation. These issues may never be entirely resolved, but as our economy shifts, new legal, financial, and organizational issues have begun to emerge, involving protection of intellectual property, doing business in the global village, transacting business via the Internet, and a renewed focus on satisfying the customer.

These economic and organizational shifts are creating new challenges. Global competition and rapid technological advancements are creating new models for business management, such as geographically dispersed workforces, flattened organizational structures, and strategic partnering among customers, vendors, suppliers, and even competitors. And companies of all sizes are developing work teams that communicate electronically instead of around a conference table or a water cooler. The virtual workplace, where there is significantly less human interaction, brings new challenges in the areas of protection of privacy, confidentiality, and copyright.

Some of the more interesting issues created by these emerging technologies and changes in the workforce are:

- How will personnel and compensation structures be different in this team-driven environment?

- In this intellectual, capital-driven economy, what steps can small and growing companies take to recruit and retain "knowledge workers"?

- What new challenges with regard to protecting a company's trade secrets, trademarks, and copyrights are created by new computer and telecommunications technologies?

- What new forms of joint venture agreements, strategic partnering agreements, joint technology development agreements, and other legal contracts will be necessary as intercompany teams, alliances, and partnerships are formed?

- What new agreements, policies, warranties, and distribution channels will be necessary as electronic communications become the principal way in which goods and services are bought and sold?

- What antitrust issues are raised by this trend toward interenterprise alliances, even among competitors? Could shared knowledge via GroupWare be tomorrow's antitrust nightmare?

- If your business is going to take advantage of these trends and attempt to earn revenues as an Internet services provider (ISP), an on-line services company, a database or content developer, a software developer, etc., then what business issues must you understand?

- How will cultural and language barriers be broken as more companies do business in the global village?

Cyberspace and Small Business

It seems as if every time you pick up a business magazine, there is at least one article about the impact the Internet and on-line services have had on the way business is conducted. The Internet has changed the way we communicate, has altered our notions of time and space, and has created countless opportunities to start new businesses or expand the horizons of existing businesses. Along the way, lawyers and the courts have tried to keep pace with the technologies by allowing the law to evolve to encompass new types of transactions, new challenges, and new forms of intellectual properties.

How and why are small-business owners using the World Wide Web? There are countless business uses, which by now include gathering information, collaborating with strategic partners, providing customers with support and information, researching competitors, providing support and data to key vendors, advertising and marketing via a "home page," publishing information, selling products and services, and buying products and services. Selling and buying products and services—typically referred to as "electronic commerce"—will increase dramatically as computer security and encryption software capabilities improve over the next five to ten years. Some adventurous companies have even offered their securities over the Internet.

Key Issues Involving the Internet

Given the pace of technological change, it is likely that some of the legal and strategic issues discussed below will be obsolete by the time this book hits your shelves. This is the risk of including topics this current in a book of this nature. For the moment, the key issues surrounding the Internet and its place in the business world include the following.

CENSORSHIP AND THE FIRST AMENDMENT In recent years, regulators, courts, and interest groups have struggled to determine how (and if) the content of the Internet should be regulated. On February 8, 1996, President Bill Clinton signed into law the Communications Decency Act (CDA), a statute designed to deter on-line pornography. However, a specially convened federal panel in Philadelphia declared the CDA unconstitutional and prohibited the Department of Justice from enforcing it. This decision, which for the moment extends the reach of the First Amendment over cyberspace, represents a battle that is likely to continue for many years. It will be difficult to achieve a balance between the regulations applicable to print or broadcast media and those that will apply to on-line content in cyberspace, especially as access to cyberspace becomes easier and more widespread. The issue was nicely summarized in the opinion of the Philadelphia court, written by Justice Stewart Dalzell: "As the most participatory form of mass speech yet developed, the Internet deserves the highest protection from governmental intrusion." As of June 1997, the case had been appealed to the U.S. Supreme Court (*Reno vs. American Civil Liberties Union No. 96-511*) which was argued March 19, 1997, but a decision had not yet been rendered.

DOMAIN NAME REGISTRATION AND TRADEMARK RIGHTS As more and more companies establish a "site" or "home page" on the World Wide Web, a company's address—or "domain name"—becomes critical. Conflicts over trademark rights and using someone else's corporate name in your domain name will continue into the future. To register a name, there is a company called InterNIC Registration Services (703-742-4777), operated by Network Solutions, Inc. (NSI), located in Herndon, Virginia, which will conduct "conflict checks" on a proposed domain name. New rules adopted by InterNIC in late 1995 help avoid disputes by requiring applicants to make an affirmative representation that they are aware of no infringements that might be in conflict with the proposed domain name. NSI has also established a formal arbitration process for resolving disputes over domain names. In addition, a trademark search should be conducted to avoid being on the wrong end of a trademark infringement lawsuit. In spring of 1997, however, the National Science Foundation announced that it will not renew the exclusive contract of NSI to register Internet domains when the agreement expires in 1998. Legal and operational issues surrounding the future of this registry were not yet resolved as of the date of publication of this book.

CREATION OF YOUR WEB SITE Various trademark and copyright issues apply to web site designs. Many small companies have attempted to incorporate attractive audio or video content into their web site, or even the logos of major corporations, to imply some type of sponsorship or affiliation, which may belong to someone else under trademark or copyright registration. In other cases, employees, freelancers, and site design firms have been hired without adequate work-for-hire or copyright assignment contracts (see Chapter 2) that would firmly place the right of ownership in the hands of the employer. Some observers have even suggested that the emerging law of trade dress protection (brought to the spotlight in 1993 in the Supreme Court case *Taco Cabana International, Inc. v. Two Pesos;* see Chapter 8) may soon apply to the design and protection of web sites and home pages.

DOWNLOADING CONTENT The Internet has provided a quick and efficient way to obtain information through electronic downloading. Again, copyright laws must be respected, especially with regard to subsequent use or republication of the downloaded data. *Copyright protection can be difficult when you cannot trace whoever originally reproduced and distributed the material.* When certain types of software are downloaded on an international basis, other laws may also apply, which may not be as readily apparent, such as United States export controls.

BULLETIN BOARD SERVICES, CHAT ROOMS, AND DEFAMATION OR INFRINGEMENT As an entrepreneur, you may have explored the use of electronic bulletin boards and chat rooms for user groups, clubs, and others with common interests. Naturally, such a forum, if not monitored, may be vulnerable to claims of defamation as well as copyright and trademark infringement, especially where the users of a bulletin board service are uploading or downloading software, games, or other information that may be proprietary or protected by trademark or copyright laws. For example, some recent cases have found the site owner liable for copyright infringement or even defamation, if basic guidelines for content and basic rules of conduct are not established.

INTERACTIVE CONTESTS AND PROMOTIONS   A wide variety of federal and state consumer protection laws must be dealt with before a contest or sweepstakes is offered via the Internet. Some companies have recently come under attack by the Federal Trade Commission and the U.S. Department of Justice for unfair trade practices, fraud, and misrepresentation because their lotteries, promotions, and contests in Cyberspace did not meet disclosure laws and other requirements at the federal and state level.

PRIVACY   One interesting development on the electronic frontier is the use and publication of one's e-mail address. As mail consumers, we can choose, through the United States Postal Service and the Direct Marketing Association, to have our names removed from mailing lists. As telephone consumers, we can have an unlisted telephone number. But if our e-mail address is shared or published without our knowledge, do we have a cause of action for invasion of privacy? The courts have struggled with this issue, but no clear, definitive answer has been determined. Regardless of how the courts resolve the issue, entrepreneurs are already hard at work developing "privacy enhancement" software that allows computer users to block certain types of unwanted advertisements from appearing on their computer monitors. Legislation has even been proposed on Capitol Hill that would force companies to disclose what kind of information they collect on visitors to their web sites and would give users a chance to remove themselves from mailing lists.

ELECTRONIC COMMERCE AND CONTRACT LAW   If a business wants to sell its products and services over the Internet, all of the rules of offer and acceptance set forth in the overview of contract law in Chapter 3 apply. The terms and conditions of a sale, return policies, warranties, limitations, etc., must be clearly published and understood by the buyer. Federal and state consumer protection and antifraud laws also apply to these electronic commercial transactions. If you will be allowing others to sell products or services from your site, then all of the issues pertaining to the appointment of sales representatives and distributors, as explained in Chapter 9, also apply.

RIGHTS OF PUBLICITY The rights of public figures—such as athletes, radio and television personalities, movie actors, etc.—have also presented certain legal issues related to the Internet, in the context of home page content, of advertising, or of subjects of electronic bulletin board chatter. For example, discussion of a public figure to promote a particular on-line service or Internet access provider may raise questions as to whether the public figure must grant permission or deserves some type of compensation much as a celebrity would be paid for an endorsement. Although there is an exception to this "right of publicity" for incidental use or for "newsworthy events or matters of public interest," in 1994 the radio personality Howard Stern challenged Delphi (an Internet services provider) over advertisements that used his picture. Delphi's advertisements were designed to promote a debate on its bulletin board on the merits of Stern's candidacy for governor of New York, and the court concluded that Stern's picture was used in the context of public debate (and thus that the use was protected), but the court left open protection of the "name and likeness" of celebrities on the Internet, much as their name and likeness are protected in the more traditional media: print and television.

TELEPHONE SERVICES Many companies are developing technologies that would allow computer users to make long-distance telephone calls. Although as of this writing no regulations had been issued by the Federal Communications Commission, a group of major telecommunications companies had argued that companies providing access to the Internet to make long-distance calls should be subject to the same regulations as traditional carriers.

JURISDICTIONAL PROBLEMS Many traditional business laws are based on geography. Disputes over which law should govern a transaction on the Internet can be more difficult, since the Internet does not really "exist" in any one fixed place—it is everywhere. As a result, when disputes arise regarding privacy, copyright and trademark infringement, or breach of contract, there are problems determining which state or even which nation should govern the transaction or dispute.

There have also been a wide variety of recent court decisions relating to cryptography, protection of source code as First Amendment speech, patent claims involving protection of microprocessor and semiconductor chips, the ability of software developers to rely on patent law for protection, the ability of software companies to enforce claims of trade secret misappropriation against former employees who developed such software, and the ability to obtain injunctions against distributors of "junk e-mail." These issues affect intellectual property law, computer law, and the emerging body of traffic laws for the information superhighway. If you plan on moving ahead with some of these exciting new ways to do business, it is definitely worthwhile to explore the legal issues thoroughly. (See Box 14-1.)

Computer Security

An issue that is indirectly related to the Internet, and is part of the downside of developments in the information age, is computer security. Many owners of small and emerging businesses simply cannot afford expensive security software, or expensive consulting firms that design intricate systems to protect against on-line theft and break-ins. But such protection is necessary, not only for security but also to prevent damage by power outages, floods, and fires. Steps that can be taken include the following:

- *Limit access to the outside world.* Some firms limit the number of computers within the office that have access to the Internet, to prevent outsiders from getting access to key databases or sensitive information. This step is sometimes referred to as "air gapping"; it creates a "space" between the outside world and your internal network and internal operating systems.

B O X   1 4 - 1

Additional Resources on Cyberspace Law

- *The Computer Industry Litigation Reporter*, published by Andrews Publications (800-345-1101).

- Cyberspace Law Institute, Washington, D.C.; attention: David Johnson (http://www.cli.org). This is a virtual think tank dedicated to exploring legal issues on the Internet.

- Virtual Magistrate, Washington, D.C.; attention: David Johnson (http://vmag.law.vill.edu:8080). This is a new project that provides an inexpensive Internet-based arbitration process for Internet-specific issues.

- Center for Democracy and Technology, Washington, D.C.; attention: Jerry Berman, Executive Director (202-637-9800). A privacy advocacy group.

- Electronic Privacy Information Center, Washington, D.C.; attention: Marc Rotenberg, Executive Director (202-544-9240).

- Creative Incentive Coalition, Washington, D.C. (202-638-2121). A public action group seeking to protect copyright law and enforcement on the Internet.

- *Develop written computer policies for your employees and contractors.* Many small and growing companies do not have adequate policies in writing to govern use of computers by their employees, their contractors, or others who have access to their system. Policies should be established regarding ownership of intellectual property, downloading data to diskettes, use of computer data or transport of diskettes, backup, electronic mail monitoring (giving rise to privacy issues), and when and how employees may be permitted to log into the system from home or another remote site.

- *Understand Your Rights and Obligations under the ECPA.* The Electronic Communications Privacy Act (ECPA) is a federal law (passed in 1986) that prevents unauthorized access to electronic communications, including e-mail via the Internet. Therefore, it is illegal under the ECPA to intercept e-mail during transmission or to wrongfully access e-mail while it is stored in a computer system. However, the ECPA does not generally protect the privacy of messages sent on internal company electronic mail systems; it treats these types of communications as ordinary interoffice memorandums that may be read by authorized employees or supervisors.

Doing Business in the Global Village

Many small and growing companies that have ventured abroad as pioneers of doing business in the global village have discovered receptive and lucrative new markets. Many countries, even developing nations, view franchising, licensing, distribution, and other methods of international expansion not only as a way to import products and services but also as a readily acceptable source of technological development and system support that introduces know-how to a fledgling business community in a cost-effective manner.

Doing business abroad is critical to the ongoing health of the U.S. economy. Every $1 billion in U.S. exports generates 25,000 jobs at home and exporting has been growing at a rate of almost 10% per annum over the past three years, according to the U.S. Department of Commerce. In a recent study of 434 manufacturing and service companies with sales ranging from $1 million to $50 million, Coopers & Lybrand found that those companies that are exporting goods and services expect to grow 25% faster than those with no plans to sell abroad.

Potential Barriers to International Expansion

When embarking on an international expansion program, small companies, especially those considering franchising, licensing, joint ventures, or technology transfer, should consider these problematic factors:

Language barriers. Although it may seem simple enough, at the outset, to translate your core marketing and operational materials into the local language, marketing the system and the product may present unforeseen difficulties if the concept itself does not "translate" well. A classic example is the Chevy Nova, which translates in Spanish-speaking countries to "doesn't move" *(no va)*—not an ideal name for a vehicle.

Marketing barriers. These types of barriers most frequently go to the deepest cultural levels. For example, although many overseas markets have developed a taste for "fast food" such as burgers and hot dogs, cultural differences may make the aspect of speed less important in some countries. Many European cultures demand the time to relax on the premises after eating a meal, rather than leaving immediately after eating, or taking a meal to go. In France, cultural differences even forced McDonald's to sell beer and wine. These cultural norms can, in turn, be affected by other factors, such as the high cost and limited availability of retail space in Singapore and Japan. To take another example, land for a large regional mall is often readily available in North America but is rare in the Middle East.

Legal barriers. A country's laws may not be conducive to the establishment of certain types of distributorship arrangements. Any one of a body of laws—governing taxes, customs, imports, and liability of corporate organizations and agencies—may prove to be a significant stumbling block. For example, laws covering technology transfer and foreign investment may "force" a given business relationship to be essentially a joint venture, when it was originally intended as a master franchise or license.

Access to raw materials and human resources. Not all countries offer the level of access to critical raw materials and skilled labor that may be needed to operate your core business. If your company requires high-trained computer technicians, you may need to locate these resources elsewhere.

Governmental barriers. A foreign government may or may not be receptive to foreign investment in general or to certain types of distribution relationships. A given country's past history of expropriation, government restrictions, high tariffs, and limitations on currency repatriation may all prove to be decisive factors in determining whether the cost of market penetration is worth the potential benefits. It may be necessary to review which tax treaties are in place between your country and the targeted nation, or even to seek governmental intervention. (For example, in the United States, the U.S. Trade Representative or the Department of Commerce's International Trade Administration might intervene.) It is also a good idea to have your corporate legal counsel, provided that they are experienced in international matters, review the laws of the targeted nation and establish a liaison with local counsel abroad.

"Commandments" for International Expansion

These potential stumbling blocks do not always mean that overseas expansion is ill-advised. On the contrary, often a thorough review of the relevant market will indicate that such expansion holds great potential. Still, a broad range of legal and strategic issues must be examined before beginning a program of international expansion. The basic commandments of successful international expansion include the following.

STRONG DOMESTIC FOUNDATION   It is important to make sure that adequate capital, resources, personnel, support systems, and training programs are in place to assist your business abroad. For example, if your business will require technical expertise, multilingual skills, etc., then you should conduct adequate research to ensure that these resources are available.

STRATEGIC PARTNERS   Experienced international executives around the world will tell you that the ultimate success or failure of the program depends on one single element: finding the right partner. Regardless of the specific legal structure selected for international expansion into a particular market, the master developer in the local market should always be viewed, philosophically and strategically, as your "partner." And, just as there should always be a dating period before a marriage or a due diligence period before an acquisition, that is also the case in selecting an international partner.

There is no substitute for face-to-face negotiations between parties. The most promising candidates for becoming your international partner will often be those with proven financial resources who have already established a successful business in the host country. What systems do you have in place for recruiting and selecting the right candidate? What procedures will you use for reviewing candidates' qualifications? What fallback plan do you have in place if you wind up selecting the wrong person or company? These are critical issues; and before you go overseas, strategies and procedures should be in place to ensure that you make the right selection. Beyond a certain point, however, only careful negotiating and contract preparation will provide any degree of protection for a business risking entry into a new market.

REALISTIC VALUATION   Many growing businesses entering overseas markets for the first time have grandiose ideas about the initial price an overseas partner will pay for the right to distribute your goods and services, license your technology, or serve as a subfranchisor. *Reality* and *patience* are the two key words here. If you overprice, you will scare away qualified candidates or leave your partner with insufficient capital to develop the market. If you underprice, you will lack the resources and incentive to provide high-quality training and ongoing support. The fee structure should fairly and realistically reflect the division of responsibility between you and your partner. Other factors influencing the structure will be currency exchange, taxes, pricing strategies, market trends, the availability of resources and personnel to provide on-site support, and which party will bear responsibility for translation of the manuals and marketing materials—as well as adaptation of the system, products, and services to meet local demand and cultural differences.

Growing businesses must be patient with regard to expectations for return on investment and profits from overseas expansion. In addition to normal economic cycles and breakeven analysis, certain countries insist on legal structures that are essentially "forced joint ventures," thereby restricting the ability of a growing business to quickly pull out capital from the targeted country. In forming the actual agreement, the company should carefully consider the structure of the relationship, the term of the agreement, and the scope and length of nondisclosure and noncompete clauses. These provisions and their enforceability will take on increased importance when they are complicated by distance and by differences in legal systems. Growing businesses should also give careful thought to structuring the financial provisions of the agreement. It is tempting to try to mitigate potential downstream losses by seeking a higher initial fee, but often a more balanced approach to fees and ongoing royalties should be considered.

TRADEMARK PROTECTION   As a general matter, trademark laws and rights are based on actual *use* (or bona fide intent to use) in a given country. There are international copyright laws, but your properly registered domestic trademark does not automatically confer any trademark rights in other countries. Be sure to take steps to ensure the availability and registration of your trademarks in all targeted markets. Also, be sure that your trademark *translates* effectively in the native language of the targeted country. Many growing businesses have had to modify their names, designs, or slogans because of problems involving translation or pirating in new targeted markets. For example, many American franchisors of automotive services, particularly oil-change services and tune-ups, had to retool trademarks and brand identities that overemphasized "speed" and "efficiency." Those qualities were attractive to the busy American consumer. It turned out, however, that in many overseas cultures, automobile owners preferred quality over speed, even if it meant the inconvenience of leaving their car in the shop for a few extra days. To them, speed meant a compromise in the care of their most treasured possession—their car—and that was unacceptable to most consumers.

ADAPTATION OF PRODUCTS AND SERVICES   The format of your proprietary products or services that have been successful in America or even Canada may or may not be successful in another country. Be sensitive to different tastes, cultures, norms, traditions, trends, and habits within a country before making final decisions on prices, sizes, or other characteristics of your products or services. Conversely, though, be careful not to change your product or service too drastically at the cost of sacrificing quality, integrity, uniformity, or consistency. Many comical stories—representing expensive lessons—can be told about North American growing businesses that learned the hard way that what works well for you at home may be very different abroad. For example, many American restaurant businesses have had to modify their serving sizes to accommodate the different eating habits of other cultures. It seems that not every

B O X   1 4 - 2

Know Your Targeted Market

Take the time to fully understand the intricacies of the various targeted markets. You can avoid costly disputes by knowing where your target market is. Different market and research studies can be conducted to measure market demand and competition for your company's products and services. Be sure to gather data on:

- Economic trends
- Political stability
- Currency exchange rates
- Foreign investment and approval procedures
- Restrictions on termination and nonrenewal (where applicable)
- Regulatory requirements
- Access to resources and raw materials
- Availability of transportation and communication channels
- Labor and employment laws
- Technology transfer regulations
- Language and cultural differences
- Access to affordable capital and suitable sites for the development of units
- Governmental assistance programs
- Customs, laws, and import restrictions
- Tax laws and applicable treaties
- Repatriation and immigration laws
- Trademark registration requirements, availability, and protection policies
- Costs and methods of resolving disputes
- Agency laws and availability of appropriate media for marketing efforts

A number of overseas growing businesses have made the mistake of awarding a single master license to a company for the development of a large country or region, only to discover that they lack the resources and the expertise to adequately develop this large territory. To avoid the problems of the "single" master licensee in large and diverse markets, we advise our international business clients to pursue a regional approach, more closely tied to the actual capability of the regional licensee and to the anticipated market demand for the products and services offered within the targeted region.

culture places value on the SuperMax Big Gulp or the Triple-X Super Sundae—some overseas markets prefer a more reasonable portion at a competitive price and will not patronize an establishment where there are likely to be leftovers, which are perceived as wasteful.

RATIONALE   Growing businesses often have widely varying reasons for selecting a targeted country or market. Sometimes they are "pulled" into a market by an interested prospect who is familiar with their concept, but this can be dangerous, especially if the company relies only on the assurances of the interested candidate that there is an actual demand for products and services.

Sources of Information

According to the International Trade Administration (ITA), exports by the United States grew 40% from 1994 to 1995, and another 30% increase was projected from 1995 to 1996. Exports to big emerging markets (BEMs)* grew 6% between 1990 and 1995. Because of increased exports, the World Bank estimates that BEMs will be six of the world's 10 largest markets by the year 2020. The ITA has created a one-stop-shop clearinghouse called the U.S. Export Assistance Center (EAC) for export information including information on acquiring loans from the Small Business Administration and the U.S. Export Import

---

*BEMs consist of the Association of Southern Asian Nations, Argentina, Brazil, the Chinese Economic Area, India, Mexico, Poland, Turkey, South Africa, and South Korea.

Bank and links to other governmental departments and agencies, including the Environmental Protection Agency and the Overseas Private Investment Corporation. Those contacting the EAC can learn:

- How to find out which international markets would welcome which products or services
- How to find agents or distributors in foreign markets
- How to get licenses and which licenses are needed for exporting
- How to get a loan

When you're ready to get started, you can call the trade information hot line at 800-872-8723 or visit one of the 20 EACs or one of the ITA's 80 domestic offices. Locations for all centers are available on the hot line, or you can visit the Trade Information Center's web site, which has almost endless links to other sites, including trade publications and financial and economic information. For additional information about resources, see Box 14-3.

The Virtual Corporation

If you were a fly on the wall of almost any corporate boardroom in the United States (or abroad) today, you would hear discussions about restructuring, rightsizing, outsourcing, shared service centers, strategic alliances, spin-outs and spin-offs, intrapreneurship, electronic commerce, virtual offices, capital formation alternatives, the global village, and other popular topics. Such phrases all point to the same basic trends:

- The world is getting smaller, not bigger.
- Companies are getting smaller, not bigger.
- Small companies are getting *smarter*, not bigger.

It is as if the entire business community had gone to a diet center and determined that "thin is in." It seems as though the

BOX 14-3

Doing Business Abroad Resource Guide

Places to Call

Trade Information Center
800-USA-TRADE
202-482-0543
TDD: 800-833-8723
Internet:
http://www.ita.doc.gov/tic

Small Business Administration
800-697-4636
202-401-9600
TDD: 202-205-7333
Internet: http://www.sbaonline.sba.gov

Bankers Association for Foreign Trade
202-452-0942

National Trade Data Bank on the Internet
800-STAT-USA
202-482-1986 to subscribe
Internet: http://www.stat-usa.gov
e-mail: stat-usa@doc.gov

U.S. Departments of Commerce and Agriculture
Journal of Commerce
800-221-3777, extension 7170

Export Assistance Center Network
800-USE-TRADE
Call for local center

Export-Import Bank of the U.S.
Export Finance Hotline
800-565-3946
Internet: http://www.exim.gov

The Bureau of Export Administration
202-482-4811
Internet:
http://www.bxa.doc.gov

International Business Exchange Network
Contact local chamber of commerce

Guidebooks, Publications, and Networks

The EAC also distributes, for a charge, guidebooks that include the following:

- *A Basic Guide to Exporting*
- *How to Build a Successful Export Business*
- *Breaking into the Trade Game: A Small Business Guide to Exporting*
- *North American Free Trade Agreement: A Guide to Customs Procedures*

(Box continued on next page)

High-Tech Exporting Assistance

Software

*   *The Export Expert* ($169.95), Columbia Cascade, Inc. 703-620-9403
*   *Quick Assistance for Export Documentation* ($895), Export-Import Trade Software, Inc. 203-396-0022
*   *Export Software:* Version II.2 ($529), Unz & Company, 800-631-3098
*   *ExportAmerica, The Complete Guide to Export for American Business* ($195), M. Thorne & Company, 360-853-7099
*   *FedEx Document Prep* (free), Federal Express Corp., download from *http://www.fedex.com/get_fedex_docprep.html* or call 800-781-3076
*   *Worldwide Express Guide* (free), DHL Worldwide Express, 800-CALL-DHL

CD-ROMs

*   *National Trade Data Base: The Export Connection* ($59 for one monthly issue; $575 for an annual subscription), U.S. Department of Commerce, 800-782-8872
*   *Eastern Europe Business Database* ($395), American Directory Corp., Order number PB93-506210INC, call National Technical Information, 703-487-4650
*   *Latin America 25,000; Asia Pacific 25,000; Western Europe 25,000; Manufacturing 25,000; Service 25,000; Worldwide 25,000* ($295 each), D-B Worldbase Services, Dun & Bradstreet Information Services, 800-624-5669
*   *PIERS (Port Import Export Reporting Service) Export Bulletin* ($175 per month), *Journal of Commerce,* 212-837-7051

Web Sites

*   TradePort, *http://www.tradeport.org/*
*   STAT-USA/Internet, *http://www.stat-usa.gov*
*   International Business Resources on the WWW, *http://ciber.bus.msu.edu/busres.htm*
*   ExporTutor, *http://web.miep.org/tutor/index.html*
*   Export Process Assistant, *http://venture.cob.ohio-state.edu:1111/tutorial/openingscr.html*

(Box continued on next page)

- NAFTAnet, *http://www.nafta.net/*
- Trade Compass, *http://www.tradecompass.com/*
- Trade Resources, *http://www.usitc.gov/tr/tr.htm*
- American Computer Resources, Inc., *http://www.the-acr.com/*
- IBEX, *http://www.ibex-gba.com/*
- I-Trade, *http://www.i-trade.com/*

ability to do more with less is critical for survival in today's competitive marketplace. Workforces are shrinking, inventories are getting smaller and forming faster, services and key functions are being outsourced, overheads are being slashed, and so on—and along the way new opportunities are being created for small and growing companies that are able to remain nimble and take advantage of these trends.

Value and Importance of Building Brand Equity

As we approach the new millennium, companies of all sizes are recognizing the cost and importance of establishing brand awareness. Campaigns and strategies to build brand recognition, brand loyalty, and brand equity have been launched by thousands of companies, on the realization that a well-established brand can be the single most valuable asset on the balance sheet. This new focus on *brand* for the year 2000 and beyond has set the stage for a variety of co-branding and brand-extension licensing transactions. Companies with strong quality-oriented brands (as well as professional sports teams, athletes, and celebrities) have sought to create new sources of revenues and to leverage their largest intangible asset—their reputation—to strengthen their income statements. To build brand awareness, companies are spending more on media advertising and promotional campaigns and less on store displays and coupons. In addition, the growth of private-label goods has plateaued. In fact, it is estimated that owners of branded products and services spent $174.1 billion in 1996 to build brand awareness, an increase of nearly 10% over 1995. See "The Brand's The Thing," by Betsy Morris—*Fortune* magazine, March 4, 1996—which stressed the importance of brands in global business.

It is estimated that in the United States alone, retail sales of *licensed* branded products surpassed $20 billion in 1992 and will reach $60 billion by the year 2000. Products born of brand-extension licensing have become staples for consumers who seek quality and value and who look for successful brand-licensed items such as Sunkist® orange soda, Hershey's® chocolate milk, and Wilson® tennis apparel. This marriage between a product and a well-recognized brand name allows trademark owners to enter into new industries without the capital investment required to actually manufacture and distribute the licensed product. Subject to strict quality control guidelines, companies with registered trademarks can penetrate new markets, build new profit centers, increase brand awareness and recognition, facilitate international expansion, and even modernize a brand's image with the appropriate brand-extension licensing strategic partners. Of course, there is a limit to what the consumer will accept. Naturally, it would do little to enhance the image or brand recognition of Ben & Jerry's® to license its name to an automobile parts manufacturer in order to produce a new line of tires. Nor would its "implied endorsement" be likely to increase sales of the tires. Yet the recent move by Starbucks to license its name for a limited new line of prepackaged ice cream seems to have been a big hit with quality-conscious consumers who knew the Starbucks name as a symbol of quality—this was evidently a natural jump to a related product.

These trends have created a whole new specialty area of law within the general intellectual-property practice, a specialty that focuses on the agreements necessary to establish and maintain brand-extension and co-branding relationships. When working on these transactions, be sure that your legal counsel has extensive experience in these areas. The legal documents necessary to effectuate these relationships, such as license and joint venture agreements, are discussed in greater detail in Chapter 9.

15

Marketing and Sales Plans

In previous chapters, we have looked at the strategic aspects of starting and growing a business. It goes without saying that building an appropriate foundation for growth is critical to a company's long-term success. But even if a company prepares an impeccable business plan, establishes an optimal capital structure, raises the funds necessary to achieve its growth plans, and recruits the management team necessary to implement these plans, a failure to grasp the crucial aspects of marketing issues will present a serious impediment to its growth and success. As the old saying goes, "You can build the best product in the world, but it will do you no good if nobody knows about it." Therefore, this chapter will be devoted to the strategic aspects of marketing practices.

Before examining the key components of marketing plans and strategies, it is crucial to understand the critical factors in developing a marketing program for your growing company.

What Is Marketing?

Marketing is the ongoing process of: (1) determining the level of consumer demand for a company's products and services; (2) matching the company's strengths and weaknesses with the established demand; (3) delivering the products and services more effectively and more efficiently than competitors; and (4) monitoring changes in consumer demand, industry trends, political and social environment, legal issues, technology, and competition in order to ensure that the company's products and services remain competitive and consistent with consumer demand.

Academics and consultants often identify the well-known "marketing mix" as the foundation of a marketing program. This mix comprises *product, price, place,* and *promotion.* All marketing plans and decisions stem from one or more of these components of the marketing mix. Some of the typical issues raised by each element of the marketing mix are as follows:

- *Product*
  1. What products and services will the company offer to the consumer?
  2. What are the various features, options, and styles that each product or service will include as being unique, of better quality, or proprietary?
  3. How will these products and services be packaged and offered to the consuming public?
- *Place*
  1. How will the company's products and services be distributed to the marketplace?
  2. What are the various advantages and disadvantages of the available distribution channels?
  3. In what geographic markets should the company's products and services be offered? (Demographics and population analysis, primary versus secondary markets, local competitor analysis, local and region consumer habits.)
- *Price*
  1. What will consumer and distributors pay for the company's

products and services at various wholesale and retail levels? How are prices determined? How does such a price relate to the company's overall marketing strategy?

2. What pricing policies will be developed with respect to discounts, allowances, and introductory or special pricing formulas? If the company does engage in introductory or promotional pricing, have such policies been reviewed by legal counsel in connection with: (a) the Robinson-Patman Act; (b) deceptive pricing regulations established by the Federal Trade Commission; (c) prohibited predatory pricing practices?

3. On what credit terms and conditions will the company's products and services be sold?

- *Promotion*

   1. What strategies will be implemented to ensure that the consuming public is *aware* of the company's products and services?

   2. What plans, programs, and strategies will be adopted for sales, advertising, and public relations?

   3. How will human and financial resources be allocated to these various advertising and promotional programs?

The importance of the last element above—*promotion*—is often overlooked by small and growing companies. Too much emphasis is usually placed on raising capital, attracting human resources, and studying the markets; and not enough time is spent on making sure that consumers will be aware of your products and services. Even the best-capitalized company producing high-quality products and services will ultimately experience business distress and failure if advertising and promotion are neglected. The old idea that "if you build a better mousetrap, the world will beat a path to your door" is simply no longer true in today's competitive marketplace unless adequate resources are devoted to informing the world that your company exists. Thus, an effective marketing program for an emerging growth company must determine not only the *characteristics* of the targeted market, but also *how* to reach this market once it is identified.

B O X   1 5 - 1

Developing Marketing Strategies: Tips and Traps

- *Never lose sight of the pitfalls of the "80/20 rule."* That is, 80% of your marketing efforts are often spent on the customers or clients yielding 20% of the annual revenues. Imagine what would happen if you did some "housecleaning" of the customers or clients that were taking up all of your time and not producing results while at the same time refocusing your efforts on the more productive and less time-consuming clients and customers with long-term growth potential.

- *Everyone is talking about "getting close to the customer."* What does it really mean? Well, it doesn't mean being so close that you could guess what they had for lunch from the smell of their breath! In today's marketplace, it means treating customers and clients (and in certain cases, even vendors) as if they truly are your strategic partners and you truly care about them and their employees. *The client and customer of the next millennium can easily detect indifference and insincerity, and they simply won't tolerate it. Long-term client and customer loyalty is a long-term challenge that you must earn every day and with every transaction.* It is the responsibility of the senior management of the company to create a culture of customer and client service. Senior management must be genuine and sincere in establishing this culture and must provide leadership through example. If a receptionist hears a CEO mistreating a customer or client, then it will be virtually impossible to get him or her to buy into the strategy.

- *Try to do more with less.* Often the most effective marketing strategy or campaign is not necessarily the most expensive or the most complex. Emerging growth companies as well as industrial giants such as Procter & Gamble are getting better results by focusing on simplification. How is it done? Try paring down unnecessary product and service lines, outsourcing post-sale functions such as training and support, cutting back on trade promotions, easing up on coupons, trimming new product launches, spinning off marginal brands, and using old-fashioned face-to-face meetings for maintaining relationships with clients and customers. Companies today are sticking with the strategies and product lines that have worked over time and are learning not to tinker with what's not broken (e.g., the launch of the "New" Coke, A-1 Steak Sauce's failed entry into poultry, or IBM's attempt to get into the copier market, a division it eventually sold to Kodak). Even the "big three" American auto manufacturers are reducing and streamlining the number of models offered and expanding brand awareness in the "old standbys" and even relaunching old brands (instead of new ones) such as the Chevy Malibu and the Plymouth Duster.

- *Don't be left behind on the information superhighway.* More and more firms are setting up web sites and learning how to use the Internet as a marketing tool. Potential clients and customers expect to be able to learn about your basic capabilities via a home page and not necessarily by paging through a thick and environmentally unfriendly 30-page brochure. For more information on this subject, see Chapter 14.

- *Don't be afraid of global markets.* Fewer and fewer companies are limiting their marketing and sales efforts to only domestic markets. Take the time to learn the challenges of doing business overseas. For more on this topic, see Chapter 14.

- *Keep your head out of the sand and your hands out of your pockets.* Successful growing companies constantly have their eyes and ears open to emerging trends in their markets, technological developments, and steps taken by their competitors. They are "hands-on" managers who don't believe in ivory towers and closely monitor the attitudes of their employees and the opinions of their "stakeholders," such as vendors, customers, staff, landlords, lenders, directors, and stockholders. Truly great entrepreneurs are *focused* 24 hours a day, seven days a week, on how to get new customers and clients as well *as* how to keep existing clients happy.

- *Make new friends but keep the old. One is silver and the other is gold.* This children's saying also applies to marketing and to the management of relationships with customers and clients. If a growth company is focused only on the silver, it will eventually fail. Your ability to attract new customers will be limited and eventually impossible if you can't hold on to, and "super-please," your existing gold customers and clients. Moreover, one of the keys to marketing and growth is getting more business from existing clients and customers. That will never happen if you are focused only on silver mining.

- *Don't forget where your bread is buttered.* This old adage is also applicable to marketing and customer service. Too often growing companies focus on the customers only, not on where the customers come from—and I don't mean their parents. The sources of client and customer referrals are relationships that must be coveted and maintained just as effectively as direct client and customer relationships. You must take the time to implement the three "R's"—that is, to: *reward* (not just tangibly but also intangibly) these referral sources, *reciprocate* wherever possible, and *refine* the scope of these relationships as they evolve. I've always felt that the *quality* of these relationships is more important than their *quantity*—it's not a business card collection contest. Rather, the key is building, enhancing, and maintaining relationships with high-quality and synergistic referral sources.

- *Don't be afraid to think outside the box.* The traditional solutions to sales and marketing problems yield traditional results. Putting your company on a rapid growth track means being willing to break through old paradigms, engage in street fighting with your competition, and approach marketing and promotion with fresh ideas and approaches. For example, instead of focusing on lowering prices to meet the competition, retool your strategy around adding value and enhancing the customer's experience. Nordstrom's strategy of focusing on the quality of the customer's experience and not on the price is very effective. The old adage "Quality is remembered long after price is forgotten" is true in many types of industries and can be a much more profitable strategy in the long run.

- *Marketing is as much about perception as it is about reality.* This is not to suggest that misleading or deceiving a targeted or existing customer is a good idea. In fact, it's a prescription for disaster. However, in many categories of products and services, the customer assumes either that the product or service is homogeneous *or* that there is an assured baseline level of quality. In these situations, the focus of the marketing effort must be on the intangible and often elusive "value-added." Although the actual value to be added to the underlying product or service must be genuine, it is often the image and the customer's perception of the image that ultimately win. Therefore, building brand image and loyalty as well as establishing market leadership is critical in today's marketplace. In fact, market leadership and consistency in the customer's experience can often triumph over quality. For example, the market leadership and worldwide consistency of McDonald's keeps sales growing, even if its hamburgers are not the best on the planet.

- *Know what business you are really in.* Ask most small-business owners what business they are in, and they'll recite the name of the business.

Joe, the owner of Joe's Italian Villa, says he sells Italian food. Mr. Berger, partner in the accounting firm Berger and Finch, says he sells accounting services to small businesses. The truth is that Joe sells food and entertainment in the medium-priced family dining category. He offers meal-replacement and time-management solutions to today's busy family. But if Joe doesn't know the business he is really in, then he'll have trouble getting and keeping loyal customers. The category (and hence the market) in which Joe operates is also a moving target. Product and service categories continue to divide and evolve, and Joe must keep track or he'll lose the race. And so will Mr. Berger, who must reposition his firm as being a solution specialist for the tax and accounting problems that a small business faces. Mr. Berger must understand that the competition for his problem-solving services is not just other small, local accounting firms but all other sources of solutions, including large and regional accounting firms, consulting firms, law firms, the Internet, books, magazines, seminars, and all other places where a small-business owner can find resources and answers to the issues and problems that may arise in the management and growth of the business.

- *Focus and discipline are not just for the military academy.* Most successful companies have stayed focused on a particular product or service category, even if it meant the sacrifice of ancillary sales or the loss of certain customers. For example, when you think about Blockbuster, you think about video rentals. Over the years, Blockbuster has also inched its way into video game rentals and a limited line of candy and merchandise, but the focus has remained on video rental (though some brand-extension—see Chapter 14—was launched with a line of music superstores). The key point is that Blockbuster could have tried to sell other products and services to the "captured customer" who spends 15 or 20 minutes choosing a video in its stores, but it had the discipline to stay focused on its *core* business, which has propelled its growth worldwide.

Key Components of the Marketing Program

Owners and managers of small and growing companies must understand the key components of a well-developed marketing program. These components fall into three distinct stages: first, marketing planning and strategy formulation; second, implementation; and third, monitoring and feedback.

Stage One: Marketing Planning and Strategy Formulation

The first stage is subdivided into (1) marketing research, (2) market analysis and segmentation, and (3) development of a marketing plan.

1. MARKETING RESEARCH Effective marketing planning begins with the development of a database of information regarding history of the company; its products, services, and personnel; trends in its industry; size of its total marketplace; characteristics of its typical customers; strengths and weaknesses of its current competitors; and various barriers to entry for prospective competitors. This information is typically the end result of *market research,* which must be conducted before the development of a formal marketing plan. Market research need not be an expensive and time-consuming process for companies that have minimal resources to devote to collecting data about the marketplace. There are essentially two sources of data in conducting market research: external and internal. Many external sources supply data virtually free of charge: state and local economic development agencies, chambers of commerce, trade associations, public libraries, local colleges and universities, and even federal agencies, such as the Small Business Administration and the U.S. Department of Commerce. Internal sources of information will include surveys and meetings with suppliers, customers, and the staff of the company in order to collect additional information regarding industry trends, consumers' preferences, and the strengths and weaknesses of current marketing efforts.

2. MARKET ANALYSIS AND SEGMENTATION The information collected during the company's market research must then be organized in order to be effective in the planning process. Unorganized data collected in a haphazard manner will be of minimal benefit to the development of marketing plans and strategies. The end result of the marketing research should be a *market analysis,* which should include information on segmentation of the company's targeted markets and trends within its industry, and an assessment of the company's direct and indirect competitors.

Key objectives of market research are *segmentation* and *targeting* of the company's market, which will serve as a starting point for market planning. Market segmentation is the process of dividing the total market into distinct groups of buyers based upon demographic variables (i.e., age, income, gender, or race); geographic location of consumers; or even social and political trends and preferences. Market targeting is the evaluation and selection of one or more of these market segments, toward which marketing efforts and resources will be directed. Once specific markets have been targeted, the company must develop plans and strategies to *position* its products and services so as to attract these desired market segments. Market positioning involves manipulation of the elements of the marketing mix in order to reach the targeted consumer effectively and efficiently.

3. DEVELOPMENT OF THE MARKETING PLAN   A well-written marketing plan becomes a blueprint for the company to follow in positioning its products and services in the marketplace in order to meet its long-term growth objectives. The marketing plan becomes an integral part of the organization's overall strategic plan. Like strategic planning, marketing planning must be an ongoing process that will allow the company to respond to changes in the marketplace, law, or technology so that its marketing strategies do not remain static or run the risk of becoming quickly obsolete. Even more important, marketing planning must be consistent with the company's overall strategies and objectives. Therefore, managers of all departments and at varying levels in the organization must be involved in the marketing planning process and kept informed of marketing strategies as they are developed on an ongoing basis.

For example, an aggressive marketing plan that is likely to triple the company's sales should not be adopted without consulting the production and finance departments. Otherwise, backlogs and uncoordinated corporate growth are likely to cripple the company.

Naturally, the contents of a marketing plan will vary for each organization in terms of topics to be addressed, relevant trends, extent of the market research, and resources that can be committed to the implementation of the plan. Nevertheless, there are certain key components that should be included in the marketing plan of any organization: executive summary; assessment of current state of affairs; discussion of current issues and opportunities; marketing objectives and strategies; execution of the program; monitoring; and alternative marketing strategies and contingency plans. These are discussed in the following paragraphs.

Executive summary. This section should provide an overview of the principal goals and strategies that the marketing department plans to adopt. The summary should be distributed to all members of the management team for review and comment *before* time and resources are devoted to the completion of the plan.

Assessment of the current state of affairs. This section must answer the classic planning question, "Where are we and how did we get here?"—but this time from a marketing perspective. Although the section is primarily historical in nature, it is also analytical because it must do more than simply tell a story; it must also explain why the company's marketing strategies have evolved in this way. This will often require a *marketing audit,* which seeks to identify and assess current marketing programs and strategies. The section should describe the company's current products and services, describe the size and growth of its marketplace, give a profile of its consumers, and assess its competitors. The importance of analyzing competitors should not be overlooked. Many entrepreneurs often make the statement "Our product or service is unique—we have no competition." Such an idea is very dangerous, because it often reveals both a misunderstanding of and a likelihood that market research has been poorly conducted. For example, suppose that a company has developed a new form of recreational activity. To the best of the company's knowledge, no other company is offering this activity to consumers. However, this could mean either or both of two things: (1) the company has not conducted sufficient market research; (2) the company has not recognized that all forms of recreation indirectly compete for whatever portion of the consumer's disposable income will be allocated for leisure activities. Therefore, direct and indirect competitors must be discovered through detailed market research and then described in the marketing plan in terms of size, financial strength, market share, sales and profits, quality of product or service, differentiation from the company's products and services, marketing strategies, and any other characteristics that may be relevant to the development of a comprehensive marketing plan.

Discussion of current issues and opportunities. This section should summarize the main opportunities and threats, strengths and weaknesses, and issues and concerns that affect the company's products and services. The principal questions to be answered in this section are, "What market trends and factors should be exploited? What external and internal barriers must be overcome before marketing strategies can be successfully implemented?" The subsection on *opportunities and threats* should address the key *external* factors in the macroenvironment affecting the company's marketing strategies, such as legal, political, economic, and social trends. The exact impact of these trends will vary, depending on the company's products and services. For example, a forthcoming recession could be a threat to automobile manufacturers because consumers will keep their cars longer, yet it could be an opportunity to a chain of movie theaters because market research has found that consumers tend to spend more on low-cost entertainment during troubled economic periods. The subsection on *strengths and weaknesses* should address the key *internal* factors in the microenvironment affecting the company's marketing strategies, such as resource limitations, research and development, organizational structure and politics, protection of intellectual property, distribution channels, service and warranty policies, pricing strategies, and promotional programs. Once the strengths, weaknesses, opportunities, and threats have been identified, the last subsection, on *issues and concerns*, should be prepared. This should discuss strategies and tactics for exploiting the company's marketing strengths and compensating for its marketing weaknesses.

Marketing objectives and strategies. This section should define the goals and objectives identified by the managers of the

320 • Running and Growing Your Business

marketing department with respect to market share, expenditures on advertising and promotion, sales volume, and profitability. It should then discuss strategies, outlining specific steps and timetables for achieving these goals and objectives. Marketing strategy is essentially the "game plan" that must be adopted with respect to targeted markets; positioning of products and services; budgets for advertising, sales, and public relations; and delegation of responsibility within the organization for specific projects. Since this section also involves dealing with projected sales and profitability, marketing managers must work closely with the finance department to ensure accuracy and consistency. As is true of all forms of planning, the statement of marketing objectives and strategies should be clear and succinct and not leave the reader (or user) hanging with regard to methodology. For example, a marketing objective of increasing sales revenue by 10% could be achieved by increasing price per unit, increasing total sales volume with the price remaining at its current level, or increasing both price and sales volume. Marketing managers must identify which course of action will be taken, on the basis of information ascertained from market research as well as data and input received from other departments within the organization.

Execution of marketing program. This section of the plan should set forth timetables for achieving specific goals and objectives, identify the persons who will be responsible for implementation, and project the anticipated resources that will be required for meeting the timetables.

Monitoring of marketing plans and strategies. This section should discuss the establishment and operation of management systems and controls designed to monitor the marketing plans and strategies implemented by the company. The relative success or failure of these programs should be measurable, so that performance can be properly assessed. Periodic reports should be prepared by the marketing department for distribution to other key members of the management team.

Alternative marketing strategies and contingency plans. This final section should address the alternative strategies available to the company in the event of changes in the marketplace that have been identified in the plan. The ability to predict these positive or negative changes and adopt alternative strategies if they occur is at the heart of effective strategic marketing planning.

Stage Two: Implementation of the Marketing Program

Once market research has been conducted and a marketing plan prepared, the second stage in the development of a marketing program is the actual *implementation* of the company's objectives and strategies. In most growing companies, a separate marketing department is responsible for the implementation of the marketing plan. This department may consist of one person or 100 people, depending on the size of the company, the nature of its business, its method of distribution, and the resources available for marketing.

The managers of a marketing department must constantly interact with other departments (such as manufacturing and research and development) as well as outside legal counsel in order to coordinate marketing efforts and to keep the marketing program consistent with the company's overall strategic plans and objectives. This will require the marketing department to establish certain procedures and controls to monitor marketing performance and to take corrective action where necessary to keep the company on its course of growth and development. These periodic performance audits should also seek to make marketing efficient by reducing unnecessary promotional expenditures and managing the costs of distribution channels. Managers of the marketing department must ensure that key members of the marketing management team are properly compensated, directed, and evaluated. Subordinate workers in the marketing department must be carefully selected, trained, and compensated so that marketing efforts at all levels stem from a secure organizational structure.

Small and growing companies typically experience four distinct phases in the evolution of the department responsible for developing and implementing marketing functions within the organization. At the inception of the company, all founders are responsible for sales and marketing efforts. During this initial phase, marketing plans are virtually nonexistent, marketing strategies are developed with a "whatever works" approach, and sales are to "anybody who will buy" the company's products and services. Eventually, the founders of the company will be too busy with other demands to continue the sales function, and as a result, a sales staff is developed—this marks a second phase. As the company reaches a third phase of its growth, all sales and marketing efforts must be centralized into a formal department. This is typically the phase when formal marketing plans start to be prepared by top marketing executives with guidance and input from managers of other departments. As the company experiences changes in its external and internal operating environment, the marketing department experiences a fourth and final phase of reorganization, during which the organizational structure is modified in order to adapt and respond to these environmental changes.

Implementation of the marketing plan will also require that responsibility for various components be vested in various dimensions within the marketing department. Typically, a marketing department will have distinct operating divisions with responsibility delegated as follows: (1) marketing research and monitoring, (2) product or service department, (3) sales, and (4) advertising and promotion. Functions, structures, terminology, job descriptions, specific responsibilities, and criteria for evaluating performance are likely to vary, however, from industry to industry. For example, a large retail chain may require a separate division within the marketing department solely for customer relations and service, and a company with a large customer base may need a database management division within the marketing department. Each operating division will be responsible for implementing a distinct component of the marketing plan. For example, the sales manager will be responsible for attracting, retaining, and compensating a qualified sales force that is capable of reaching the targeted markets identified in the marketing plan. The sales manager must then develop sales and follow-up methods, presentation materials, and related sales tools and programs for the sales force to use in reaching the targeted markets. Policies must be developed for determining how geographic territories will be allocated among the sales force, sales compensation formulas, performance quotas, and techniques for evaluation.

Stage Three: Marketing Program Monitoring and Feedback

Once marketing plans are developed and implemented, the third stage of the marketing program is reached: systems must be put into place to monitor the performance of the marketing department as well as to gather intelligence about markets and competitors. The market research division is usually responsible for acquiring data and intelligence, which are sometimes used as the first step in the development of the marketing plan and at other times are used in tracking the performance of marketing efforts in order to modify and refine marketing plans. In either case, systems must be developed to gather and process customer data, market characteristics and trends, and competitive analyses, and to monitor general business, economic, legal, political, and technological conditions. These intelligence-gathering systems are indispensable tools of a well managed marketing department and the overall organization.

A comprehensive system for monitoring and review will help the marketing department to identify strengths and weaknesses of the plans and strategies initially adopted and implemented, measure the performance of marketing efforts, refine plans to adapt to changes in the marketing macroenvironment, and totally eliminate marketing strategies that have been a complete failure.

The key components of an effective monitoring and intelligence-gathering system include: (1) acquiring and maintaining sufficient computer capability to manage and organize market data; (2) tracking the development and problems of competitors; (3) remaining active in industry groups and trade associations; (4) regularly reading trade journals and industry publications; (5) meeting with key suppliers and customers in order to understand industry trends and preferences; (6) buying the products of competitors to observe pricing, packaging, labeling, and features; (7) keeping track of the information that may be readily available from federal, state, and local governments; and (8) staying abreast of political, economic, social, and legal trends and developments affecting marketing plans and strategies.

Legal Aspects of Implementing Marketing Strategies

The legal consequences of sales and marketing decisions as a company grows must be carefully considered before actual plans and strategies are implemented. Failure to understand these laws will not only disrupt implementation but also could subject the growing company and its officers, directors, and managers to substantial civil and even criminal penalties. Owners and managers of growing companies should have a working knowledge of three categories of legal restraints on marketing practices:

1. Federal and state antitrust laws

2. Consumer protection (advertising, packaging, labeling, and warranty) laws established by federal regulatory agencies such as the Federal Trade Commission (FTC) and the Food and Drug Administration (FDA)

3. State and common-law principles of unfair competition and related business torts

An Introduction to Antitrust Laws

The federal antitrust laws, beginning with the Sherman Act of 1890, the Clayton Act of 1914, the Federal Trade Commission Act of 1914, and the Robinson-Patman Act of 1936, have been designed to promote a free-market system and protect against restraints of trade. Conflicts have arisen, however, between the two themes at the heart of antitrust policy. On one hand, political theory supported a body of law that promoted equality and fair play among businesses. Under this view, the interests of the smaller business are paramount, even if the end result is economic inefficiency. This view essentially states that the interests of the small business owner override the interests of the consumer. On the other hand, antitrust laws have also been developed based upon economic theory. Economists view antitrust as a body of law designed to protect competition and production efficiency, with the emphasis on the consumer, not on the interests of individual competitors. No matter which theory is currently at the forefront, owners and managers of growing companies adopting aggressive strategies in order to expand market share must be aware of the pricing, customer relations, marketing practices, and distribution methods that will not be tolerated.

Essentially, two general categories of restraints are prohibited by antitrust laws. The first category, *vertical restraints,* are those placed by a manufacturer on a distributor or by a wholesaler on a retailer. These are restraints on trade that develop between firms at *different* levels in the production and distribution network, such as if a manufacturer attempts to impose overly burdensome restrictions on a particular distribution channel. Examples include *resale price maintenance,* such as an attempt by a manufacturer to fix the prices at which a retailer can offer its products, *geographic and customer limitations,* such as limiting a distributor to an exclusive territory; *exclusive dealing arrangements,* such as forcing a distributor to sell only the manufacturer's products; *tying,* which forces distributors to buy products A and B when all they really want is B; and *price discrimination,* such as selling to one wholesaler in a given area under terms and conditions that are designed primarily to drive out regional competition. In certain cases, these arrangements are contractual and voluntary—as in a franchise agreement—or are necessary to protect against "free-riders," who threaten product quality and pricing formulas. However, if it is determined that a growing company is implementing these restraints in bad faith, merely to protect and expand its market share, antitrust claims are likely to be triggered.

The second category of practices prohibited by antitrust laws is *horizontal restraints.* Here the law is concerned with practices by firms operating at the same level in the distribution chain and doing business in generally the same markets. The laws are designed to protect against the concentration of large portions of market strength and market share in one or only a few firms. Monopolistic practices, such as predatory pricing (underselling rivals in order to acquire or preserve market share), refusals to deal, price fixing among market leaders (in order to squeeze out smaller firms and create greater barriers to market entry), production and output agreements, and other forms of collusion among market leaders, and restrictions on mergers and acquisitions, all generally fall within the category of horizontal restraints.

Specific Marketing Practices Under Federal and State Antitrust Laws

Penalties for failure to obey federal and state antitrust laws can be severe, and in the past have included criminal sanctions, injunctions, and damages for lost profits—in certain cases, treble damages. This discussion of specific marketing practices that run afoul of the antitrust laws should be of interest not only to the growing company seeking to avoid these sanctions, but also to the entrepreneurs who feel they may have been injured by such practices by a competitor.

A variety of specific marketing, distribution, and pricing practices are closely scrutinized by federal and state antitrust laws. For example, suppose that a growing company has adopted a marketing strategy that calls for entry into new geographic markets, either by acquiring other manufacturers of the product or by developing a below-cost pricing structure in the new territories. Although such a strategy appears on its face to be perfectly legitimate, it may trigger horizontal restraint problems under the Sherman Act or predatory pricing problems (if an anticompetitive intent is proved) under the Robinson-Patman Act, both of which carry civil and even criminal penalties. Therefore, it is the responsibility of the marketing department of a company to develop strategies and objectives that comply with applicable antitrust laws and to recognize when legal counsel must be consulted.

The following specific practices have been deemed to be anticompetitive or in restraint of trade under federal and state antitrust laws and therefore should be considered in developing marketing strategies.

MONOPOLISTIC PRACTICES   It may seem ironic that a capitalistic society that fosters entrepreneurship and business growth also has laws penalizing companies that manage to acquire substantial market power. Nonetheless, antitrust legislation has attempted, over the last century, to draw a line between practices that were permissible because market power has been achieved by a superior product or business skill and practices that must be condemned as anticompetitive and harmful to our economy and society because market power has been achieved by a conscious effort on the part of a growing company to reduce output and raise prices. The current approach for striking this balance involves applying a test called the "rule of reason" to the conduct in question. The "rule of reason" will examine all relevant facts and circumstances in an attempt to determine whether the particular act by the company was exclusionary and harmful to competition or whether the act should be permitted as actually fostering and promoting competition.

A variety of acts could be deemed to be monopolistic in nature, such as price discrimination, refusals to deal, certain restrictions on customers and territories, mergers of rivals, tying arrangements, and conspiracies among competitors. Some of these will be discussed in greater detail below. Courts have consistently ruled that size and growth alone, even at the expense of competitors, are *not* enough to determine guilt under the antitrust laws; rather, there must be some wrongful intent or illegal conduct by which the company seeks to either obtain or sustain market power.

PRICE-FIXING   The Sherman Act specifically prohibits "contracts, combinations or conspiracies" in restraint of trade. Under Section 1 of the Sherman Act, if two or more competitors conspire to fix prices or methods of price computation (e.g., base-point pricing) at a certain level, such conduct is per se illegal. This means that such practices will not be tolerated by the courts regardless of the facts and circumstances, even if prices are fair, reasonable, and in the best interests of all competitors within the industry or geographic area. This per se approach not only affects any agreements among competitors as to price, but also covers any terms and conditions of sale, such as credit terms, shipping policies, and trade-in allowances. Another practice closely related to horizontal price-fixing is known as "conscious parallelism," whereby companies will follow the acts of a dominant market leader, such as a change in price or sales terms, even in the absence of a formal agreement to fix prices among competitors.

Similar principles apply to attempts at price-fixing in a vertical chain of distribution, generally known as resale price maintenance (RPM). Attempts by a company to impose RPM policies on its distributors and retailers are also per se illegal, with a few limited exceptions for nonprice vertical restraints, such as unilateral refusals to deal, customer restraints, and designation of exclusive territories. Perhaps the most noted exception to the per se illegality of vertical price-fixing is the "unilateral refusal to deal" rule, which allows an objective decision by a manufacturer that it will not deal with distributors who cut prices below suggested levels, provided that the decision to refuse to deal is both truly unilateral (i.e., not at the urging of another distributor) and not the result of threats or intimidation. The only other well recognized exception to the per se rule against RPM arises when a manufacturer essentially retains ownership of a product by distributing on a consignment basis. These consignment arrangements make the reseller a mere "agent" of the manufacturer and thus create a legal and business justification for controlling prices.

PRICE DISCRIMINATION   Most issues of price discrimination arise under the Robinson-Patman Act, when a seller offers its otherwise uniform products at different prices because of the size or geographic location of the buyer. The Robinson-Patman Act is designed both to ensure fair pricing among the various buyers of the seller's products and to protect against pricing strategies intended to drive out local competition.

Here again, the antitrust laws attempt to draw a line between competitive practices, which will be encouraged, and anticompetitive practices, which will be prohibited. For example, the Robinson-Patman Act does not expressly prohibit a seller from charging a lower price to a customer if its actual costs of the sale are lower because of the quantities purchased by the buyer or the geographic proximity of the buyer. Similarly, a seller is permitted to drop its prices under certain circumstances if necessary to meet changing market conditions—for example, in order to compete with a rival's equally low price—as long as products are not sold below cost. As with certain related monopolistic practices, Robinson-Patman issues must be considered not only in terms of direct pricing but also in terms of nonprice considerations such as promotional allowances and credit.

VERTICAL NONPRICE RESTRAINTS   A variety of restraints by manufacturers affecting distribution channels can trigger antitrust considerations. The three most common forms are tying, exclusive dealing, and territorial and customer restrictions.

Tying is an arrangement in which the sale or lease of product X (which the buyer wants) is conditional on the buyer's also purchasing product Y (which the buyer does not necessarily want). Recent cases have set forth a clear test for distinguishing when a tie-in arrangement will be permitted and when it will be prohibited, although the exact elements of the test vary among jurisdictions. A threshold condition for finding an illegal tying arrangement has always been that the seller must have sufficient market power and must exercise enough coercion to truly force the buyer to purchase product Y as a condition of getting product X.

Exclusive dealing involves a situation in which a buyer contracts to purchase all of its requirements of a given product exclusively from a particular seller. When the buyer is entering into such an arrangement merely to protect its requirements for a given product in a period of uncertain supply, it would clearly be wrong to classify such an agreement as anticompetitive. However, if an exclusive dealing contract is designed to suppress competition, then it will be examined by the court in light of all relevant facts and circumstances under the "rule of reason" test.

Territorial and customer restrictions usually involve attempts by sellers to divide a targeted market up into distinct territorial segments and grant a geographic area or certain customers exclusively to a given buyer. Courts have struggled with the antitrust implications of such arrangements primarily because of the dual effect on competition that territorial and customer restraints tend to have: interbrand competition (competition among different manufacturers) is generally increased at the same time that intrabrand competition (competition among different retailers of the same manufacturer) is generally decreased. The courts have attempted to balance this conflicting effect on competition by analyzing all of the surrounding facts and circumstances in the analysis of a territorial or customer restraint under the "rule of reason" test.

A Word on State Antitrust Statutes

As a general rule, state antitrust statutes closely parallel the principles codified in the federal antitrust laws; however, specific rules and regulations often will vary widely from state to state. Nevertheless, certain trends have emerged recently at the state level that owners and managers of growing companies should consider when developing marketing and distribution strategies.

First, as federal enforcement of the antitrust laws becomes more relaxed, many state attorney generals have become that much more vigilant in their enforcement of civil and criminal state antitrust statutes. These statutes are being used as vehicles to enforce economic and political positions regarding antitrust policies within a given state's jurisdiction, as well as to pursue white-collar and organized criminals whose business practices may be, among other things, in restraint of trade. A second important trend has been the willingness of state courts and juries to interpret state antitrust statutes more broadly, and exceptions to antitrust violations more narrowly. For example, arguments concerning economic efficiency may not be very effective in persuading a jury in a case where a large local employer is being adversely affected by the trade practices of an unknown out-of-town conglomerate. Third, many recent state "antitakeover" statutes designed to protect local business have also fostered an environment in which proposed mergers are being challenged on anticompetitive grounds by state antitrust enforcement officials more often than in the past.

Developing an Antitrust Compliance Program

As a company's growth leads it into new product lines and expanded geographic territories and gives it an increased market share, the need to establish and maintain a formal antitrust compliance program becomes increasingly important—in fact, it is a virtual necessity for avoiding antitrust problems and penalties.

Implementation of an antitrust compliance program should begin with an *antitrust audit*, which consists primarily of a questionnaire circulated to all key employees responsible for decisions about marketing, distribution, and pricing. The purpose of the questionnaire is to identify existing company policies, objectives, activities, contracts, practices, or even attitudes that could create problems under the antitrust laws if not promptly corrected. The audit should address the following issues:

1. Does the company have an oral or written understanding with any direct or indirect competitor with respect to pricing, warranties, discounts, shipping and credit terms, promotional contributions, or service policies in connection with any of the company's products?

2. What are the exact product and geographical markets in which the company competes? What is its share of each of these markets?

3. Has the company experienced any actual or threatened antitrust litigation or investigation in the past? What were the specific company practices upon which these claims were based? What steps, if any, have been taken to resolve any of the problems previously identified?

4. How are the company's pricing policies developed? Is the same product ever sold to different customers at different prices? What is the rationale or justification for such a price disparity?

5. What distribution channels have been selected for marketing the company's products and services? What oral or written agreements have been developed with wholesalers and retailers? Do any of these agreements include specific provisions or understandings as to price or territorial or customer restrictions? Does the company engage in dual distribution? Are any buyers of the company's products or services forced to purchase unwanted products and services as a condition of dealing with the company?

6. To what trade associations does the company belong? What types of information are exchanged among members? Why?

The answers provided by the managers of the company should be reviewed by legal counsel in order to determine whether a change in policy or practice should be implemented.

The other key component of the initial antitrust audit is document review. Legal counsel should be brought in to review all customer sales contracts, licensing agreements, distributorship contracts, joint venture agreements, documents regarding prior litigation, employment agreements, trade association bylaws, minutes of board meetings and shareholders' meetings, merger and acquisition agreements, customer lists, agreements with sales representatives, marketing and business plans, internal memorandums, correspondence with competitors and suppliers, customer leasing agreements and service contracts, invoices, and any other document used in connection with the company's dealings with suppliers, consumers, or competitors. These will then be analyzed by legal counsel from the perspective of antitrust law.

Once all of the operating policies and marketing strategies of the company have been reviewed by legal counsel, an antitrust compliance manual should be prepared. The compliance manual should provide an overview of federal and state antitrust laws as well as a more detailed discussion of those areas of law that directly or indirectly regulate or otherwise affect the company's business practices. The company's policies regarding antitrust compliance should be widely disseminated to all employees through the manual, bulletins, antitrust compliance seminars, orientation meetings for new employees, and small-group workshops.

An effective compliance program is especially important in the area of antitrust law, where the actual *intent* of the company and its personnel will be closely examined in connection with its conduct. Effective antitrust compliance will also require careful record keeping when sales and marketing personnel interact with customers, suppliers, and competitors. Top management must be committed to the implementation of the antitrust compliance program. The time and resources invested in the establishment and maintenance of such a program will usually far outweigh the costs of civil and criminal penalties that the company, and even its individual officers and directors, may face in the event of an antitrust violation.

An Introduction to Consumer Protection Laws

There are an almost infinite number of federal, state, and local consumer protection laws that directly and indirectly affect planning and decision making with regard to marketing and distribution. This section is intended not to address all of these laws but rather to ensure that owners and managers of growing companies will carefully review legal restrictions on manufacturing, packaging, and labeling, false advertising, and related consumer protection laws, when developing marketing strategies. In addition to laws of general applicability, there are a variety of industry-specific regulations in businesses such as textiles, pharmaceuticals, and food products that have been developed by the FTC, the FDA, and other federal and state regulatory agencies.

Consumer protection laws of general applicability to growing companies generally fall into one of two categories:

1. Laws affecting design and production
2. Laws affecting sales and advertising

LAWS AFFECTING DESIGN AND PRODUCTION Companies of all sizes and in all industries that manufacture consumer or industrial products have a legal as well as a social responsibility to offer products that are safe for their intended use. This commitment to product safety will begin with the design of the product by the research and development department for its intended purposes. It will then become the responsibility of the manufacturing department to ensure that products are made without defects or hazardous parts. Finally, the marketing department will have the responsibility for ensuring that the product is packaged in a manner that is not misleading, either in terms of its range of capabilities or in terms of the instructions for use.

Laws regarding the safety of consumer products have attracted significant attention in the last decade as a result of increases in litigation (resulting in excessive awards of damages to plaintiffs) and increases in insurance costs (resulting in excessive and even inaccessible insurance rates for small companies). At state and local levels, the laws governing product liability, negligence, and personal injury determine the manufacturer's responsibility to produce safe products and the penalties for failure to do so. Liability may be imposed because of an act of negligence by a company, because of a breach of a warranty, or even as a result of "strict liability"—a theory that forces a manufacturer to pay damages even if there was no intent to produce a faulty product and no breach of the duty of reasonable care, which is at the heart of all negligence law. The scope and limitation of these state laws are constantly changing; therefore, manufacturers of consumer products, especially at the small-business level, should pay careful attention to the state product liability laws in the various jurisdictions where their products are manufactured and distributed.

At the federal level, most consumer product safety laws are developed by the Consumer Product Safety Commission (CPSC), the FDA, and the FTC. The CPSC was created in the early 1970s as part of the Consumer Products Safety Act in order to develop federal regulations designed to reduce the hazards posed to consumers by unsafe products. CPSC regulations now affect the design, manufacture, and marketing of a wide variety of consumer products offered by small and growing companies. CPSC has the power and authority to:

1. Inspect a company's manufacturing facilities

2. Publicize information about companies and products that it has determined are in violation of its regulations

3. Force a manufacturer to order a recall, pay a refund for, or offer to replace a hazardous product

4. Establish regulations for minimum standards of safety and quality control for specific products

5. Completely ban a given hazardous product from the marketplace

A second major federal regulator in this area is the Food and Drug Administration (FDA). The principal statute enforced by the FDA is the Federal Food, Drug, and Cosmetic Act (FFDCA). The FFDCA is intended to ensure that:

1. Food products are pure and wholesome, safe to eat, and produced under sanitary conditions.

2. Drugs and medical devices are safe and effective for their intended uses.

3. Cosmetics and beauty aids are safe and made from appropriate ingredients.

4. Packaging and labeling of all types of food, drug, and cosmetic products are truthful, informative, and not deceptive. In addition, the Fair Packaging and Labeling Act (FPLA) regulates the contents and placement of information required on the packaging of all consumer and industrial products. The FDA is also charged with the regulation of manufacturing and distribution of certain biological products and electronic devices.

The FFDCA prohibits interstate distribution or international importation of products that are either adulterated or misbranded. An adulterated product is defined by the statute as one that is defective, unsafe, filthy, or produced under unsanitary conditions. A misbranded product is defined by the statute as one that includes false, misleading, or incomplete packaging or labeling. A variety of federal regulations and court cases have attempted to interpret the scope of these two broad prohibitions as applied to the facts and circumstances surrounding each alleged violation of the statute. If a product requires approval by the FDA, the FFDCA also prohibits its distribution prior to such approval, the refusal or failure of a company to provide the FDA with reports, and the refusal by a manufacturer to allow FDA officials to inspect facilities regulated by the statute.

LAWS AFFECTING SALES AND ADVERTISING   Sales and advertising campaigns are usually developed by growing companies in order to to the following:

- Introduce the marketplace to the company's products and services
- Build goodwill and consumer loyalty
- Increase the company's revenues and profits once a market is developed

Advertising must communicate the various benefits, features, and competitive advantages of the company's products and services clearly, concisely, and accurately. Companies that include false or misleading information in their advertising materials are likely to rapidly lose market share, consumer goodwill, and the dedication of the distribution network. In addition, it is likely that suppliers, creditors, consultants, shareholders, and lenders will become disenchanted with a company—that is, its credibility and reputation will suffer—if deceptive practices play a role in its advertising. But the costs of false and deceptive practices go beyond problems affecting the operation and management of the company from a business perspective. These types of practices also trigger legal problems at federal and state levels, because of the consumer protection laws regulating advertising and sales strategies.

At the heart of the legal regulation of sales and marketing practices is the FTC, which, through Section 5 of the Federal Trade Commission Act, has the authority to prohibit all unfair or deceptive acts or practices in interstate commerce. In order for the FTC to bring a formal enforcement action against a company for a deceptive act, three elements must be present: (1) There must be a representation, commission, or practice that is likely to mislead the consumer. (2) The specific act will be analyzed from the perspective of the consumer acting reasonably under the circumstances. (3) The act in question must be material. The broad nature of these elements vests the FTC with considerable discretion in determining whether an unfair or deceptive act or practice has occurred.

The primary "safe harbor" available to a growing company in developing aggressive sales and marketing strategies is known as "puffing." Puffing has been referred to as the "sellers' privilege to lie their heads off, so long as they say nothing specific, on the theory that no reasonable person would be influenced by such talk." In order to fall within the parameters of this safe harbor, the contents of the specific advertisement should discuss the company's products and services using only subjective opinions, superlatives, or exaggerations and should not claim to be based upon any specific facts unless such facts have been reasonably substantiated.

To avoid a claim for false or deceptive advertising under federal law or the various state laws, these general guidelines should be followed:

- Federal and state regulators put a premium on accuracy, full disclosure, and the ability to substantiate claims. Claims that are made about a company's products or services, regardless of whether they are made in a radio advertisement or a written brochure, must be backed up with facts, test results, letters of opinion, market surveys, and testimonials from customers that support and substantiate the representations made to the general public.

- An informed sales staff will not only build customer loyalty but will also help to avoid claims of misrepresentation or deception. Sales training meetings, manuals, and marketing information systems, implemented on a regular basis, will keep the sales staff up to date on product developments and capabilities.

- Avoid sales gimmicks. Very few successful growth companies were ever built on "bait and switch" techniques, liquidation sales, or giving away cheap gifts or prizes.

- A material omission can be just as damaging as an affirmative misrepresentation. Leaving important information out of an advertisement or brochure concerning the side effects of a product, a disclaimer of warranty as to a particular service, or a condition of obtaining a particular benefit can cause regulators or consumers to bring a claim of deception.

An Overview of Unfair Competition Law and Related Business Torts

In addition to federal and state antitrust and consumer protection laws, there is a broad and growing body of state and local *unfair competition* laws that must be considered in developing marketing plans and strategies. The nature and scope of the laws of unfair competition will vary from state to state. Most jurisdictions recognize some form of the following business torts as usually falling into the category of unfair competition: trade libel; disparagement of a competitor's product; interference with existing or prospective contractual relations; misappropriation and infringement of intellectual property (as discussed in Chapter 8); passing off; invasion of privacy; commercial bribery; price-fixing; price discrimination; and the enforceability of equitable servitudes and covenants. Although a detailed state-by-state analysis is beyond the scope of this book, owners and managers of growing companies should be aware of the following general principles when developing marketing plans and strategies:

TRADE LIBEL AND PRODUCT DISPARAGEMENT   If one company makes a false and malicious statement to the public regarding the reputation or products of one of its competitors, then it may be liable for any pecuniary losses suffered by the competitor as a result of the libel or disparagement. Therefore, although comparative advertising is permitted and even encouraged by federal and state regulations, statements about a competitor should either be very carefully substantiated or fall within the safe harbor of "puffery," in order to avoid the risk of an action for disparagement or libel.

INTERFERENCE WITH CONTRACTUAL RELATIONS   Although the antitrust laws are designed to foster competition, excessive competitive zeal in approaching your competitor's customers and suppliers will not be tolerated by state courts. Improper solicitations of a competitor's customers or suppliers that are designed to encourage a breach of an existing contract or even a prospective contract could result in a civil cause of action by the competitor. In determining whether the alleged act or practice was improper, most courts will consider the nature of the conduct, the proximity of the conduct to the alleged interference, the current status of the relationship that was interfered with, and the interests of the third-party supplier or consumer that dealt with the competitor. The bottom line is that there is a large gray area separating a legitimate effort to take business away from a competitor and an improper attempt to induce a breach of contract. Marketing and advertising strategies must, therefore, be developed to strike this delicate balance, and sales staffs must be provided with guidelines as to what conduct is acceptable and what is not. Note that recently the tort of interference has become a part of the growing body of labor and employment law when an employer attempts to recruit a competitor's employees.

PASSING-OFF   This common-law business tort is closely related to infringement of trademarks and misappropriation of trade secrets in that it attempts to penalize a company that copies the packaging, design, name, shape, appearance, taste, color scheme, or general physical characteristics of a competitor's products or services, when the intent is to confuse the consumer as to source of origin. Therefore, although competitors are all equally entitled to ensure that their products and services offer attractive features and are attractively presented, no competitor is entitled to confuse the public by posing as another company.

EQUITABLE SERVITUDES AND COVENANTS An attempt by a seller to restrict the use of a product following the sale is an equitable servitude, which is generally unenforceable as an illegal restraint of trade. Similarly, an unreasonable covenant against competition following the termination of an employment or franchise relationship will not be tolerated by most state courts. If a company has a legitimate business justification for the use of such covenants or servitudes, then it will also bear the burden of proving the reasonableness of the provision when challenged.

A wide variety of federal and state laws directly and indirectly affect the marketing plans and strategies of growing companies. Legal counsel should be retained to work closely with the marketing department and advertising agency in order to ensure that aggressive campaigns developed to foster rapid growth are structured within the bounds of the law.

A P P E N D I X

Resource **D**irectory for the **G**rowing **B**usiness

Federal Agencies

U.S. Small Business Administration (SBA)
409 Third Street, S.W.
Washington, D.C. 20416
(800) 827-5722

Offers a wide variety of financing programs, workshops and seminars, management and technical assistance, etc.—typically through its many district offices.

Export-Import Bank (Eximbank)
811 Vermont Avenue, N.W.
Washington, D.C. 20571
(800) 565-3946

Offers financing assistance for potential exporters and companies of all sizes interested in doing business abroad.

U.S. Department of Commerce (DOC)
Herbert C. Hoover Building
14th Street & Constitution Ave., N.W.
Washington, D.C. 20230
(202) 482-2000

Offers a variety of programs and services relating to economic development, international trade, and minority business. The U.S. Patent and Trademark Office (800-786-9199) is a division of the

DOC that processes federal patent and trademark applications and publishes various resources on the protection of intellectual property.

In addition to the agencies above, all major federal departments and agencies have an Office of Small and Disadvantaged Business Utilization (OSDBU), which is responsible for ensuring that an equitable share of government contracts are awarded to small and minority businesses. Some sample OSDBU phone numbers within selected agencies include:

Department of Agriculture
(202) 720-7117

Department of Justice
(202) 616-0521

Office of Personnel
Management
(202) 606-2180

Department of Defense
(703) 614-1151

Agency for International
Development
(703) 875-1551

State Agencies

Although a comprehensive state-by-state directory is beyond the scope of this chapter, virtually every state has at least one office or agency that is responsible for coordinating programs and assistance for small and minority-owned businesses. These various state programs offer a wide range of services, from technical assistance to advocacy to financial support. Each state "houses" the small-business division in a slightly different place, but a good place to start is with a call to the state's Department of Commerce or Department of Economic Development. A few states, such as California (916-324-1295), Connecticut (860-258-4200), Illinois (217-524-5856), and Minnesota (800-657-3858) have a stand-alone Office of Small Business. Many states offer training programs, seminars, publications, and even tax breaks to foster and encourage the growth of small businesses. The chambers of commerce in each state are also an excellent starting point for determining the availability and extent of small-business development programs in a given region.

▌rade Associations

There are literally thousands of trade associations, networking groups, venture clubs, and other organizations that directly or indirectly focus on the needs of small-business owners, entepreneurs, growing companies, women-owned businesses, minority-owned businesses, importers and exporters, and virtually every other group that shares common interests. Some of the more established groups with a genuine nationwide presence and solid track record include:

U.S. Chamber of Commerce
1615 H Street, N.W.
Washington, D.C. 20062
(202) 659-6000

The U.S. Chamber of Commerce represents 215,000 businesses, 3,000 state and local chambers of commerce, 1,200 trade and professional associations, and 72 American Chambers of Commerce abroad. It works with these groups to support national business interests and includes a Small Business Center (202-463-5503).

Alliance of Independent Store Owners and Professionals (AISOP)
P.O. Box 2014 Loop Station
Minneapolis, MN 55402
(612) 340-1568

AISOP was organized to protect and promote fair postal and legislative policies for small-business advertisers. Most of its more than 4,000 members are independent small businesses that rely on reasonable third-class mail rates to promote their businesses and contact customers in their trade areas.

American Entrepreneurs Association
2392 Morse Avenue
Irvine, CA 92714
(800) 482-0973

The American Entrepreneurs Association was established to provide small-business owners with benefits and discounts that are generally reserved for big businesses, such as express shipping, health insurance, and discount long-distance telephone rates.

American Small Business Association (ASBA)
1800 North Kent Street, Suite 901
Arlington, VA 22209
(800) ASBA-911

ASBA's membership base consists of small-business owners with 20 or fewer employees. ASBA members have access to the same advantages that larger corporations enjoy through member benefits and services.

International Franchise Association (IFA)
1350 New York Avenue, Suite 900
Washington, D.C. 20005
(202) 628-8000

The IFA serves as a resource center for current and prospective franchisees and franchisors, the media and the government. The IFA has promoted programs that expand opportunities for women and minorities in franchising.

National Association of Development Companies (NADCO)
4301 N. Fairfax Drive, Suite 860
Arlington, VA 22203
(703) 812-9000

NADCO is the trade group of community-based, nonprofit organizations that promote small-business expansion and job creation through the SBA's 504 loan program, known as Certified Development Companies (CDC).

National Association of Manufacturers (NAM)
1331 Pennsylvania Avenue, N.W., Suite 1500 North
Washington, D.C. 20004
(202) 637-3000

NAM serves as the voice of the manufacturing community and is active on all issues concerning manufacturing, including legal system reform, regulatory restraint, and tax reform.

National Association for the Self-Employed (NASE)
2121 Precinct Line Road
Hurst, TX 76054
(703) 683-1601

NASE helps its members become more competitive by providing over 100 benefits that save money on services and equipment. NASE's members consist primarily of small-business owners with few or no employees.

National Association of Small Business Investment Companies (NASBIC)
1199 N. Fairfax Drive, Suite 200
Alexandria, VA 22314
(703) 683-1601

National Federation of Independent Business (NFIB)
53 Century Boulevard, Suite 300
Nashville, TN 37214

600 Maryland Avenue, S.W., Suite 700
Washington, D.C. 20024
(800) 634-2669
(800) 552-6342
NFIB disseminates educational information about free enterprise, entrepreneurship, and small business. NFIB represents more than 60,000 small and independent businesses before legislatures and government agencies at the federal and state level.

National Small Business United (NSBU)
1155 15th Street, N.W., Suite 710
Washington, D.C. 20005
(202) 293-8830
The NSBU is a membership-based association of business owners that presents small business's point of view to all levels of government and the Congress.

National Venture Capital Association
1655 Fort Myer Drive, Suite 700
Arlington, VA 22209
(703) 351-5269
The National Venture Capital Association's mission is to define, serve, and promote the interests of the venture capital industry, to increase the understanding of the importance of venture capital

to the U.S. economy, and to stimulate the flow of equity capital to emerging growth and developing companies.

National Association of Investment Companies (NAIC)
1111 14th Street, N.W., Suite 700
Washington, D.C. 20005
(202) 289-4336

NAIC is the industry association for venture capital firms that dedicate their financial resources to investment in minority businesses.

National Association of Women Business Owners (NAWBO)
1100 Wayne Avenue, Suite 830
Silver Spring, MD 20910
(301) 608-2590

NAWBO uses its collective influence to broaden opportunities for women in business, and is the only dues-based national organization representing the interests of all women entrepreneurs in all types of business.

National Association for Female Executives (NAFE)
30 Irving Place, 5th Floor
New York, NY 10003
(212) 477-2200

Through education and networking programs, NAFE helps women share the resources and techniques needed to succeed in the competitive business world.

National Business League (NBL)
1511 K Street, N.W., Suite 432
Washington, D.C. 20005
(202) 737-4430

NBL is primarily involved in business development among African Americans and serves as a voice for black business on Capitol Hill and in the federal government.

U.S. Hispanic Chamber of Commerce
1030 15th Steet, N.W., Suite 206
Washington, D.C. 20005
(202) 842-1212

The Hispanic Chamber advocates the business interests of Hispanics and develops minority business opportunities with major corporations and at all levels of government.

In addition to the above, there are a variety of special purpose or industry-specific trade associations or foundations. These include:

Young Entrepreneurs' Organization (YEO)
1321 Duke St., Suite 300
Alexandria, VA 22314
(703) 519-6700

National Foundation for Teaching Entrepreneurship to Handicapped and Disadvantaged Youth, Inc. (NFTE)
120 Wall Street, 29th Floor
New York, NY 10005
(212) 232-3333

Opportunity International
360 W. Butterfield Road
Elmhurst, IL 60126
(708) 279-9300

American Farm Bureau Federation
225 W. Touhy Avenue
Park Ridge, IL 60068
(312) 399-5700

American Financial Services Association
919 18th Street, N.W., Third Floor
Washington, D.C. 20006
(202) 296-5544

Association of American Publishers
1718 Connecticut Avenue, N.W., Suite 700
Washington, D.C. 20009
(202) 232-3335

National Association of Convenience Stores
1605 King Street
Alexandria, VA 22314
(703) 684-3600

National Restaurant Association
1200 17th Street, N.W.
Washington, D.C. 20036
(202) 331-5900

Council of Growing Companies
8260 Greensboro Drive, Suite 260
McLean, VA 22102
(800) 929-3165

American Electronics Association
1225 Eye Street, N.W., Suite 950
Washington, D.C. 20005
(202) 682-9110

American Society of Association Executives (ASAE)
1575 Eye Street, N.W.
Washington, D.C. 20005
(202) 626-2723

Information Industry Association
555 New Jersey Avenue, N.W., Suite 800
Washington, D.C. 20001
(202) 639-8262

National Association of Wholesaler-Distributors
1725 K Street, N.W., Suite 300
Washington, D.C. 20006
(202) 872-0885

National Retail Federation
325 Seventh Street, N.W., Suite 1000
Washington, D.C. 20004
(202) 783-7971

Small-Business Resources in Cyberspace

Over the past few years, hundreds of web sites have been developed to provide resourceful support to small-business owners and entrepreneurs. Web sites come and go quickly and change often, so use one of the popular search engines and enter key words that will narrow the scope of your search or particular resource need. Here are some web sites worth visiting:

Name	Internet Address	Main Features
IdeaCafe	http://www.ideacafe.com/welcome.html	Small-business meeting place
Legaldocs	http://legaldocs.com	Low-cost legal forms
Venture Capital Institute	http://vcinstitute.org	Wide range of venture capital resources
Small Business Resource Center	http://www.webcom.com/~seaquest	Offers dozens of tips to help make a small business a success
NetMarquee Family Business Net Center	http://www.nmq.com/fambiznc	Offers articles and newsletters covering management issues of family-owned businesses
Dun & Bradstreet Information	http://dbisna.com	A comprehensive source of financial and demographic information
Invest-O-Rama	http://www.investorama.com	Offers a directory of investment-related information on topics such as the stock market, brokerage firms, mutual funds, and dividend and reinvestment plans
The American Association of Individual Investors	http://www.aaii.org	Offers a basic guide to computerized investing, and articles from the *AAII Journal* and *Computerized Investing*

NETworth	http://www.networth.galt.com	Offers information and links to mutual fund companies and online access to fund prospectuses
EDGAR	http://www.sec.gov/edgarhp.htm	A database that contains all corporate annual and quarterly reports (and exhibits) filed with the Securities and Exchange Commission
Investment Brokerages Guide	http://www.cs.cmu.edu/%7Ejdg/invest_brokers	Offers links to full service and discount and online brokerages worldwide
The Wall Street Journal's Interactive Edition	http://www.update.wsj.com	Allows users to access news and financial information about specified companies
Inc. Online	http://www.inc.com	Allows users to (1) build their own web sites; (2) read the current issue or browse through *Inc.* magazine's extensive archives; and (3) interaction with other entrepreneurs, experts, and *Inc.* editors
"Ask the Lawyer"	http://www.fairmeasures.com	A new web site that offers practical advice for complying with employee law and preventing lawsuits
IFA Online	http://www.entremkt.com/ifa	Offers *IFA's Franchise Opportunities Guide*, *Franchising World*, bulletin boards, calendar of events, and more for franchisers and franchisees

Business Journal	http://www.amcity.com (home page)	
	http://www.amcity.com/toolstogrow	Features expert advice for small businesses on topics such as sales and marketing, technical issues, business financing, and tips on shopping for business products and services
CareerMosaic	http:///www.careermosiac.com	Offers a database of national job offerings
E-Span	http://www.espan.com	Used by human resource professionals to post jobs worldwide. Provides reference materials for human resource practitioners
Monster Board	http://www.monster.com	Offers information on a variety of issues, from hiring to staffing to other related topics for human resource executives
Online Career Center	http://www.occ.com	A nonprofit consortium for corporations posting job openings
Interbiznet's	http://www.interbiznet.com/ibn/top25.html	Lists top 25 recruiting sites
The Internet Mall	http://www.internetmall.com/4mplymntsrvcs.htm	Offers links to resume services, city job banks, career counselling, and publications
JobHunt	http://www.rescomp.stanford/edu/jobs	A commercial site that distributes electronic resumes
CareerPath	http://www.careerpath.com	Launched by *The Boston Globe, Chicago Tribune, Los Angeles Times, The New York Times, San Jose*

		Mercury News, and *The Washington Post,* it divides hundreds of listings by journal and by field of interest
OfficeNET	http://www.officenet1.com	Offers administrative, secretarial, and professional support services
SHRM (Society Human Resource Management)	http://www.shrm.org	Lists a variety of services and products for human resource professionals
SBA Women in Business	http://www.sba.gov/womeninbusiness	
American Society of Association Executives	http://www.asaenet.org	
Income Opportunities Magazine	http://www.incomeops.com	
Span Link Communications	http://www.spanlink.com	
BusinessLink On-Line	http://www.buslink.com	
Switchboard	http://www.switchboard.com	
Marketing Tools Magazine	http://www.marketingtools.com	
Small Business Express	http://www.gnn.com/gnn/met.a/finance/smallbus/index.htm	
Herring Magazine	http://www.herring.com	
Info Franchise News, Inc.	http://www.infonews.com/franchise	

I N D E X

ABOUT THE AUTHOR

ANDREW SHERMAN represents over 150 emerging growth businesses as a principal shareholder in the Washington, D.C., office of Greenberg Traurig, a Florida-based national law firm. He has been a featured speaker at over 200 conferences worldwide, including seminars sponsored by *Inc.* magazine, the Young Entrepreneur's Organization, and the International Franchise Association. As an adjunct professor at the MBA programs at Georgetown University and the University of Maryland, Sherman teaches courses on growth strategies, corporate finance, and business planning. He is the author of five books on the legal and strategic aspects of business growth, capital formation, and franchising.